W9-AXX-155

The Master Teacher

Expand Your Skills and Share Your Talents to Improve Your School

Steve Springer, Brandy Alexander, and Kimberly Persiani-Becker, Ed.D.

Illustrated by Steve Springer and Brandy Alexander

New York   Chicago   San Francisco   Lisbon   London   Madrid   Mexico City
Milan   New Delhi   San Juan   Seoul   Singapore   Sydney   Toronto

The McGraw·Hill Companies

Copyright © 2009 by The McGraw-Hill Companies, Inc. Interior illustrations copyright © 2009 by Steve Springer and Brandy Alexander. All rights reserved. Printed in the United States of America. Except as permitted under the United States Copyright Act of 1976, no part of this publication may be reproduced or distributed in any form or by any means, or stored in a database or retrieval system, without the prior written permission of the publisher.

1 2 3 4 5 6 7 8 9 10 11 12 13 14 15 16 17 18 19 20 21 22 23 24   QPD/QPD   0 9

ISBN 978-0-07-149681-0
MHID   0-07-149681-5
Library of Congress Control Number: 2008940596

Interior design by Village Bookworks, Inc.

McGraw-Hill books are available at special quantity discounts to use as premiums and sales promotions or for use in corporate training programs. To contact a representative, please visit the Contact Us pages at www.mhprofessional.com.

This book is printed on acid-free paper.

Contents

Introduction   xi
The Evolution of the Master Teacher   xii
The Master Teacher   xiv

I

Personal Development Goals

1

Attending Professional Development Conferences 3

Types of Professional Development Education Conferences   4
Conference Reminders   8
Conference Checklist   9
Conference Tools   10
Conference Planner   11
Staff Conference Log   12
Personal Conference Log   13
Conference Notes Organizer   14

2

Presenting at Conferences 15

Preparing a Conference Presentation Proposal   15
Presentation Proposal Resource Sheet   17
Presentation Checklist   20
Agenda   21
Presentation Day Checklist   22

© The McGraw-Hill Companies, Inc.

3
Conferences to Choose From 23

National Council of Teachers of Mathematics (NCTM)   24
National Council of Supervisors of Mathematics (NCSM)   25
National Reading Conference (NRC)   26
International Reading Association (IRA)   27
National Association for Bilingual Education (NABE)   28
National Council of Teachers of English (NCTE)   29
California Association for Bilingual Education (CABE)   30
National Center for Family Literacy (NCFL)   31
International Society for Technology in Education (ISTE)   32
School Science and Mathematics Association (SSMA)   33
National Association for Research in Science Teaching (NARST)   34
National Council for the Social Studies (NCSS)   35
Council for Exceptional Children (CEC)   36
Hawaii International Conference on Education   37
Association for Moral Education (AME)   38

4
Pursuing Higher Education (and Getting Your Paperwork Together!) 39

Personal Inventory   40
Personal Goals   41
Establishing Goals for Continuing Education   42
Personal Profile   43
Tips from Experience   45

5
Professional Programs to Explore 46

Salary Point Courses   46
Salary Point Tracker   47
Master's Degree   48
Ed.D. or Ph.D.   52
Advanced Degree Application Checklist   53
National Board Certification   54

© The McGraw-Hill Companies, Inc.

II
Showing Leadership in Your School

6
Organizing Teams and Meetings with Your School Staff 57

Organization 58
Topic Ideas 59
Participant Survey 60
Goals 61
Meeting Planner 62
Meeting Agenda 63
Sample Meeting Agenda 64
Sign-In Sheet 65
Meeting Log 66
Materials Request Form 67

7
Planning and Leading Professional Developments 68

Features of a Professional Development 69
The Do's of Professional Developments 70
Plan Your Topic Using a Professional Development Inventory 71
Schedule the Professional Development 72
Create Your Professional Development Agenda 73
Professional Development Planner 74
Professional Development Checklist 75
Professional Development Sign-In Sheet 76
Professional Development Action Plan 77
Professional Development Evaluation 78
Professional Development Materials List 79

8
Presentation Techniques and Topics 80

Professional Development Presentation Techniques 80
Professional Development Topics by Curricular and School-related Area 86
Professional Development Planner 93
Sample Professional Development Plans 94

© The McGraw-Hill Companies, Inc.

9
Mentoring New Teachers 104

Setting Up an Agenda for Meetings   104
Mentor Teacher Checklist   105
Planning Benchmarks and Goals   106
Planning Formal and Informal Observations   107
Counseling Strategies   108
Meeting Agenda (New Teacher–Mentor Teacher)   109
Feedback and Needs Assessment Worksheet (New Teacher)   110
Observation Feedback Form (Mentor Teacher)   111

10
Supporting a Student Teacher 112

How Do You Know If You Are Ready to Support a Student Teacher?   112
Important Characteristics of a Cooperating Teacher   113
How Shall I Prepare for a Student Teacher?   114
What Do I Do When My Student Teacher Arrives?   115
Informing the Student Teacher About School Policy: A Checklist   117
Student Teacher Responsibilities   118
Cooperating Teacher Responsibilities   119
Role in Supervising   120
Initial Days: Observation   121
Conferencing   122
Effective Conferences   123
Professional Issues   124
Self-reflection (Cooperating Teacher)   125

11
Student Teaching Forms and Resource Documents 128

Student Teaching Meeting Agenda   128
Classroom Observations (Student Teacher)   129
Observation Feedback Form (Cooperating Teacher)   130
Reflective Journal (Student Teacher)   131
Self-reflection (Student Teacher)   132
Student Teaching Timetable   133
Student Teaching Weekly Planner   134
Observation Log (Cooperating Teacher)   135
Conference Log (Cooperating Teacher)   136
Informal Observations (Cooperating Teacher)   137
Reflective Journal (Cooperating Teacher)   138

© The McGraw-Hill Companies, Inc.

III
Leadership Outside the Regular Classroom

12
Planning, Organizing, and Leading After-school Programs 141

After-school Program Survey   143
After-school Program Academic Needs Review   144
After-school Program Planner   145
Sample After-school Program Planner   146
After-school Program Home Letter   147
After-school Program Permissions and Waivers   147
After-school Program Daily Routine Planner   148
Sample After-school Program Daily Routine Planner   149
After-school Program Attendance Sheet   150
After-school Program Roster   151
After-school Program Teacher Sign-In Sheet   152
After-school Program Cancellation Notification   153
After-school Program Assessments   154
After-school Program Progress Report   155
After-school Program Evaluation (Teachers)   156
After-school Program Evaluation (Students)   157
After-school Program Checklist   158

13
After-school Program Ideas 159

Reading Tutoring After-school Program   160
Math Tutoring After-school Program   161
Computer Lab After-school Program   162
After-school Chess or Game Club   163
Art After-school Program   164
After-school Homework Club   165

© The McGraw-Hill Companies, Inc.

14
Getting Parents Involved 166

Ways to Communicate   168
Sample Parent Newsletter   170
Parents at Home   172
Parents at School   173
Parents in the Classroom   174
Parent Volunteer Considerations   175
Parent Volunteer Form   176
Parent Volunteer Planner (Volunteer)   177
Parent Volunteer Sign-In Sheet   178
Parent Volunteer Certificate of Recognition   179
Parent Nights   180
Parent Night Workshop Planner   181
Parent Night Workshop Agenda   182
Parent Night Workshop Sign-Up Sheet   183
Parent Night Workshop Tickets   184
Parent Night Themes   185
Homework Passes   189

15
Incentive Programs 190

Incentive Program Survey   192
Incentive Program Planner   193
Sample Incentive Program Planner   194
Behaviors and Rewards   195
Rewards and Incentives   196
Incentive Tickets   197
Student Recognition (Student of the Week)   198
Movie Day   200
Sports Day or Activity Day   202
Jobs and Responsibilities   204
Incentive Program Notification   206
Incentive Program Roster   207
Incentive Program Student Tracker   208
Certificate of Recognition   209
Sports Day/Activity Day Instructor Sign-Up Sheet   210
Sports Day/Activity Day Student Sign-Up Sheet   211

© The McGraw-Hill Companies, Inc.

16
Fund-raising 212

Fund-raising Survey 213
Fund-raising Checklist 214
Advertising Your Fund-raiser 215
School Fund-raiser Planner 216
Sample School Fund-raiser Planner 217
Sale of Products 218
Flea Market 219
Walk-a-thon 220
Performance 222
Pancake Breakfast 223
Sock Hop 224
Collection Drive 225
Fund-raising Solicitation Letter 226
Fund-raising Resource Documents 227
Donation Receipt 228
Volunteer Sign-Up Sheet 229
Silent Auction Bid Sheet 230
Tickets 231
Volunteer Job Schedule 232
Certificate of Participation 233
Pledge Form 234

17
Grant Writing 235

Through the Eyes of the Funder 236
Grant-writing Tips 237
Components of a Grant Proposal 240
Grant-writing Resource Documents 242
Grant Survey 245
Grant Research Organizer 246
Grant Inventory Worksheet 247
Grant Application Worksheet 248
School Profile Organizer 249
Introduction/Overview Organizer 250
Needs Statement Worksheet 251
Goals Organizer 252
Methods and Design Organizer 253
Measurable Results Organizer 254
Budget Planner 255
Expenditure Tracker 256
Activity Tracker 257
Timeline Planner 258

© The McGraw-Hill Companies, Inc.

18
Preparing for a Formal Evaluation 259

Important Preparation Tips   259
7-Step Lesson Plan   260
Evaluation Lesson Checklist   261
Lesson Plan Labels   262
Lesson Plan Label Descriptions   263
Glossary of Terms Used in Lesson Plans   266
Teacher Evaluation Overview   271
Classroom Environment Checklist   272
Teacher Self-evaluation Checklist   273
Teacher Self-reflection   274
Teacher Responsibilities   275
Time Management   276
Daily Schedule and Daily Agenda   277
Homework   279
Small Group Instruction   280
Sample Lesson Plan: Auto-Bio-Poem   281
Sample Lesson Plan   284
Lesson Plan Template   286
Auto-Bio-Poem Format   288
Sample Auto-Bio-Poem   289

© The McGraw-Hill Companies, Inc.

Introduction

The Master Teacher is a resource for teachers who take on various out-of-the-classroom responsibilities and school-wide leadership roles. Why "Master" Teacher? Why not "Veteran," "Experienced," or "Seasoned" teacher? While all of those terms describe excellent teachers, the Master Teacher we refer to is the teacher who has a comprehensive approach—a global perspective that encompasses the classroom, the school, the community, and education as a lifelong journey. Master Teachers strive to grow in their craft and service.

A Master Teacher, then, for the purpose of this book, is a teacher who goes above and beyond the basic responsibilities and obligations of a classroom teacher. This may mean taking on one role beyond the classroom— or it may involve taking on many additional roles at one time. The Master Teacher is able to handle the challenges that come with additional roles and responsibilities.

The Master Teacher addresses responsibilities such as being a mentor teacher, leading staff developments, heading a committee, or serving as grade-level chair. Many of these roles bring great satisfaction. They empower the teacher and open the door for professional growth.

The Master Teacher covers the basics of organization and strategies by providing practical checklists and reproducibles. It is not only directed to those who are already Master Teachers, but it has practical tips for new and veteran teachers as well.

Wherever you are in your educational career, *The Master Teacher* will serve you well. In addition to providing an excellent overview of roles beyond the classroom, it is like an experienced teacher who gives good advice.

© The McGraw-Hill Companies, Inc.

The Evolution of the Master Teacher

Teachers grow and evolve, each one developing his or her own styles and strengths. Every teacher is different: Some establish a style relatively quickly, while others take longer. There is no one right way or absolute timeline for this. Below is a very loose timeline that represents the growth of a teacher. Keep in mind that it will vary from teacher to teacher.

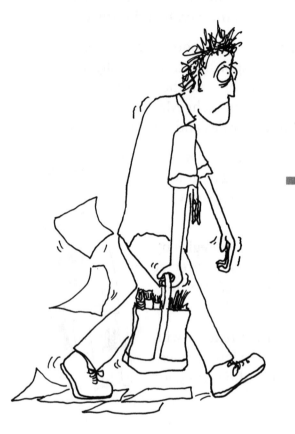 

First-year Teacher

• Learns the curriculum
• Establishes classroom management
• Learns school and district record keeping
• Develops lesson plans
• Gets to know staff

Second- and Third-year Teacher

• Expands curricular knowledge
• Improves classroom management
• Works with grade level

© The McGraw-Hill Companies, Inc.

Fourth-year and Beyond Teacher

- Comfortable with curriculum
- Established lesson planning
- Knows school and district procedures

Master Teacher

- Ready to move into roles beyond the classroom
- Involved in school
- Takes an active role
- Assumes leadership roles
- Presents at conferences and workshops

© The McGraw-Hill Companies, Inc.

The Master Teacher

Master Teachers take on many responsibilities and roles at the school site and within the educational community. They are often the leaders in their schools and districts. Some take on numerous roles, others may take on just a few. Whether you take on one or many additional roles, it is important to realize that going beyond classroom duties and responsibilities can provide a richer teaching experience, creating new knowledge and skills and keeping teaching exciting.

Mentoring
- Guiding new teachers
- Goal setting
- Planning
- Classroom management

Formal Evaluations
- Planning lessons
- Goals
- Environment

Conferences
- Selecting conferences
- Organizing information

Student Teachers
- Modeling lessons
- Modeling classroom management
- Assisting in planning and implementation

Collaboration and Working Together
- Grade-level chairperson
- Departmental chairperson
- Leading
- Decision-making

Fund-raising
- Organizing fund-raisers
- Community solicitation
- Implementation

Presenting
- Presenting at conferences or workshops
- Planning presentations

Higher Degrees
- Pursuing expertise in a specific area of education

Professional Development
- Leading and organizing district trainings and staff developments

Grant Writing
- Finding grants and writing grant proposals
- Implementing grants

Parent Involvement
- Creating programs that increase parent involvement
- Creating parent programs and classes

Time Management
- Developing grade-level or school schedules

Professional Portfolio
- Systematically building portfolio

Incentive Programs
- Targeting needs
- Creating school-wide incentive programs

After-school Programs
- Planning and organizing an after-school program
- Leading implementation of a program

Parent Nights
- Organizing a Parent Night

© The McGraw-Hill Companies, Inc.

I

Personal Development Goals

1 Attending Professional Development Conferences 3

2 Presenting at Conferences 15

3 Conferences to Choose From 23

4 Pursuing Higher Education (and Getting Your Paperwork Together!) 39

5 Professional Programs to Explore 46

Attending Professional Development Conferences

As a teacher—especially a master teacher—you have no doubt attended many professional development meetings for your school district. Perhaps you have National Board Certification or a graduate degree by now. However, no matter how much experience you have as a teacher, it is important to remember that professional growth for a master teacher is ongoing.

You can continue to build your professional skills by belonging to a nationally recognized education organization or attending—and even presenting at—national professional development conferences. Not only will this help you develop new skills, but it will enhance what you are already doing as you read about, listen to, participate in, or lead workshops of interest. Attendance at a conference may also earn you credit units required for renewing credentials or advancing on the salary scale.

The section that follows includes information about many national professional education organizations and conferences. Because information in this area is continually changing, it is important to keep up-to-date by searching the Internet or otherwise actively seeking out additional organizations and conferences. Networking with other teachers, administrators, parents of school-age children, authors, and researchers is a great way to help you stay current in the field, help build your curriculum repertoire, and give you ideas that will help you maintain an exciting, active classroom.

At least one national organization or professional development conference for each curricular area has been included here, as well as others of more general interest. Remember to find out about regional conferences, too, so that you can attend conferences held closer to where you live and work. The website information included in this book for each organization or conference is accurate as of the date of publication.

© The McGraw-Hill Companies, Inc.

Types of Professional Development Education Conferences

There are many conference opportunities worldwide. Here we present a selection of conferences hosted annually by well-known professional education organizations in the United States. To find other conference opportunities in your area of interest, network with other teachers from your area, read union and teacher publications, and search the Internet.

Specific information about each of these conferences, which can be easily reproduced for fellow teachers, is found in Chapter 3.

Math

Math conferences provide an excellent opportunity to learn the newest teaching methodologies. They may also offer an opportunity to learn more about hands-on approaches using manipulatives, games, and even technology. Vendors may be on hand with books, software, and other math-related resources.

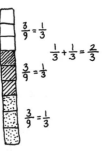

National Council of Teachers of Mathematics (NCTM): http://www.nctm.org

National Council of Supervisors of Mathematics (NCSM): http://ncsmonline.org

Reading

Reading conferences may cover everything from phonics and primary reading instruction to comprehension and vocabulary development. These conferences typically attract teachers and other professionals who are experts in the field.

Participants can learn the latest methodology and theory of reading instruction, as well as practical applications. Vendors are often on hand with teacher resource materials and even the newest children's books. In addition, you will have an opportunity to learn about current research in the field and soon-to-be-published materials from the publishers of reading and language arts curricula.

National Reading Conference (NRC): http://www.nrconline.org

International Reading Association (IRA): http://www.reading.org

© The McGraw-Hill Companies, Inc.

Bilingual Education

Bilingual education conferences typically offer sessions or workshops in instructional methodologies and on facilitating the transition of students into mainstream English classes. They may also have sessions on managing a bilingual program or on the criteria for assessing a student's English language development (ELD) level. Because there are many different testing procedures and recordkeeping systems for bilingual programs, keeping up-to-date is important for coordinators, as well as for teachers and administrators. Conferences are a great place to network and to learn the very latest approaches to meeting the needs of the bilingual student. At larger conferences, vendors sell teacher resources and realia that support bilingual education.

National Association for Bilingual Education (NABE): http://www.nabe.org

National Council of Teachers of English (NCTE): http://www.ncte.org

California Association for Bilingual Education (CABE): http://www.bilingualeducation.org

Literacy

It is not usually considered important to include families at academic conferences; however, the National Conference on Family Literacy sponsored by the organization below is one that parents, as well as teachers, administrators, and researchers, will find beneficial. It is important for families, parents, and caretakers to be aware of the current trends and ideas in literacy and to be involved in their child's learning. Literacy conferences showcase new and interesting materials, strategies, and research.

National Center for Family Literacy: http://www.famlit.org/conference

© The McGraw-Hill Companies, Inc.

Technology

Technology conferences focus on making technology a bigger part of today's twenty-first-century classrooms. The conference listed below is appropriate for K–12 teachers and college professors as well as for teacher education candidates. Research, new software, and connections between curriculum and technology are introduced and presented. Because today's competitive global academic environment is at the forefront for educators, parents, and administrators, conferences such as this one are critical to making sure that all learners are exposed to the newest strategies and materials.

International Society for Technology in Education (ISTE): http://www.iste.org

Science

Science instruction at both the K–12 level and the college level is recognized as one of the most important subject areas in our world today. Science conferences introduce cutting-edge techniques, updated curricula, hands-on learning tools, and current research. They are appropriate for teacher education candidates, teachers, and college professors.

School Science and Mathematics Association (SSMA): http://www.ssma.org

National Association for Research in Science Teaching (NARST): http://www.narst.org

Social Studies

Social studies conferences present interesting ideas about how to approach this subject area in ways that keep the students actively engaged in learning. Teachers, administrators, paraprofessionals, and teacher aides who attend can find strategies and new ideas to enhance current curricula, and can work together to align them to district standards. Sessions may demonstrate best teaching practices, introduce the latest technology, or demonstrate how to incorporate fiction and nonfiction books into history lessons. Vendors often attend with the latest books and teacher resources to enhance social studies instruction.

National Council for the Social Studies (NCSS): http://www.ncss.org

© The McGraw-Hill Companies, Inc.

Special Education

Special education conferences provide opportunities to learn about specific educational topics through a series of sessions based on multiple strands such as the Division for Research, Division for Early Childhood, Division for Learning Disabilities, Division on Visual Impairments, The Association for the Gifted, and Teacher Education Division, among others. Internationally recognized experts in special and general education and related disciplines are invited, and they often serve as keynote speakers, addressing the most current, research-based information on topics of interest. Remember to check out the exhibit area for new curriculum ideas, children's literature, and an opportunity to meet some of the keynote speakers in person.

Council for Exceptional Children (CEC): http://www.cec.sped.org

General Education

There are many conferences that focus on a variety of education issues—math, reading, writing, technology, science, social studies, special education, character and moral education, best practices, new curriculum ideas, utilizing outdoor learning environments, higher education, children's literature, and much more. The general education conferences open the door to all of these education areas and house them in one conference that is not specific to any curricular area in particular. These conferences are great places to network, deliver presentations, and learn from veterans in the field.

Hawaii International Conference on Education: http://www.hiceducation.org

Association for Moral Education (AME): http://www.amenetwork.org

© The McGraw-Hill Companies, Inc.

Conference Reminders

While not all of these organizations and conferences are meant for everyone, it is important to consider which of them fit your interests for professional growth. While it may be recommended that certain professionals in the field of education attend certain conferences, it doesn't mean that you can't attend if your job isn't mentioned; anyone can attend conferences of interest. Attending conferences will add to your current repertoire and will increase your experience.

Regional conferences may be more reasonable financially than national conferences because of reduced travel expenses and lower registration fees. Regional and state conferences are often held more than once a year, and the location typically varies. The most current information for regional conferences should be available online.

Presenting at conferences sometimes nets you a free day pass for the day you present. If you plan to present, you'll need to be aware of proposal guidelines and submit a proposal before the deadline. Consider asking another colleague to present with you; this can reduce the preparation time for each presenter and enhance each one's delivery of the presentation to the audience.

Sponsoring organizations may offer group rates if a number of people from one institution are attending. You should talk to your administrator at the beginning of

each year to find out if there is funding available for conference attendance and to ask about joining an organization relevant to your school's mission. It is important to plan your conference schedule early in the school year; fees are based on deadlines and typically increase for registration after a deadline or on the day the conference begins.

© The McGraw-Hill Companies, Inc.

Conference Checklist

Here is a list of considerations related to attending conferences. Information about many of these will be available on the conference website.

 ☐ *Complete conference registration and payment; be aware of deadlines.*

Registration is usually handled online, but may also be available by fax and/or mail.

 ☐ *Make hotel and car reservations, if necessary.*

Most conferences offer special arrangements for recommended hotels, airlines, and shuttle services. Make these plans early, because designated slots tend to fill up fast.

 ☐ *Preview sessions.*

A complete program, minus any last-minute changes, can usually be downloaded online or requested by mail. This gives you an opportunity to choose which sessions you'd like to attend, plan for lunch and/or dinner receptions, and learn about the exhibit participants.

 ☐ *Arrive early to sign-in and select sessions.*

On the day or evening before the conference's first full day, you can usually sign in, pick up your program to check the schedule for any changes, and pay any additional fees that may be required for such things as breakfast, luncheons, dinner receptions, etc.

 ☐ *Bring money for vendor purchases.*

Plan to bring additional money to conferences promoting large exhibit halls, because this is a great place to purchase new, innovative teacher and curricular resources, newly published texts, conference bags, and T-shirts.

© The McGraw-Hill Companies, Inc.

Conference Tools

The following pages will help you focus and organize your conference experience. Selecting appropriate conferences and keeping track of those you attend is important to maximize your conference experience.

Conference Planner *page 11*

With so many conferences, it is important to narrow your focus and align it with your professional goals. Use this planner to help you choose which conferences to attend. List the training you have had, and articulate your strengths and what your goals are. Knowing your strengths and future goals is important when selecting the appropriate conference. This page can be used individually or as part of a professional development.

Staff Conference Log *page 12*

A compiled list of conferences that staff members have attended in the past is a great resource and a very helpful way to network. Those who have attended past conferences can recommend specific conferences or presenters, which will save you a lot of time when you are deciding which conference(s) to attend. The list can be maintained and updated as staff members attend conferences throughout the year.

Personal Conference Log *page 13*

Keeping track of the conferences you have attended yourself is important. You should include this log in your professional portfolio. A conference log is an excellent way to document conferences attended, with specific information about each one. Some states may require this information for the renewal of credentials, which often requires a specific number of professional development hours.

Conference Notes Organizer *page 14*

A conference notes organizer provides a way to document each session you attend at a conference, including contact information for the presenter, so that you will have the information when you need it afterward. These sheets serve as further documentation for your professional development; you may be able to use them for documentation if you plan to receive Continuing Education Units from a sponsoring university (you will need to submit them to your district office).

© The McGraw-Hill Companies, Inc.

Conference Planner

Name	Date

Where have you been?
What training have you had? What conferences have you attended?

Where are you now?
What are your goals? (Write three short-term and three long-term goals.)

Short-term goals (1–12 months)   **Long-term goals** (1–5 years)

Interests and strengths
What do you enjoy teaching? What are your strengths? (Math, Reading, Writing, Grammar, Computer Technology, Science, Social Studies, Literature, Art, Music, Theatre Arts, Dance, Physical Education, Sports, Special Education, Bilingual Education, Self-esteem)

School goals and roles
What roles do you have at school? What is the current academic goal for your school site this year?

Where are you going?
What do you want to do? What conferences would meet your needs? (NOTE: Refer to the conferences attended resource sheet if you have already completed it.)

© The McGraw-Hill Companies, Inc.

Staff Conference Log

School _____

District _____

Group _____

Conference name	Attendee	Focus/ Audience	Dates	Location	Contact information

© The McGraw-Hill Companies, Inc.

Personal Conference Log

Professional education conferences
I have attended

Conference name	Location	Dates	Sessions/ Workshops	Presenter	Hours	Credits

© The McGraw-Hill Companies, Inc.

Conference Notes Organizer

Conference _____ Dates _____

Session or workshop title _____

Conference day _____ Time _____ Presenter _____

Notes

Contact information

Phone _____

E-mail _____

Website _____

Address _____

_____

Related resources mentioned (books, websites, etc.)

Session or workshop title _____

Conference day _____ Time _____ Presenter _____

Notes

Contact information

Phone _____

E-mail _____

Website _____

Address _____

_____

Related resources mentioned (books, websites, etc.)

© The McGraw-Hill Companies, Inc.

2

Presenting at Conferences

Preparing a Conference Presentation Proposal

Consider It

At the beginning of the school year, determine your top professional learning goals for the year. You might consider, for example, developing technology skills, incorporating moral and character education into the curriculum, meeting the needs of students with special needs, or utilizing math manipulatives in the classroom. Then plan to attend one or more conferences that will further these goals.

During the first few days of the school year, when teachers come together for one or more days of professional development presentations, make a point to get together with other teachers who have professional interests similar to yours. Since you and some of your colleagues may be considering attending conferences, this is a good time to share your experiences with other teachers. Talk with them about the idea of presenting at a conference. After all, one of the most rewarding parts of attending a conference is presenting a workshop of your own. However, because presenting at a conference for the first time can be intimidating, some of you might choose to do this together. If you are working on a higher education degree, consider asking one of your professors to present with you, because it's likely that he or she has a good deal of experience presenting and could also help with the proposal submission.

Plan It

Spend some time researching conferences of interest. Once you have found them, pay close attention to the conference titles for the year, because the title gives you a clear picture of that conference's theme. If you and your colleagues have an idea about teaching practices or curriculum that fits a conference theme, you are ready to write your proposal. Make sure your idea is feasible: Can you conduct your session in the allotted time? Can you transport what you need? Is the necessary equipment available?

15

© The McGraw-Hill Companies, Inc.

Propose It

You will want to review the conference proposal guidelines. The guidelines not only explain all the requirements for submission, but also spell out the discipline strands so that you can choose more specifically which workshop or session topic you'd like to present.

Submit It

You will want to do this right at the beginning of the year, because many submission deadlines occur between July and November for a conference date six months later. If your school year begins in July, you will want to do this right away for a conference date of February or March. If your school year starts in September, you may not have enough time to submit a proposal for that academic year, and you may actually find yourself planning for the following year.

Most conference websites ask you to apply and submit materials online, but many offer you the option to submit them by mail or fax. If you plan to mail them, pay very close attention to the deadline. If materials are not received prior to the deadline, there is a chance that your submission won't even be opened. Online or fax submission is best.

When you are ready to submit your conference proposal, you may also choose to register for the conference itself. If you are selected as a presenter, you may not have to pay the registration fee for the day you present. This could save you a significant amount of money, especially if you are only planning to attend on the day you present. Otherwise, if you plan to attend the entire conference (highly recommended), this is a good time to register.

Be sure to look at the registration form for specifics, since conference registration fees typically increase after the "early registration" deadline. When registering, also consider whether your school will pay for or reimburse fees; *always* ask if this is a possibility. Your principal may be more likely to allocate funds if a group rate will allow sending four or five teachers. If you are currently a student working on an advanced degree or if you are taking courses related to the field of education, you could register as a student and pay reduced registration fees. If you know you will be able to attend on only one day, you can save money by registering at the one-day rate.

16

© The McGraw-Hill Companies, Inc.

Presentation Proposal Resource Sheet

The following presentation proposal resource sheet shows the information that is typically required on an application form for a potential conference presenter. Some proposal applications may ask for more information and some may ask for less, but it's a good idea to have this information ready. Fill out this resource sheet and save it so it can be re-used for other conferences.

Primary presenter

Sponsoring organization member ☐ Yes ☐ No

Name _____ Title _____

District/Organization/Agency _____

Type of agency ☐ School ☐ District ☐ County ☐ University

Home address _____ Home phone _____

Work phone _____ Fax _____ E-mail _____

Secondary presenter

Sponsoring organization member ☐ Yes ☐ No

Name _____ Title _____

District/Organization/Agency _____

Type of agency ☐ School ☐ District ☐ County ☐ University

Home address _____ Home phone _____

Work phone _____ Fax _____ E-mail _____

Title of presentation _____
Short, simple, "catchy"—Let the audience know what the presentation is about, for example, "Hands-on Elementary Math," "Read It, Write It!", "Classroom Reactions, a Hands-on Approach to Physical Science," etc.

Strand choice _____
You may be asked to choose a specific discipline, or strand. Conference organizers use this information to schedule workshops of similar interest throughout the conference rather than at the same time. This allows multiple opportunities for conference attendees to participate in workshops of interest. The following strands are examples of typical teacher education conferences.

Administration and Leadership	Early Childhood Education	Research
Anti-Bias Curriculum	English Language Development	Special Needs Education
Assessment and Evaluation	Health Education	Technology
Children's Literature	Parent and Community Involvement	Teacher Preparation
Curriculum	Para-Educators	… and many others
Cooperative Learning	Policy Making	

© The McGraw-Hill Companies, Inc.

Language of presentation

☐ English ☐ Other language (please specify) _____

Type of presentation

Consider conference guidelines, materials, set-up, environment, transport, number in attendance, time, and audience. Practice full presentation for timing and practicality.

☐ Demonstration   ☐ Hands-on workshop
☐ Lecture   ☐ Research
☐ Panel discussion ☐ _____
☐ Group interaction

Grade level

☐ Preschool   ☐ 9–12
☐ K–2   ☐ Adult education
☐ 3–5   ☐ College
☐ 6–8   ☐ All levels
☐ K–8

Intended audience

☐ Administrators   ☐ Teachers   ☐ Researchers
☐ Policy makers   ☐ Para-educators ☐ All
☐ Professors   ☐ Support staff
☐ Parents   ☐ Librarians

Level of audience

☐ New to field   ☐ Experienced   ☐ Both

Room set-up requested

☐ Theatre style (chairs only)
☐ Banquet style (round tables)
☐ Classroom style (rectangular or square tables)

Scheduling

These are the days I **cannot** present my workshop/session:

☐ Monday ☐ Tuesday ☐ Wednesday ☐ Thursday ☐ Friday ☐ Saturday ☐ Sunday

Technology

☐ My workshop/session requires having a computer with Internet access.
☐ I need an overhead projector.
☐ I need a VCR/DVD player.
☐ I need _____.

Presentation time preference

☐ 90 minutes   ☐ 3 hours
☐ 2 hours   ☐ _____

© The McGraw-Hill Companies, Inc.

Please provide a brief description of your presentation.
This should be to the point, explaining the purpose of your presentation. Describe what you plan to accomplish. What do you want the attendees to take away with them? What new and interesting tools or ideas do you think the attendees will learn from you? You may also want to mention the theme of the conference.

Please explain how the proposed presentation is aligned with or promotes the conference vision.
Review the conference title. What is the theme for the year? How do you see your presentation fitting into that theme? Be clear about how your presentation will meet the goals of the conference.

Finally, you will upload your research paper if you are submitting to a research conference.

Research title _____

Other documents specific to the session or presentation (agendas, end evaluations, handouts, etc.)

© The McGraw-Hill Companies, Inc.

Presentation Checklist

Now that your proposal has been accepted and you have been given a time slot on the conference schedule, you need to start planning your presentation. Use the following checklist to organize your presentation.

☐ **Send notification of your acceptance to attend and present at the conference.**

You will receive the news by e-mail, phone, or mail. The name, phone number, and e-mail address of that year's contact person will be sent to you. Don't forget to let them know whether you will or will not be able to present, and confirm your technology needs with the contact person as well.

☐ **Register.**

If you haven't done so already and were waiting to see if you were accepted, you should now register yourself and any colleagues attending the conference with you. You will find specific information about this on the website.

☐ **Make travel arrangements.**

If you will be flying to the conference location or need to reserve a hotel room, make these arrangements sooner rather than later. Go to the conference website to see if there are any discounts for travel before you book it yourself. This is a good way to save money, especially if you can share a room or rental car with those traveling with you.

☐ **Review your proposal.**

It's been a while since you submitted it, so re-familiarize yourself with your original idea and make any subtle changes. Be careful not to make too many changes, since you were accepted based on what you submitted.

☐ **Materials.**

One to two weeks before your presentation, pull together all necessary materials (for example, handouts, books, business cards) and make enough copies to hand out to your audience.

☐ **Presentation.**

Create your PowerPoint presentation or overhead transparencies. Be sure to make at least 20–25 copies to share with those who attend your presentation. If more than that attend, you can always request e-mail addresses and send materials out later.

☐ **Attire.**

Choose your presentation attire in advance. It would be appropriate to wear something that could be worn for a job interview but is still comfortable. You need to be able to "work the crowd" and move around, yet still appear professional.

© The McGraw-Hill Companies, Inc.

Agenda

It's important to create an agenda for your presentation. This is a good way to organize your time, and it also gives the audience a "heads-up" about what they will find in your presentation. Typically, presentations last for 90 minutes to 3 hours. Your preference for the length of your presentation is usually included in the presentation proposal. It is highly recommended that you choose a 90-minute time block for your first few presentations. Agendas vary depending on the length and content of the presentation. Below is a basic agenda resource sheet that can be used as a guide. When you attend other conference sessions, you will no doubt get additional ideas for future presentations and agendas.

Agenda Resource Sheet

1 · Ice breaker (10–15 minutes)
The ice breaker should be related to your presentation. It can be as simple as sharing something like a relevant comic, a short "Dear Abby" column, or a picture book. The point of the ice breaker to set the stage for your presentation and get the audience thinking about your topic. (See more suggestions for ice breakers in Chapter 8.)

2 · Review of your focus/purpose/goal (5–10 minutes)
You might hand out a piece of paper with your focus/purpose/goal written at the top and room for note taking at the bottom.

3 · Presentation (15–20 minutes)
PowerPoint presentation or overhead presentation.

4 · Activity (20–25 minutes)
Demonstration, hands-on interactive collaboration in groups, whole group contribution after small group discussions, etc.

5 · Q & A (20–30 minutes)
Depending on how much time you have left, this is a good time for whole group sharing and reflections or questions and answers. Always allow enough time for your participants to get to the next workshop or session.

A Few Things to Keep in Mind

1. On the chance that your agenda might not work as anticipated when you are presenting, make decisions prior to presentation day about quick adjustments you would be willing to make if you needed to eliminate elements. Also, have two or three additional elements ready to add in case your presentation goes too quickly.

2. If a colleague who is scheduled to present with you can't make it, decide whether or not you can present by yourself. If you decide you need to withdraw as a conference presenter, let the conference contact person know right away so the reserved room can be used for someone else or another proposal can be substituted for yours.

3. Read your audience. If they are ready to move on, move on. If they seem to be asking several clarification questions, slow down and review with them what you have done so far.

© The McGraw-Hill Companies, Inc.

Presentation Day Checklist

Highlight all items that apply to your presentation, including any that you have added to the ones listed here. The day of your presentation, check off items as you verify that you have them.

Conference title _____ Contact _____

Conference address _____ Phone _____

_____ Fax _____

General items and materials

- ☐ Business cards
- ☐ Resource books
- ☐ Handouts
- ☐ Laser pointer
- ☐ Tape
- ☐ Chart paper
- ☐ Posters
- ☐ Markers
- ☐ Tissues

- ☐ Water
- ☐ Pens
- ☐ Scissors
- ☐ Activity supplies
- ☐ Prizes (candy, stickers, teacher materials, etc.)
- ☐ Post-its
- ☐ _____
- ☐ _____
- ☐ _____

Activity supplies

- ☐ Construction paper (for example)
- ☐ _____
- ☐ _____
- ☐ _____

- ☐ _____
- ☐ _____
- ☐ _____
- ☐ _____

Presentation essentials

- ☐ PowerPoint presentation
- ☐ Overheads
- ☐ CDs/DVDs
- ☐ Flash drive
- ☐ Video
- ☐ _____
- ☐ _____

Equipment

- ☐ Camera
- ☐ Video recorder
- ☐ Laptop
- ☐ Projector
- ☐ VCR/DVD player
- ☐ T.V.
- ☐ _____
- ☐ _____

© The McGraw-Hill Companies, Inc.

3

Conferences to Choose From

The following pages provide detailed information on conferences of the following organizations.

National Council of Teachers of Mathematics (NCTM) *page 24*

National Council of Supervisors of Mathematics (NCSM) *page 25*

National Reading Conference (NRC) *page 26*

International Reading Association (IRA) *page 27*

National Association for Bilingual Education (NABE) *page 28*

National Council of Teachers of English (NCTE) *page 29*

California Association for Bilingual Education (CABE) *page 30*

National Center for Family Literacy (NCFL) *page 31*

International Society for Technology in Education (ISTE) *page 32*

School Science and Mathematics Association (SSMA) *page 33*

National Association for Research in Science Teaching (NARST) *page 34*

National Council for the Social Studies (NCSS) *page 35*

Council for Exceptional Children (CEC) *page 36*

Hawaii International Conference on Education *page 37*

Association for Moral Education (AME) *page 38*

© The McGraw-Hill Companies, Inc.

National Council of Teachers of Mathematics (NCTM)

Conference focus

Math workshops, math books, math resources, math manipulatives, and math technology.

Who should attend?

Teachers
Teacher assistants
Teacher education candidates
Parents
Math coaches/coordinators

Conference description

This conference is the perfect venue for those interested in mathematics. It typically includes over 300 presentations with workshops led by math teachers or others who have background and expertise in mathematics. You will participate in interactive sessions and Q&A sessions, and math products and texts will be available for purchase. Every discipline, grade level, and teaching focus is addressed at the annual conference, with most of the same material covered on a smaller scale at the regional conferences.

Exhibitions

View mathematics education books, teaching resources, games, manipulatives, and technology and services. You will get fresh ideas, valuable information and resources, and see demonstrations of how products work.

Presentation opportunities

Submit proposal online.

Proposal deadline

About six months before the conference date, but could be earlier. Check website for details.

Dates

Annual conference	April
Regional conferences	October and November

Location

April 22–25, 2009	Washington, DC
April 21–24, 2010	San Diego, CA
April 13–16, 2011	Indianapolis, IN
April 25–28, 2012	Miami, FL
April 17–20, 2013	Denver, CO
April 9–12, 2014	New Orleans, LA
April 15–18, 2015	Boston, MA
April 14–16, 2016	San Francisco, CA

Accommodations

Check the website for recommended hotels and local airports, as well as a variety of rental car services, public transportation information, and shuttle and taxi services. You will also find travel discount codes should there be any.

Approximate costs

Member	$225
Non-member	300
Attendee	150
Presenter	160
Exhibitor	75
Student	100–150

Contact

Address	National Council of Teachers of Mathematics 1906 Association Dr. Reston, VA 20191-1502
Phone	972-349-7476 (International) 888-241-8406 (Domestic)
Fax	972-349-7715
Website	http://www.nctm.org
E-mail	See website.

© The McGraw-Hill Companies, Inc.

National Council of Supervisors of Mathematics (NCSM)

Conference focus

Hear about current research from some of the leaders in the field of mathematics at lectures by keynote speakers and major session leaders. Attend special interest group meetings and view sponsor displays.

Who should attend?

Teachers
Teacher education candidates
Math professors
Math coaches/coordinators

Conference description

Organizations and conferences such as this one provide support for leaders in mathematics education. There is an enormous need today for math teachers who can provide instruction of math curriculum that is aligned to the standards. Many districts have put in place large numbers of math coaches to serve as math support staff, in addition to lead teachers in mathematics. Teachers attending this conference will hear about a variety of perspectives, learn about best practices, examine research and trends in mathematics education, and have an opportunity to talk with each other about what their school sites, teacher education programs, and districts are doing to encourage math learning and instruction.

Exhibitions

View mathematics education books, teaching resources, games, manipulatives, and technology and services. You will get fresh ideas, valuable information and resources, and see demonstrations of how products work.

Presentation opportunities

Submit proposal online.

Proposal deadline

About six months before the conference date, but could be earlier. Check website for details.

Dates

Annual conference   April
Regional conferences   October and November

Location

Changes annually. Check website for details.

Accommodations

Check the website for recommended hotels and local airports, as well as a variety of rental car services, public transportation information, and shuttle and taxi services. You will also find travel discount codes should there be any.

Approximate costs

Member	$175
Non-member	275
Member, one day	90
Non-member, one day	105

Contact

Address	NCSM Member and Conference Services
	6000 East Evans Ave #3-205
	Denver, CO 80222
Phone	303-758-9611
Fax	303-758-9616
Website	http://ncsmonline.org
E-mail	ncsm@mathforum.org

© The McGraw-Hill Companies, Inc.

National Reading Conference (NRC)

Conference focus

The conference focuses on current results in classrooms across the country with regard to reading and literacy development. It includes keynote speakers, research paper sessions, lectures on research of current trends and issues in regard to literacy, and special session formats.

Who should attend?

Elementary/Secondary teachers
Administrators
Professors
Policy makers
Literacy coaches/coordinators

Conference description

The NRC is for individuals who share an interest in literacy and literacy instruction. Attendees will listen to keynote speakers, visit paper sessions, attend lectures on research of current trends and issues that pertain to literacy, and be exposed to other session formats. In addition to attending the annual conference, educators might consider ordering the NRC quarterly journal, the Journal of Literacy Research (JLR), and the NRC Yearbook, which offers papers of previous presenters. These publications help new and veteran teachers continue learning from one another through print.

Exhibitions

See website for updated information.

Presentation opportunities

Submit proposal online.

Proposal deadline

About six months before the conference date.
Check the website or call for details.

Dates

Annual conference   First week of December

Location

Throughout the United States.

Dec. 2–5, 2009   Albuquerque, NM

The 2008 conference was held in Orlando, FL.

Accommodations

Check the website for recommended hotels and local airports, as well as a variety of rental car services, public transportation information, and shuttle and taxi services. You will also find travel discount codes should there be any.

Approximate costs

Member	$200–275
Non-member	230–300
Graduate student	100–120
One-day rate	125–175

Contact

Address	National Reading Conference
	7044 S. 13th Street
	Oak Creek, WI 53154
Phone	414-908-4924
Fax	414-908-4924
Website	http://www.nrconline.org
E-mail	customercare@nrconline.org

© The McGraw-Hill Companies, Inc.

International Reading Association (IRA)

Conference focus

Literacy research, theory, and instructional practice from early literacy instruction to teacher preparation.

Who should attend?

K–16 teachers
Researchers
Students
Parents
Literacy coaches/coordinators
Tutors

Conference description

At this conference, researchers and practitioners share information about current studies in the field of teaching reading through best practices. Conferences also feature leaders in the field on today's hottest literacy topics.

Exhibitions

This annual conference has more than 1,000 exhibits where educators can find out about the latest resources for reading professionals.

Presentation opportunities

Submit proposal online.

Proposal deadline

About 9 to 11 months before conference date. Check the website for details.

Dates

Annual conference	Usually in May
Regional conferences	October, November, and December

Location

Throughout the United States.

February 21–25, 2009	Phoenix, AZ
May 3–7, 2009	Minneapolis, MN
May 2–6, 2010	Los Angeles, CA
May 8–12, 2011	Orlando, FL
April 29–May 3, 2012	Chicago, IL
May 5–9, 2013	Anaheim, CA

Accommodations

Check the website for recommended hotels and local airports, as well as a variety of rental car services, public transportation information, and shuttle and taxi services. You will also find travel discount codes should there be any.

Approximate costs

Member	$ 275–385
Non-member	385–465
One-day rate	110–215
Exhibitor	1,465–1,515
Student	125–175

Contact

Address	International Reading Association Headquarters Office 800 Barkside Road PO Box 8139 Newark, DE 19714-8139
Phone	800-336-7323 302-731-1600
Fax	302-737-0878
Website	http://www.reading.org/
E-mail	customerservice@reading.org

© The McGraw-Hill Companies, Inc.

National Association for Bilingual Education (NABE)

Conference focus

This annual conference explores topics of interest to teachers, administrators, and parents, such as second language acquisition, bilingual education, assessment and accountability, teacher training, and special education.

Who should attend?

Teachers
Teacher assistants
Teacher education candidates
Parents
Consultants
Administrators
Professors

Conference description

This conference represents both English language learners and bilingual education professionals. This organization proudly represents more than 20,000 bilingual and English as a Second Language (ESL) teachers, administrators, paraprofessionals, university professors and students, researchers, advocates, policymakers, and parents.

Exhibitions

Textbook publishers, children's books and authors, job fairs, non-profit organizations, commercial exhibitors.

Presentation opportunities

Submit proposal online.

Proposal deadline

About six months before the conference date. Check the website for details.

Dates

Annual conference   February

Location

Throughout the United States.

February 18–21, 2009   Austin, TX
February 3–6, 2010   Denver, CO

Accommodations

Check the website for recommended hotels and local airports, as well as a variety of rental car services, public transportation information, and shuttle and taxi services. You will also find travel discount codes should there be any.

Approximate costs

Member	$ 250–350
Non-member	325–425
Member, one day	115–165
Non-member, one day	180–230
Commercial exhibitor	1,250
Non-profit exhibitor	850
Job fair employer	650

Contact

Address	National Association for Bilingual Education
	1313 L. Street NW, Suite 210
	Washington, DC 20005
Phone	202-898-1829
Fax	202-789-2866
Website	http://www.nabe.org
E-mail	nabe@nabe.org

© The McGraw-Hill Companies, Inc.

National Council of Teachers of English (NCTE)

Conference focus

This annual conference's goal is to improving the teaching and learning of English and the language arts at all levels of education.

Who should attend?

Teachers
Teacher assistants
Teacher education candidates
Parents
Consultants
Administrators
Professors

Conference description

This conference offers opportunities for teachers to continue their professional development and provides a framework for understanding concepts that affect the teaching of English. At the annual conference, K–12 teachers, college faculty, administrators, and other educational professionals gather to hear award-winning speakers, attend relevant sessions, share best practices, and hear about the latest teaching materials.

Continuing Education Credits: One unit possible through UC San Diego. See the website for more information.

Exhibitions

With more than 300 display booths, you will have the opportunity to preview textbooks and instructional materials. There will be more than 160 publishers and distributors of educational and professional materials displaying their latest products.

Presentation opportunities

Submit proposal online.

Proposal deadline

About six months before conference date. Check website for details.

Dates

Annual conference   November

Location

Throughout the United States.

November 19–22, 2009   Philadelphia, PA
November 18–21, 2010   Orlando, FL
November 17–20, 2011   Chicago, IL

Accommodations

Check first with the Housing Bureau, but if they are full, check the website for recommended hotels and local airports, as well as a variety of rental car services, public transportation information, and shuttle and taxi services. You will also find travel discount codes should there be any.

Approximate costs

Member	$210–240
Non-member	275–305
Student member	90
Student non-member	100
One-day workshops, member	125
One-day workshops, non-member	150
One-day workshops, student	75

Breakfast, luncheon, and reception arrangements are also available for registration for additional fees.

Contact

Address	National Council of Teachers of English
	1111 W. Kenyon Road
	Urbana, IL 61801-1096
Phone	800-369-6283 ext. 3673
Fax	217-328-0977
Website	http://www.ncte.org

© The McGraw-Hill Companies, Inc.

California Association for Bilingual Education (CABE)

Conference focus

Students need to be academically prepared, multilingual, multi-culturally competent, technology and information literate, civic oriented, and prepared to be advocates for their communities in order to be productive members of a diverse society in the twenty-first century.

Who should attend?

K–12 teachers
Administrators
Parents
Teacher assistants
Professors
Adult educators

Conference description

This conference offers opportunities to learn to promote equity and educational achievement for students with diverse cultural, racial, and linguistic backgrounds. The variety of workshops, keynote speakers, and authors, plus the exhibit hall, is what makes this conference so successful. It's not just for teachers in California, but for any educator who is interested in tools and ideas to help develop language for those who find schooling and participation in our educational system and society difficult due to language needs.

Exhibitions

Display booths, offering a variety of texts to be previewed as well as instructional materials and resources. Exhibits of children's books, publishers, and distributors of educational and professional materials displaying their latest products.

Presentation opportunities

Submit proposal online.

Proposal deadline

About six months before conference date. Check website for details.

Dates

Annual conference   March

Location

San José, CA
Los Angeles, CA
Long Beach, CA

Accommodations

Check the website for recommended hotels and local airports, as well as a variety of rental car services, public transportation information, and shuttle and taxi services. You will also find travel discount codes should there be any.

Approximate costs

Member	$295–415
Non-member	395–515
Student/parent/TA (member)	160–279
Student/parent/TA (non-member)	175–285
One-day workshops (member)	160–190
One-day workshops (non-member)	215–245
One-day workshops (student/parent/TA)	100–120
One-day workshops (non-member (student/parent/TA))	115–135

Contact

Address	California Association for Bilingual Education
	16033 E. San Bernardino Road
	Covina, CA 91722
Phone	626-814-4441
Fax	626-814-4640
Website	http://www.bilingualeducation.org
E-mail	info@bilingualeducation.org

© The McGraw-Hill Companies, Inc.

National Center for Family Literacy (NCFL)

Conference focus

This annual conference explores topics of interest to teachers, administrators, and parents. Typical topics presented are second language acquisition, bilingual education, assessment and accountability, teacher training, and special education.

Who should attend?

Elementary teachers
Early childhood education (ECE) teachers
Policy makers
Practitioners
Librarians
Social workers
Professors

Conference description

The National Conference on Family Literacy is for those interested in strategies that work well for diverse family populations. Sessions include transformative practice, research, and policy as they relate to family literacy. Many of the sessions appeal to a culturally, racially, and ethnically diverse audience; often they encourage attendee participation. These sessions are relevant to literacy programs working with parents, children, and families. They also offer tangible strategies and resources to use in one's own programs and classrooms.

Continuing Education Units: Jefferson Community and Technical College, which is a fully accredited institution, will award units. See website for more details.

Exhibitions

The National Conference on Family Literacy features an exhibit area that showcases the best in educational resources for children, adults, and families.

Presentation opportunities

Submit proposal online.

Proposal deadline

About three to four months before the conference date.

Dates

Annual conference   End of March

Location

Throughout the United States.

The 2008 annual conference was held in Louisville, KY.

Accommodations

The website recommends hotels and local airports, as well as a variety of rental car services, public transportation information, and shuttle and taxi services. You will also find travel discounts.

Approximate costs

Early registration $385
Late registration   425

You also may attend pre-conference training sessions, family literacy institutes, and discussion luncheons for additional fees.

Contact

Address   National Center for Family Literacy
            325 West Main Street Suite 300
            Louisville, KY 40202

Phone   502-584-1133

Fax   502-212-4840

Website   www.famlit.org/conference

E-mail   conference@famlit.org

© The McGraw-Hill Companies, Inc.

International Society for Technology in Education (ISTE)

Conference focus

The International Society for Technology in Education is dedicated to professional development, advocacy, and leadership innovation.

Who should attend?

K–12 teachers
Teacher assistants
Graduate students
Administrators
Professors

Conference description

The conference shows how school leadership can be made more effective by showcasing the effective use of technology in PreK–12 and teacher education.

This conference is an opportunity for educators to find support as they look to transform education by including technology in their teaching, planning, assessments, and administrative responsibilities.

Continuing Education Units: CEUs are available for this conference. See website for specific details.

Exhibitions

The exhibit hall features well-known vendors displaying hardware, software, educational and technical publishing materials, and services emphasizing the use of computers by education professionals.

Presentation opportunities

Submit proposal online.

Proposal deadline

About six months before the conference date, but could be earlier. Check website for details.

Dates

Annual conference   June

Location

Throughout the United States.

The 2008 conference was held in San Antonio, TX.
The 2007 conference was held in Atlanta, GA.

Accommodations

Check the website for recommended hotels and local airports, as well as a variety of rental car services, public transportation information, and shuttle and taxi services. You will also find travel discounts here.

Approximate costs

Member	$205–255
Non-member	285–335
Student	125
One-day rate	135–175
Guest	75

Contact

Address	National Educational Computing Conference International Society for Technology in Education 1277 University of Oregon Eugene, OR 97403-1277
Phone	800-280-6218 (US and Canada) 541-346-3537 (International)
Fax	541-346-3545
Website	http://www.iste.org
E-mail	iste@iste.org

© The McGraw-Hill Companies, Inc.

School Science and Mathematics Association (SSMA)

Conference focus

Current science and mathematics ideas for integration across curricular areas led by keynote speakers and other professionals in the field.

Who should attend?

Science/Math teachers
Teacher education candidates
Administrators
Science/Math coaches/coordinators
Professors

Conference description

This conference is dedicated to the improvement of instruction at all levels in and between science and math, as well as other curricular areas, by providing leadership in the field. The conference goals usually include three strands: teacher education, research, and meeting the needs of K–16 teachers. Teacher education candidates and professors will be exposed to issues related to the preparation and enhancement of teachers; K–16 teaching ideas and activities are presented through hands-on experiences and through current research in the field.

Exhibitions

See website for updated information.

Presentation opportunities

Submit proposal online.

Proposal deadline

About six months before the conference date, but could be earlier. Check website for details.

Dates

Annual conference   Each fall (September–December)

Location

Throughout the United States.

The 2008 conference was held in Raleigh, NC.
The 2007 conference was held in Indianapolis, IN.

Accommodations

Check the website for online hotel reservations and local airport recommendations.

Approximate costs

Member	$100–235
Non-member	150–285
K–12 teacher	70–175
Full-time student	50–145

Contact

Address	School Science and Mathematics Association
	College of Education
	Oklahoma State University
	245 Willard
	Stillwater, OK 74078
Phone	405-744-7396
Fax	405-744-6290
Website	http://www.ssma.org
E-mail	office@ssma.org

© The McGraw-Hill Companies, Inc.

National Association for Research in Science Teaching (NARST)

Conference focus

Hear from some of the leaders in the field of science who are committed to ensuring that all learners—children and adults—have the opportunity to achieve science literacy.

Who should attend?

Science teachers
Teacher education candidates
Professors in the field of science

Conference description

The goals of this conference are to introduce multiple perspectives in approaching science teaching and learning. Researchers present their current studies, best practices, and cutting-edge instructional ideas. Policy makers are encouraged to promote and establish these transformative and innovative techniques as they plan for future science learning.

Exhibitions

See website for the individual year's exhibition announcements.

Presentation opportunities

Submit proposal online.

Proposal deadline

Six to nine months prior to the conference date is standard for proposal submission. Science teachers, researchers, and policy makers sharing best practices, current innovative research in the field, and upcoming policy changes are of most interest.

Dates

| Annual conference | March or April |
| Regional conferences | Held throughout the year. |

Check website for detailed information.

Location

Throughout the United States. The 2008 conference was held in Baltimore, MD. The April 2007 conference was held in New Orleans, LA.

Accommodations

Check the website for recommended hotels and local airports, as well as a variety of rental car services, public transportation information, and shuttle and taxi services. You will also find travel discount codes should there be any.

Approximate costs

Member	$200
Non-member	320
Student member	105
Student non-member	145
One-day rate	105

Contact

Address	National Association for Research in Science Teaching
	12100 Sunset Hills Road, Suite 130
	Reston, VA 20190-3221
Phone	703-234-4138
Fax	703-435-4390
Website	http://www.narst.org
E-mail	info@narst.org

© The McGraw-Hill Companies, Inc.

National Council for the Social Studies (NCSS)

Conference focus
To provide leadership, service, and support for all social studies educators.

Who should attend?
Elementary/Secondary social science teachers
Professors of history, geography, economics,
    political science, sociology, psychology,
    anthropology, and law-related education

Conference description
This conference covers the full range of social studies subjects at all grade levels. It focuses on the needs of elementary teachers, novice teachers, and urban educators. Also included are the perspectives of international educators. The conference offers more than 500 sessions, workshops, poster presentations, and clinics.

Exhibitions
This conference is the premier venue to discover products and services for your social studies students. You will find tools to implement new ideas and have an opportunity to meet with people ready to talk about education and the classroom. The exhibit area includes children's books, publishers, and authors.

Presentation opportunities
Submit proposal online.

Proposal deadline
About six months before the conference date, but could be earlier. Check website for details.

Dates
Annual conference	November or December
State and regional meetings	Offered throughout the year. Check the website for your closest meeting place.

Location
Throughout the United States.

November 13–15, 2009	Atlanta, GA
November 19–21, 2010	Denver, CO
December 2–4, 2011	Washington, DC
November 16–18, 2012	Seattle, WA

Accommodations
Check the website for recommended hotels and local airports, as well as a variety of rental car services, public transportation information, and shuttle and taxi services. You will also find travel discount codes should there be any.

Approximate costs
Member	$225
Member, one day	130
Student member	70
Non-member	300
Non-member, one day	175
Student non-member	85
Student non-member, one day	65

Contact
Address	National Council for the Social Studies 8555 Sixteenth Street Suite 500 Silver Spring, MD 20910
Phone	301-588-1800
Fax	301-588-2049
Website	http://www.ncss.org
E-mail	registration@ncss.org

© The McGraw-Hill Companies, Inc.

Council for Exceptional Children (CEC)

Conference focus

Examples of conference strands include but are not limited to Division for Research (DR), CEC Pioneers Division (PD), Division for Early Childhood (DEC), Division for Learning Disabilities (DLD), Division on Visual Impairments (DVI), The Association for the Gifted (TAG), and Teacher Education Division (TED).

Who should attend?

Special education teachers
Administrators
Parents
Special education teacher assistants
Resource specialists

Conference description

Participants will have the opportunity to engage in sessions related to specific educational topics through a series of conceptually and developmentally sequenced sessions based on multiple strands. Attendees may choose to attend all strand sessions or one or two sessions of a strand. Internationally recognized experts in special and general education and related disciplines will bring the most current, research-based information on topics of interest.

Continuing Education Units: When participants attend all sessions of a strand, they are eligible to earn CEUs.

Exhibitions

Exhibits are geared to those who work with exceptional children—students with disabilities and students with gifts and talents. Decision-makers from all areas of the special education field, including administrators, teachers, professors, researchers, and related service providers in the field, will be represented. The Career Center, located in the exhibit area, offers one of the most comprehensive placement services in the field of special education.

Presentation opportunities

Submit proposal online.

Proposal deadline

About six months before conference date. Check website for details.

Dates

Annual conference   April

Location

The 2008 conference was held in Boston, MA.

Accommodations

Check website for suggestions.

Approximate costs

Member	$277–327
Non-member	449–489
Student	157–207
Retired member	157–207
One-day rate	157–389

Contact

Address	Council for Exceptional Children
	1110 North Glebe Road, Suite 300
	Arlington, VA 22201
Phone	888-232-7733
TTY	866-915-5000
Fax	866-915-5000
Website	http://www.cec.sped.org
E-mail	See website.

© The McGraw-Hill Companies, Inc.

Hawaii International Conference on Education

Conference focus

This conference is held for academicians and professionals from education and related fields from all over the world to share best practices in a variety of education areas of interest.

Who should attend?

K–12 Teachers
Administrators
Parents
Teacher assistants
Professors
Teacher education candidates

Conference description

The main goal of the Hawaii International Conference on Education is to provide an opportunity for professionals from various education-related fields from all over the world to come together and learn from each other. It's also a place for education professionals with cross-disciplinary interests related to education to meet and interact with members inside and outside their own particular areas of interest and expertise.

Exhibitions

Several advertisers and exhibitors will be on site. Freebies, raffles, and opportunities to preview education materials will be available.

Presentation opportunities

Submit proposal online.

Proposal deadline

Four to six months before the conference date.

Dates

Annual conference   January

Location

Honolulu, HI

Accommodations

Check the website for recommended hotels and local airports, as well as a variety of rental car services, public transportation information, and shuttle and taxi services. You will also find travel discount codes should there be any.

Approximate costs

All participants and attendees $390–440

Breakfast and luau can be registered for at an additional cost.

Contact

Address	Hawaii International Conference on Education P.O. Box 75036 Honolulu, HI 96836
Phone	808-542-4931
Fax	808-947-2420
Website	http://www. hiceducation.org
E-mail	education@hiceducation.org

© The McGraw-Hill Companies, Inc.

Association for Moral Education (AME)

Conference focus

This conference is meant to offer a forum for professionals who fill positions in moral education. It also serves to foster discussion, training, and research in moral education for those in the field.

Who should attend?

K–12 teachers
Administrators
Researchers
Policy makers
Professors

Conference description

This organization is most concerned with supporting moral and character education in practice for the elementary, secondary, and college classroom. This is a gathering not only for teachers, but also for all those associated with these audiences in the field of education. Its main concern is the current educational practice that values the worth and dignity of each individual as a moral agent in the twenty-first century.

Exhibitions

Each year, a keynote speaker who is recognized for innovative and transformative research in the field of moral and character education delivers the Kohlberg Memorial Lecture.

Presentation opportunities

Submit proposal online.

Proposal deadline

About six months before conference date. Check website for details.

Dates

Annual conference   Varies from year to year.
                     Check website.

Location

Throughout the United States and internationally.

July 2–4, 2009   Utrecht, The Netherlands

The 2008 conference was held in Notre Dame, IN.
The 2007 conference was held at New York University
    in Greenwich Village, NY.
The 2006 conference was held in Fribourg, Switzerland.

Accommodations

Check the website for recommended hotels and local airports, as well as a variety of rental car services, public transportation information, and shuttle and taxi services. You will also find travel discount codes should there be any.

Approximate costs

All participants and attendees $125–200

Lunches and dinner receptions can be registered for at an additional cost.

Contact

Contact varies from year to year.

See website for current contact information.

Website   http://www.amenetwork.org

© The McGraw-Hill Companies, Inc.

Pursuing Higher Education (and Getting Your Paperwork Together!)

There may come a time in your teaching career when you decide to focus on professional advancement. There are many ways to do this. You can continue attending and presenting at professional conferences and leading professional developments and staff meetings at your school site, or you may be ready to take on a bigger challenge. Some of you may consider taking courses offered through the district to better enhance your personal teaching practice or expertise in a particular area, or to learn new things such as creating an inclusive environment or differentiating instruction effectively. You may decide that you're ready to begin work toward a master's degree, doctoral degree, or National Board Certification. In most cases, these efforts will lead to an increase in pay, which is an added bonus.

Only you can decide how much you should attempt to do. A good approach is to start out slowly and see how your students react to your energy level. If you and your students are doing well, you might decide to add another class the next quarter or you might choose to take an online class. But don't forget your responsibilities to your students—they come first. If you are tired from going to class at night or on weekends and have little energy left for your students, you're actually doing the opposite of what better teaching practices tell you to do! Start slowly, use time off to your advantage, and let your students see how excited you are about being a lifelong learner.

Before making a decision about any program, decide how much time you can invest per quarter, semester, or year, and then choose a program that fits this timeline. Be realistic—you need to avoid depleting both your finances and the time you have available for your students, your family, and yourself. This is also a good time to update your résumé. See how much you have done already, and try to envision where you would like to be in three to five years. Talk with your principal to find out if he or she has any recommendations about a specific program, about the benefit of choosing a degree versus certification, or about other issues related to your specific job in the school or district.

© The McGraw-Hill Companies, Inc.

Personal Inventory

Taking classes or working toward an advanced degree in order to grow professionally is a big responsibility. You should begin with an inventory of the different areas of your life and how important they are to you. This will help you to know if you have the time (or can make the necessary adjustments to create the time) needed for a new professional commitment. Remember, this won't take forever, but it could take a few years, and you need to be sure that you can give it the time and energy it needs while still maintaining an acceptable lifestyle for yourself. Use this form to inventory your commitments and responsibilities.

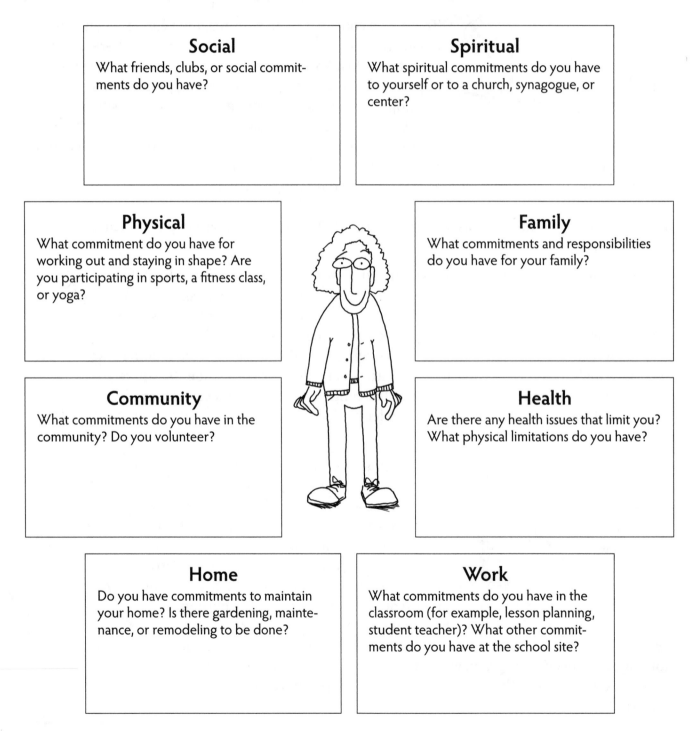

Social
What friends, clubs, or social commitments do you have?

Spiritual
What spiritual commitments do you have to yourself or to a church, synagogue, or center?

Physical
What commitment do you have for working out and staying in shape? Are you participating in sports, a fitness class, or yoga?

Family
What commitments and responsibilities do you have for your family?

Community
What commitments do you have in the community? Do you volunteer?

Health
Are there any health issues that limit you? What physical limitations do you have?

Home
Do you have commitments to maintain your home? Is there gardening, maintenance, or remodeling to be done?

Work
What commitments do you have in the classroom (for example, lesson planning, student teacher)? What other commitments do you have at the school site?

© The McGraw-Hill Companies, Inc.

Personal Goals

It is important to set goals and to establish a vision of where you want to be. Review that vision often; keeping this vision in mind will help you accomplish your goals. Establish three short-term goals, three mid-range goals, and three long-term goals (career intentions). Keep goals realistic and practical.

Short-term goals   What are my immediate and short-term (6 months to a year) goals?

1.

2.

3.

Mid-range goals   What are my mid-range (1 year to 3 years) goals?

1.

2.

3.

Long-term goals (career intentions)   Where would I ultimately like to see myself (beyond 3 years)?

1.

2.

3.

© The McGraw-Hill Companies, Inc.

Establishing Goals for Continuing Education

Be realistic in setting your goals, taking into account all outside responsibilities in your life. This checklist will help you focus; it can be changed at any time.

Who?

Name _____ Years of service _____

What?

I will …

☐ Take school site trainings/professional developments (PDs) (to enhance my craft and grow professionally)

☐ Take salary point classes (to grow professionally and receive salary points to move up the pay scale)

☐ Take university level classes (to grow professionally or to study an area of interest)

☐ Enter a master's program (to obtain a master's degree in an area of interest, possibly moving out of a classroom position)

☐ Enter an Ed.D. or Ph.D. program (to obtain a doctorate in a specific area of study)

How?

I will accomplish this by …

☐ Taking trainings, professional developments, or courses as available

☐ Taking _____ classes or courses per quarter

☐ Taking _____ classes or courses over the summer

☐ Enrolling in a university program and following their timeline

☐ Enrolling in an online program and taking _____ courses each quarter or semester

---

Why?	**When?**	**Where?**
☐ To enhance my teaching	☐ This quarter	☐ School site
☐ For a pay increase	☐ Next quarter	☐ Local district site or office
☐ For an advanced degree	☐ This summer	☐ University or college
☐ For a special interest	☐ Next year	☐ Online

© The McGraw-Hill Companies, Inc.

Personal Profile

As you apply to different programs, you will find that the applications require a lot of personal information. Tracking down this information can take time, but if you organize the information ahead of time, it will be much easier when you fill out the applications. Make copies of everything, and keep a file of any required documents.

Full name _____ Date of birth _____

Address

Street _____

City, State, Zip _____

Phone _____

Alternate phone _____

Fax _____

E-mail _____

School district

School _____

City, State, Zip _____

Phone _____

Fax _____

Education

☐ B.A.   ☐ B.S.   College/University _____
                                          Name   City, State   Month/Year graduated

                                 Major _____ Cumulative GPA _____

☐ M.A.   ☐ M.S.   College/University _____
                                          Name   City, State   Month/Year graduated

                                 Program _____

Qualifications/Credentials

Teaching credential   ☐ Current   ☐ Expired   Date _____

☐ _____ Preliminary   ☐ _____ Professional Clear
   State   State

☐ Other _____

Exams/Tests (Request copies of scores from required tests online at the testing websites.)

☐ GRE/MAT _____   ☐ MSAT _____   ☐ CSET _____
         Date   Date   Date

☐ PRAXIS _____   ☐ Single subject _____   ☐ SSAT _____
     Date   Date   Date

© The McGraw-Hill Companies, Inc.

Financial aid/Grant (Fill out contact information and gather necessary paperwork.)

Am I applying for financial aid? ☐ Yes ☐ No

Contact information Website _____

Phone _____ Fax _____

Documents I may need in applying

☐ Annual income ☐ Utility statements ☐ Address information (last ten years)

☐ Bank statements ☐ Tax returns ☐ Employment history

Transcripts (Official and sealed! Request copies from your institution of learning. NOTE: It may take a few weeks, so request early.)

_____	_____	_____
Institution	Dates attended	Date of Request
_____	_____	_____
Institution	Dates attended	Date of Request
_____	_____	_____
Institution	Dates attended	Date of Request

Letters of recommendation/References (at least 3 professional references—not family or friends)

_____	_____
Name	Title
_____	_____
Phone E-mail	Address
_____	_____
Name	Title
_____	_____
Phone E-mail	Address
_____	_____
Name	Title
_____	_____
Phone E-mail	Address

Work experience (List all work experience that relates to your field of study.)

Personal statement/Résumé (Check each item required.)

☐ Résumé (generally one page; includes personal information, education, work history, and professional experience)

☐ Letter of intent (a letter to the selection committee explaining why you want to attend)

☐ Personal statement (a personal document about yourself illustrating why you are a good candidate)

☐ _____ (other possible writing required by the program or institution)

© The McGraw-Hill Companies, Inc.

Tips from Experience

✔ Research program styles (face-to-face, on-line, hybrid).

✔ Research university programs (for example, private school education, multicultural and international education, curriculum and instruction, administration and leadership, technology education, bilingual education, special education).

✔ Apply early for admission. Some universities only accept a certain number of students per year.

✔ Apply to several programs. Some programs only accept a limited number of students.

✔ Apply for financial aid and possible scholarships at least a year in advance. Delaying can lead to missed opportunities.

✔ Speak with colleagues to find out how they managed their own professional program together with the workload at school.

✔ Plan your coursework schedule with a timeline that is realistic. Taking on too much or too little can create major stress as you try to finish your program in a timely manner. Be sure to take a realistic class load: Whether you're taking one class per session or more than that, don't overextend yourself. The goal is to finish, not burn out.

© The McGraw-Hill Companies, Inc.

5

Professional Programs to Explore

Salary Point Courses

In many districts, teachers are able to acquire the professional development points necessary for credential renewal and salary increases by attending courses offered within their district. The courses may include classroom management strategies, technology, and cultural diversity, or even a program that involves summer travel abroad with other teachers from the district. Upon completion of the course work, points are awarded that advance the teacher on the salary schedule. Every 12 to 15 points accumulated on the salary schedule merits a salary increase. Each year, teachers earn salary increases based on number of years in the classroom, but acquiring professional development points as well warrants a more significant increase. These professional development courses are also a great way to stay abreast of current curricular programs, assessment techniques, and changes in the field, in addition to earning more money. Attending professional development courses through the district is a good way to keep current in the field and network with other teachers while sharing best practices.

Salary Point Checklist

☐ Undergraduate degree

☐ Transcripts showing higher degree courses

☐ List of professional development courses taken and copies of any certificates earned to share with district office

☐ Proof of conferences attended and any continuing education units earned from attendance

© The McGraw-Hill Companies, Inc.

Salary Point Tracker

Document course work for salary points and credential renewal. (Keep all class receipts, documentation, syllabi, and agendas.)

Course/class title	Instructor	Provider	Start date	End date	Points	Emphasis/Focus

© The McGraw-Hill Companies, Inc.

Master's Degree

Why might you want to earn a master's degree? Earning an M.A. can help enhance current teaching practices and open the door to additional opportunities. A traditional M.A. program offers regular face-to-face courses. In today's fast-paced world, many universities offer online M.A. programs, while others offer a hybrid program in which some classes are taken online and others are taken face-to-face or "on ground."

Face-to-Face M.A. Program

The traditional M.A. program involves attending classes in a standard university setting. If you are still new to the classroom, you will most likely benefit from being in a setting with other new teachers and might choose an M.A. program where all or most of the classes are face-to-face.

Online M.A. Program

All course work is offered via the Internet in an online M.A. program. It usually involves discussion boards where students post responses to readings. Contact is maintained through online discussions and e-mail. All assignments are submitted online. If you have been teaching for ten or more years, you might find that an online program will meet your needs, because you already have extensive experience with curriculum, administrators, and subject matter.

Hybrid M.A. Program

For those teachers who are very busy—whether at your school site, at home, or with community commitments—but benefit from having opportunities to work with others while studying, a hybrid program might work best. When life is less busy, you might prefer to take classroom courses; other times might be better suited for online courses. This kind of program is a good compromise, providing multiple ways to take courses.

NOTE: It's really up to you to decide which program will work best for you. If you are not necessarily good at time management, you might need a more structured face-to-face program, but if you are a self-starter and technology savvy, you might opt for an online program.

Programs That Require Thesis vs. Comprehensive Exams

You will likely be required to either write a thesis or take comprehensive exams, depending on the program or institution of higher learning you've chosen. Whichever is required, it will be the culmination of your learning experience through the program.

Some programs allow you to choose which you would prefer—a thesis project or comprehensive exams. Comprehensive exams are structured to assess your knowledge of all the concepts you learned, all the theorists you studied, and all the practical applications you have been exposed to. If you organize information well and perform

© The McGraw-Hill Companies, Inc.

well on essay exams, this might be a good choice for you. For those who enjoy research and write well, a thesis might be a better choice. If you choose to write a thesis, you should select a topic early in your program. Knowing your topic early allows you to be doing research as you complete your course work, rather than beginning your research and writing only after your course work has been completed.

Fields of Study

Following are some possible areas of study. Most universities provide a wide range of choices in the field of education. Do your research and ask around for other ideas. You may even be able to work with a school to tailor a program specifically aligned to your goals.

Language Arts/Reading

An M.A. in Language Arts/Reading will prepare you for a position as a reading specialist teacher or a literacy coach. A review of programs at several universities across the nation shows that course work might include but is not limited to the following:

- Reading/Language Arts Assessment and Instruction for Classroom Teachers
- Principles and Practices of Teaching Writing
- Issues and Trends in Children's and Young Adult Literature
- The Use of Multicultural Children's and Young Adult Literature
- Emergent Literacy
- Developing English Reading/Language Arts Skills in Cross-Cultural Environments
- Reading/Language Arts Across the Curriculum

Math or Science

An M.A. in Math or Science will prepare you for a position as a coach or lead teacher in one of these curricular areas. A review of programs at several universities across the nation shows that course work might include but is not limited to the following:

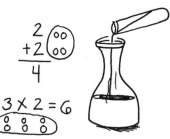

- Curriculum and Teaching of Mathematics
- Teaching Mathematics for Early Childhood
- Special Topics in Mathematics for Elementary Teachers: Metric Measurement, Problem Solving, Geometry, or Logic
- Math Assessment and Instruction for Mathematics
- Use of a Calculator in Teaching Mathematics
- Computer Applications for Teaching Mathematics

© The McGraw-Hill Companies, Inc.

Special Education

An M.A. in Special Education will prepare you to work with children with special needs or in an out-of-the-classroom position such as a resource specialist. Areas of focus could include speech therapy, reading specialist, one-on-one teacher, or special education coordinator. A review of programs at several universities across the nation shows that course work might include but is not limited to the following:

- Behavior Analysis in School, Home, and Agency Settings
- Behavior Interventions for Severe Behavior Problems
- Teaching Students with Moderate to Severe Disabilities
- Educating Individuals with Serious Emotional Disturbances
- Educating Students with Autism
- Teaching Functional Communication
- Foundations of Special Education
- Problems and Practices in Special Education

Technology

An M.A. in the area of Educational Technology will prepare you for a position such as a technology coordinator or a computer lab specialist. A review of programs at several universities across the nation shows that course work might include but is not limited to the following:

- Computer Systems in Education
- Survey of Instructional Media and Teaching
- Instructional Applications of Interactive Video
- Video Technology in Education
- Technology Leadership in Schools
- Internet and the World Wide Web in Education

Leadership

An M.A. in Educational Leadership will focus on leadership and organization, eventually leading to an Administrative Credential. A review of programs at several universities across the nation shows that course work might include but is not limited to the following:

- Educational Leadership
- School Law
- Instructional Leadership
- School Management
- School Finance

© The McGraw-Hill Companies, Inc.

English Language Instruction

An M.A. in English Language Instruction is for those who want to work with English Language Learners, either children or adults. A review of several university programs shows that course work might include but is not limited to the following:

- Methods for Teaching Second Languages
- Teaching in Bilingual/Cross-cultural Schools
- Instructional Strategies for Urban School Environments
- Developing English Reading/Language Arts Skills in Bilingual/Cross-cultural Settings
- Children's Reading Materials in Languages Other than English
- Theories of Teaching and Learning Second Languages

A Master's Degree for a Master Teacher

It's not necessary to earn a master's degree to be a successful and engaging teacher. However, an M.A. does open the door to additional opportunities, especially once you have been in the field for a while and are ready for a challenge or a change of pace— and a pay increase as you earn more points for the salary schedule is always a benefit.

No matter which master's degree option you choose, take your time and enjoy your learning. If you will be writing a thesis as part of the M.A. program, incorporate your thesis or research interests into each of your courses whenever possible. This will make it much easier when the time comes to write your thesis, because you will have built a body of information and data to draw upon. In addition, as you read your course texts, begin a list of significant quotations from them. This will help you build a resource of material to cite in your thesis as well as in the writing you do for your courses.

More than anything, once you make the commitment to begin a master's degree, stay focused, follow your program plan, and don't be afraid to ask for help. Enjoy the process! Take advantage of every opportunity to develop your skills and to become more of the master teacher you already are.

Master's Degree Checklist

- ☐ Undergraduate degree (Most master's degree programs require an undergraduate degree.)
- ☐ GRE scores or other necessary test scores (Most programs have a minimum required score.)
- ☐ Accredited college or university (The desired institution is accredited and recognized by your district.)
- ☐ Class schedule (The schedule works with your teaching schedule.)
- ☐ Online (The accredited institution's program and your computer skills are adequate for course work online.)
- ☐ Finances (tuition and financial aid)

© The McGraw-Hill Companies, Inc.

Ed.D. or Ph.D.

A doctoral degree provides the same opportunities as the master's degree, and then some. Many teachers with doctoral degrees often end up mentoring or teaching others how to be teachers, whether at their school site, in their district, or at the college level. Universities offer a variety of programs, especially in the field of leadership, for those who have identified the position of principal as a long-term goal. Even though districts have intern programs today, where teachers can earn Administrative Credentials, a doctorate in this field paves the way for more opportunities and preferred locations. Salary increases due to points earned and degrees acquired are an additional benefit.

Dissertation

Doctoral programs require dissertations. For those who enjoy research and write well, a dissertation will be right up your alley. You will want to select a topic early in your program. Knowing your topic early allows you to do research as you complete your course work, rather than beginning your research and writing after your course work has been completed.

Fields of Study

Following are a few examples of specific areas of study for a doctoral program in the field of education; it is important to research others. You may even be able to work with an institution to create your own area of study.

- Private School Education
- Multicultural and International Education
- Curriculum and Instruction
- Administration and Leadership
- Technology Education
- Bilingual Education
- Special Education

Ed.D./Ph.D. Checklist

☐ Doctoral degree in an area of study (This is generally, but not always, a related field; check with your specific program.)

☐ GRE scores or other necessary test scores (Most programs have a minimum required score.)

☐ Accredited college or university (The desired institution is accredited and recognized by your district.)

☐ Class schedule (The schedule works with your teaching schedule.)

☐ Online (The accredited institution's program and your computer skills are adequate for course work online.)

☐ Finances (tuition and financial aid)

© The McGraw-Hill Companies, Inc.

Advanced Degree Application Checklist

Below are items you may need for the application process for the advanced degree programs discussed in this chapter. Highlight the items that you are required to have, and then check them off as you complete them. You may want to attach this form to the front of a folder where you file all your documents as you collect them.

☐ Completed application

☐ Letters of recommendation: _____ are needed.

_____   _____
Name   Title

_____   _____   _____
Phone   E-mail   Address

_____   _____
Name   Title

_____   _____   _____
Phone   E-mail   Address

_____   _____
Name   Title

_____   _____   _____
Phone   E-mail   Address

☐ Transcripts (original transcripts, sealed copies)

Ordered: _____   _____
         Date   Institution

Ordered: _____   _____
         Date   Institution

☐ District/School site employment verification _____   _____
                                                Date   Institution

☐ Exam/Test results   ☐ GRE   ☐ MAT   ☐ MSAT   ☐ CSET   ☐ SSAT

☐ PRAXIS _____   ☐ TESOL
         Subject

☐ Statement of purpose

☐ Autobiography

☐ Philosophy statement

☐ Letter of intent

☐ Résumé (current)

☐ Financial aid: Contact _____

☐ Grants list: Contact _____

© The McGraw-Hill Companies, Inc.

National Board Certification

National Board Certification certificate areas, which are determined by the National Board for Professional Teaching Standards (NBPTS), are designed to help candidates demonstrate the knowledge, skills, disposition, and commitment of accomplished teachers. Since 1987, more than 55,000 teachers have achieved National Board Certification. Certificates are valid for a period of ten years and must be renewed if you wish to maintain your designation as a National Board Certified Teacher. Maintaining certification requires, for example, that you participate in leading professional developments and mentoring new teachers. There is usually a financial benefit for those who hold such certification.

NBPTS offers 25 certificate areas, one of which will certainly meet your needs. The following list is a sampling of the certificate areas; you should visit their website (http://www.nbpts.org) to see the entire list and find one that fits your area of expertise.

- Art
- English as a New Language
- English Language Arts
- Exceptional Needs Specialist
- Generalist
- Library Media
- Literacy: Reading–Language Arts
- Mathematics
- Music
- Physical Education
- School Counseling
- Science
- Social Studies–History
- World Languages Other than English

National Board Certification Checklist

☐ Timeline for completion

☐ Finances (tuition/financial aid)

☐ Notification to principal

☐ Parent notification

☐ Develop work groups with other teachers seeking National Board Certification

© The McGraw-Hill Companies, Inc.

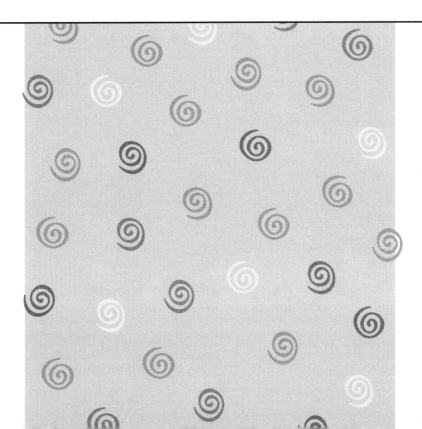

II

Showing Leadership in Your School

6 Organizing Teams and Meetings with Your School Staff 57

7 Planning and Leading Professional Developments 68

8 Presentation Techniques and Topics 80

9 Mentoring New Teachers 104

10 Supporting a Student Teacher 112

11 Student Teaching Forms and Resource Documents 128

6

Organizing Teams and Meetings with Your School Staff

Serving as the chairperson for a grade level or a specific curricular area is a great way to develop leadership skills. At most school sites, principals require teachers to designate a grade-level or departmental chairperson. This chairperson works with the teachers in that group and may also be designated to work with the support staff, depending on the school. He or she is typically a liaison between the administrator and the teachers and may help to plan professional developments and training for the entire school. Serving as chairperson is a great opportunity for professional growth.

The chairperson is responsible for creating a cohesiveness and consistency of approach among the teachers within his or her grade level or department. This teacher is responsible for creating an agenda for each meeting, establishing a long-range action plan for the year, and leading the scheduled meetings. The chairperson also brings back information to the group from the administrator, school planning committees, and parent organizations.

Considerations

Do I have the time?	Would this take time from my other commitments?
Is my classroom under control?	Can I work well with my administrator and fellow teachers?
Am I well organized?	
Am I an effective planner?	Could this experience help me in my professional growth?

© The McGraw-Hill Companies, Inc.

Organization

It takes time and creativity to plan and organize a grade-level, department, or committee meeting. Some schools encourage grade-level or departmental groups and committees to meet once a week, twice a month, or once a month. Some schools even have set days when students get out an hour early so that meetings can take place at that time. Today's teachers have little time available for meetings, but one of the scheduling options below should work for you and your school. Be sure to clear each meeting with your administrator.

Whether a meeting is mandated or not, teacher buy-in is critical to the meeting's success. You can build trust by starting on time, sticking to the agenda, and following through. Demonstrate your commitment by honoring your teachers' time. Motivate them by providing refreshments (candy, fruit, cookies). School funding may be available to cover costs, or you can rotate the responsibility for refreshments among group members.

Before School

If your school doesn't have set meeting times for grade-level or departmental groups and committees, you might meet in the morning before school. (It doesn't hurt to provide doughnuts and coffee for motivation.)

During School

If there is a critical issue to discuss or topic deadline to meet, the principal may have your groups or committees meet during school hours. Students must be supervised by at least one credentialed teacher; this can be accomplished by rotating supervising teachers. Students may be supervised on the playground or in an auditorium or classroom where they can watch an educational video.

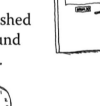

At Lunch

If necessary, a meeting at lunchtime is an option. While no one likes extensive meetings, checking in with your group or committee members once a week or so, especially if there is something significant to discuss, is necessary to make sure you are all on the same page.

After School

If your school doesn't have an established meeting schedule, you might want to ask group or committee members to meet in your classroom for an hour after school to take care of any pressing business.

Locations

Consider holding meetings in group or committee members' classrooms on a rotating basis. This gives teachers a chance to visit other teachers' classrooms and get ideas, as well as to showcase what they are doing in their own classrooms. It's also an equitable way to hold meetings, so that preparing the classroom for visitors isn't the responsibility of the same teacher every time.

© The McGraw-Hill Companies, Inc.

Topic Ideas

Meeting as a grade-level or a departmental group can really build a team, and sharing collective knowledge can increase performance across the grade level or department. There are many areas you can focus on, from lesson planning and sharing lesson ideas to test preparation and scoring assessments. The primary goal is to get everyone on the same page so that there is consistency across the grade level or department, and the same quality of instruction is being delivered in all classrooms.

Following is a list of just a few topics and ideas that can be discussed. Get to know your group and what they want. Their buy-in is the key to your success!

- ✔ Plan for grade-level and subject-specific group members to observe one another or perhaps other teachers who are innovative and critically conscious, both at your school site and elsewhere.
- ✔ Plan for grade-level or subject-specific field trips.
- ✔ Plan for fund-raising for your grade level or department—or for the whole school.
- ✔ Engage in long-range curriculum planning.
- ✔ Share best practices and highly recommended lesson plans.
- ✔ Review new curricula for possible implementation.
- ✔ Share books and materials across the classrooms.
- ✔ Discuss upcoming annual reviews (for example, possible lessons, pre-conference with principal, post-conference with principal).
- ✔ Discuss difficult students and strategies that have been found to be useful in meeting student needs.
- ✔ Prepare for holiday festivals.
- ✔ Prepare for annual standardized testing.
- ✔ Plan team teaching ideas.
- ✔ Score writing samples or select anchor papers that correspond to the grading rubric or scoring system.

59

© The McGraw-Hill Companies, Inc.

Participant Survey

Please complete the following survey. This survey coupled with mandated obligations will assist in setting goals and planning.

Name	Date

Meeting goals
List three specific academic goals to focus on.

1.

2.

3.

Meeting goals
List three school or classroom goals to focus on.

1.

2.

3.

Meeting logistics
When do you prefer to meet?
☐ Before school ☐ After school ☐ During school ☐ At lunch ☐ Other _____

Where do you want to meet?
☐ Designated classroom ☐ Various classrooms (rotate location) ☐ Library ☐ Other _____

How often would you prefer to meet?
☐ Weekly ☐ Biweekly ☐ Monthly ☐ Semester ☐ Other _____

List ideas for student supervision during meetings (if applicable).

Write any other comments or concerns (continue on back if necessary).

© The McGraw-Hill Companies, Inc.

Goals

Write out established group goals. For academic goals, write out the learning standards they support. Include what will be needed to achieve each goal—materials, support, etc.

Group _____

Meeting days _____

Location _____

Facilitator _____

Goal
Standards

Materials

Goal
Standards

Materials

Goal
Standards

Materials

© The McGraw-Hill Companies, Inc.

Meeting Planner

Detail plans for the year to accomplish goals set by the group.

Group _____

Planning year _____

August	September	October	November

December	January	February	March

April	May	June	

© The McGraw-Hill Companies, Inc.

Meeting Agenda

An agenda is meant to keep the group on task so it can accomplish the goals set forth in the meeting. Sticking to the agenda is the key to success. You should fill in the time (in minutes) allowed for each topic. Enter each topic and its talking points on the form. Below is a blank agenda to show how you might organize a group meeting. A sample agenda follows.

Group _____ Date _____

Facilitator _____

Goals/Objectives for today

Time	Topic	Talking points/Notes

Guidelines

✔ One person speaks at a time.

✔ Be respectful and listen when others are speaking.

✔ Stay on task.

✔ Avoid side conversations and turn off all cell phones.

✔ Additional items of concern will be covered if time permits, otherwise they will be moved to the next meeting's agenda.

© The McGraw-Hill Companies, Inc.

Sample Meeting Agenda

This agenda is meant to keep us on task so we can accomplish the goals set forth in our meeting. Sticking to our agenda is the key to our success.

Group _1st Grade Team Meeting_	Date	_Tuesday, 10/12/12_
Facilitator _Brandy Alexander, Grade Level Chair_		

Goals/Objectives for today

Review student writing samples for first grading period with previously developed scoring rubric (5-point scale)

Plan fund-raising booth for Fall Harvest Festival

Time	Topic	Talking points/Notes
2:30–2:45	Review past business and any grade-level concerns.	Discussion about playground rules and rotating recess duty schedule. We will check with principal to see if we can go from 3 to 2 teachers on duty.
2:45–3:30	Each teacher shares a "proficient," "basic," and "below basic" writing sample to make sure all teachers are scoring the same way.	Most of the teachers were having trouble distinguishing between a score of "3" and a score of "2." We changed the rubric language to better serve the level of writing the students are producing.
3:30–3:45	Plan fund-raising booth for the Fall Harvest Festival on Saturday, October 30.	Teachers decided to do a face-painting booth. Each of us will supply one of the necessary materials to make this successful. Each teacher will spend one half-hour at the festival painting faces. Check with the PTA about materials reimbursement. The booth will charge $2.50 for face painting.
3:45–4:00	Closure. Review today's meeting and confirm fall festival participation.	Teachers have signed up for materials and times for the fall festival.
4:00–4:15	Plan for the next grade-level meeting.	Next week we will share three more writing samples and make final preparations for the fall festival.

© The McGraw-Hill Companies, Inc.

Sign-In Sheet

Welcome! Please sign in as documentation of your participation. Thank you!

Sign-In	
Group _____ Date _____	
Facilitator _____	

Name	Title
1.	
2.	
3.	
4.	
5.	
6.	
7.	
8.	
9.	
10.	
11.	
12.	
13.	
14.	
15.	
16.	
17.	
18.	
19.	
20.	

© The McGraw-Hill Companies, Inc.

Meeting Log

Complete log and attach an agenda. Use the back for additional notes if needed.
Save for documentation purposes.

Group _____ Date _____

Facilitator _____

Recorder _____

Meeting goals/objectives

1.

2.

3.

Topic

Notes/Talking points

Topic

Notes/Talking points

Topic

Notes/Talking points

© The McGraw-Hill Companies, Inc.

Materials Request Form

Follow school policy for requests.

	Office Use Only
	Funding source _____
	Initial _____

Group _____ Date _____

Facilitator _____

Item name	Item number	Catalog/Website	Page number	Quantity	Price

Proposed purpose (Include use, curricular relevance, standards supported, goals, etc. that apply.)

Item name	Item number	Catalog/Website	Page number	Quantity	Price

Proposed purpose (Include use, curricular relevance, standards supported, goals, etc. that apply.)

Item name	Item number	Catalog/Website	Page number	Quantity	Price

Proposed purpose (Include use, curricular relevance, standards supported, goals, etc. that apply.)

Item name	Item number	Catalog/Website	Page number	Quantity	Price

Proposed purpose (Include use, curricular relevance, standards supported, goals, etc. that apply.)

© The McGraw-Hill Companies, Inc.

7

Planning and Leading Professional Developments

Throughout the year, teachers must engage in professional development meetings. These meetings are arranged by school principals to ensure that teachers are kept up-to-date in the field—learning about new curricular programs, hearing guest speakers, and learning about new classroom strategies that will benefit their students. Meetings might be held every week on a designated day, every two weeks, or once a month, depending on the school.

Depending on your district or school, these sessions may be called Professional Trainings, Teacher In-Service, Teacher Trainings, Staff Development, or Professional Developments, but for the sake of this book we will refer to them as Professional Developments (PDs).

A school or district conducts Professional Developments that align with its vision and goals. Some may be mandated by the district or could be part of a grant commitment. School support staff, administrators, outside providers, district personnel, and teacher volunteers often organize and lead the trainings.

One of the school's best and most accessible resources for facilitating Professional Developments is its current teaching faculty. Teachers not only have the respect and trust of their colleagues, but they also have a very real sense of what is realistic and what is needed to succeed in the classroom. Your experience and expertise make *you* the perfect candidate for developing and leading training sessions.

The first step toward doing this is to talk with your principal about leading a professional development meeting. Find out how the training topics are decided, if there is a planning committee, and whether the district requires that a teacher be trained before presenting a training session to his or her school. Once you have

the approval of your administrator to create school-generated training sessions, you may need to find others at your grade level or across grade levels to help you plan and implement your idea. You'll need to decide goals, pull together resources, create an agenda, set a date, and make all necessary preparations for the meeting.

© The McGraw-Hill Companies, Inc.

Features of a Professional Development

Professional Developments need to be well thought out and have teacher buy-in to be successful. This page summarizes and outlines the four key steps in the process of developing and leading a Professional Development.

Think

Brainstorm.
Set goals.
Assess needs.
Survey staff and determine needs.
Investigate district mandates.

Follow through

Establish next steps; create
    action plan.
Establish clear expectations.
Monitor progress.
Schedule follow-up meetings.
Consider follow-up PDs.

Plan

Set date.
Set goals with clear expectations.
Establish agenda.
Pull resources together.
Gather materials.
Copy handouts.
Purchase refreshments.
Secure location and equipment.
Notify participants.
Walk through presentation.

Present

Prior to presentation

Set up location.
Test equipment.
Prepare handouts.
Mentally walk through
    presentation.

Presentation

Stick to agenda as much
    as possible.
Pace yourself, not too fast
    or too slow.
Keep participants on task.
Be flexible and ready to
    adjust.
Don't take it personally!

© The McGraw-Hill Companies, Inc.

The Do's of Professional Developments

Do practice your presentation prior to conducting the training. Walk yourself through every step. Make any necessary adjustments to the agenda. This is essential to make sure that you have enough time to get through each element. It also allows you the opportunity to add anything you think might be missing.

Do test all equipment and power sources prior to the presentation. *Never* assume everything will work. Plug every piece of equipment in and turn them all on! Connect laptops to projectors, click through PowerPoint presentations, and play videos. There is nothing worse than scrambling in front of an audience because your projector isn't working properly.

Do stick to your agenda and avoid getting pulled off task by questions and side conversations. Maintain a good pace as you move through your agenda. This honors the time commitment made by your participants.

Do be organized. Have enough of everything you plan to use, from materials and handouts to supplies and refreshments. Being prepared not only helps facilitate the Professional Development, but it adds to your level of professionalism.

Do dress professionally. While this seems like a "no-brainer," you are more apt to elicit teacher participation if you appear professional and confident.

Do confirm the time and location for your session. It can be frustrating when you think you are supposed to set up in the auditorium but you were really supposed to set up in the library.

Do be sure to start on time. It is inevitable that some teachers will get sidetracked when parents show up to speak with them after school or when they have to call a student's home or offer assistance to a child at the end of the day. Nevertheless, you want to honor those who are on time. Those who come in later can catch up.

Do remember that teachers in attendance are most likely people you work with on a daily basis. They also have a lot of experience. Treat them like your equals, ask for their ideas, and validate their experience. This will go a lot further than "teaching down" to them.

© The McGraw-Hill Companies, Inc.

Plan Your Topic Using a Professional Development Inventory

List Professional Developments you have recently attended, your instructional strengths, instructional weaknesses, and areas in which you want to improve. For each curricular area of interest, jot down any ideas you may have for Professional Developments. Sharing this inventory with your grade-level group and administrator is a great way to start off the school year's planning. If you are a grade-level chairperson, you might consider adding discussion of this inventory to your first grade-level planning meeting of the year, especially if your principal requires groups or committees to take turns planning and leading Professional Developments.

Math	Reading	Writing
Science	**Professional developments**	**Physical Education**
The Arts	**Strengths**	**Special Education**
Social Studies	**Weaknesses**	**Special Programs**
Health	**Areas to improve**	**Intervention**
	Technology	

© The McGraw-Hill Companies, Inc.

Schedule the Professional Development

Some schools or districts have established meeting times for Professional Developments; in others, it can vary. Teachers interested in offering Professional Developments to their colleagues will need to work within the school or district framework.

Most schools schedule their Professional Developments after school, whether once a week, twice a month, or once a month. Some schools even have set days when students get out an hour early so that Professional Developments can take place at that time. If your school does not have an established schedule for Professional Developments, you will want to work with your administration to schedule one at a time when you think the teachers you especially want to reach will be able to attend.

Start of the School Year

Many districts schedule Professional Developments for teachers and staff one to five days before students begin the school year. Presenting a Professional Development during this contractual time is beneficial because it takes place at a time when teachers are being paid. While most teachers don't mind volunteering their time, some are more likely to participate and be engaged if these meetings are held at a time when they are getting paid.

© The McGraw-Hill Companies, Inc.

Create Your Professional Development Agenda

It's important to create an agenda for your professional development presentation. This is a good way to organize your time, and it also gives the audience a "heads-up" about what they will find in your presentation. Typically, presentations last for 30 to 90 minutes. At the beginning of the school year, a professional development presentation might even be a half day or all day. For your first professional development presentation, you might want to limit yourself to 90 minutes or less.

Agendas vary depending on the length and content of your presentation. Below is a guide to creating a basic agenda. Draw upon your own experiences in attending professional developments as you work to create an agenda that best suits you.

Professional Development Agenda Tips

1 · Ice breaker (10–15 minutes)

The ice breaker should be related to your presentation. It can be as simple as sharing a relevant comic, a short "Dear Abby" column, or a picture book. See Chapter 8 for more suggestions. The point of the ice breaker is to set the stage for your presentation and get the audience thinking about your topic, or to get the group involved and ready to participate if the professional development requires it.

2 · Review of your focus/purpose/goal (5–10 minutes)

Hand out a piece of paper with your focus/purpose/goal written at the top and room for note taking at the bottom.

3 · Present research (5–10 minutes)

Your research piece can be an article, video, or recording. It should be related to your topic's goals. This research piece should serve as validation and motivation for the professional development presentation. Participants can work collaboratively, discuss, and share their thoughts with the group. Keep the group on topic during the discussion.

4 · Presentation (10–15 minutes)

Make your presentation clear, simple, and easy to follow. Have clear expectations. This may be broken up with activities that support each section. It may include a PowerPoint presentation or overhead presentation, but keep the words to a minimum and the graphics rich, because what is most important is what you will be saying.

5 · Activities (20–30 minutes)

This time can be spent in hands-on, interactive collaboration in small groups or in whole group contributions after small group discussions. It could also involve a series of activities that alternate with the presentation itself. These activities should be purposeful and engaging.

6 · Q & A and action plan (20–30 minutes)

Depending on how much time you have left, this is a good time for whole group sharing and reflections or a question-and-answer session. Hand out your action plan sheet and discuss different options for following through on the goals set forth in this professional development.

A Couple of Reminders

✔ Always have a back-up activity or an extra research piece in case your presentation goes too quickly.

✔ Read your audience. If they are ready to move on, move on. If they are asking several clarification questions, slow down and review with them what you have done so far.

✔ Relax and enjoy, and let the presentation flow. Every group is different. Don't take anything personally.

73

© The McGraw-Hill Companies, Inc.

Professional Development Planner

Professional development name

Date	Location

Presenter

Description of presentation

Goals	Research piece

Ice breaker

Activity

Materials

© The McGraw-Hill Companies, Inc.

Professional Development Checklist

Prior to the Day of the Professional Development

- [ ] Approved by administration
- [ ] Calendar date and time set
- [ ] Agenda set
- [ ] Support material (research piece, video)
- [ ] Packets/Handouts
- [ ] Location (seating, AC/heat, parking)
- [ ] Equipment (VCR/DVD, laptop, projector, overhead)
- [ ] Materials/Supplies (markers, pens, Post-its)
- [ ] Refreshments (purchase items/supplies, coffeemaker)
- [ ] Presentation walk-through (practice entire presentation)

Day of the Professional Development

- [ ] Location (doors open, lights, restrooms, contact person)
- [ ] Tables and chairs (set-up)
- [ ] Room temperature (comfortable)
- [ ] Handouts (agenda, support pages, evaluation in order and stapled)
- [ ] Technology and equipment (tested and ready)
- [ ] Materials (on tables and ready)
- [ ] Sign-in sheet and nametags
- [ ] Personal needs (tissue, water)
- [ ] Refreshments (food, treats, cups, napkins, plates)

© The McGraw-Hill Companies, Inc.

Professional Development Sign-In Sheet

Sign-In

Training _____ Date _____

Name	Sign in	Sign out
1.		
2.		
3.		
4.		
5.		
6.		
7.		
8.		
9.		
10.		
11.		
12.		
13.		
14.		
15.		
16.		
17.		
18.		
19.		
20.		

© The McGraw-Hill Companies, Inc.

Professional Development Action Plan

Articulate a plan for the follow-through on what you learned from this professional development. Establish clear, realistic expectations. Keep them simple. Set up to three goals for each time period listed. Post these goals and revisit them at the end of each time period in order to make any necessary adjustments.

Today	
One month	
Three months	
One year	
Long-term	

© The McGraw-Hill Companies, Inc.

Professional Development Evaluation

An evaluation is important. It shows you what worked, what didn't work, and where improvement is needed. This will help you in planning and leading future Professional Developments. Keep the evaluation short and simple.

Keep the questions positive. Negative questions are not the purpose of an evaluation. The evaluation gives you feedback and is not meant to leave anyone thinking negatively about the time they have spent with you. A sample evaluation follows for you to use as a guide.

Professional Development Evaluation
What was the most informative or useful information you learned today?
Based on your own experience, do you have any additional ideas to add to the content of this Professional Development?
Do you know where you are going from here? Do you have established goals?
Are there any questions you have concerning the next steps? Thanks!

© The McGraw-Hill Companies, Inc.

Professional Development Materials List

The following is a list of materials that are commonly used in professional development presentations. This can be used as a guide, and you can highlight any items that you expect to use and then check them off as you have them accounted for on the day of the presentation. Add any additional materials that you may need.

- Post-its
- Chart paper and stand
- Masking tape
- Nametags
- Markers
- Handouts
- Refreshments
- VCR/DVD/TV
- VHS tapes, DVDs
- Laptop
- LCD Projector
- Overhead projector
- Overhead transparency
- Overhead markers
- Sign-in sheet (if required)
- Participation certificates
- Official hour logs or credit log
- Pens and pencils
- Note paper
- Tissues
- Paper towels
- Spray cleanser
- Art supplies
- CD player
- CDs
- Flash drive
- Digital camera
- Camcorder

© The McGraw-Hill Companies, Inc.

8

Presentation Techniques and Topics

Professional Development Presentation Techniques

Ice Breakers

Ice breakers are an excellent way to open a meeting, especially if the group is going to be interacting or working in small groups. It quickly establishes a cohesive learning environment and can produce a strong sense of purpose and participation. Below you will find some easy ice breakers that are excellent ways to kick off a professional development session!

Four Corners Name Tags

Have white 8½″ × 11″ sheets of paper and colored pencils, crayons, or markers available. Ask participants to fold a sheet of paper into thirds to make a name tent, and then tell them to write their name in the center of one panel. Ask the participants to think of four ways they identify themselves (for example, teacher, Canadian, mother, runner, African-American, father, gardener), and then to write one of those four terms in each corner of their nametag. Once they have done this, ask them to introduce themselves through their identity nametag. This gives the participants an opportunity to know a bit about others in the room.

Name Game

Everyone sits in a circle. The first person starts by saying his or her name; the second person repeats the first person's name and then adds his or her own name. Each person in the circle repeats the growing list of names, always ending with his or her own, until the final person in the group—in this case, the presenter—repeats the names of everyone in the entire group.

© The McGraw-Hill Companies, Inc.

Get Yourselves Organized

State that you want to divide the participants into groups of three to five people each. Then give the instruction to "organize yourselves in 60 seconds"—without giving more detailed instructions or guidelines. At the end of 60 seconds, the presenter asks each group to explain how they organized themselves (for example, by height, birth date, city of residence). Direct the groups to organize themselves two more times, each time asking them to explain how they've chosen to organize themselves. If you have a really large group, you may need to give them suggestions (for example, by height, shoe size, color of shirt, length of hair, month of birth).

Paper Towel Roll

Ask your participants to sit in a circle. The presenter shows a paper towel roll (use one with smaller sheets) to the group and instructs them to take as much as they want as the roll is passed around. Once the roll has been around the circle, the group is told that for each sheet of paper they took, they must tell the group something about themselves that the other people don't know. The presenter goes first, and talk proceeds around the circle.

Commercials That Fit

Participants are told to think about their personal or professional lives, and then to think of a famous commercial jingle that appropriately describes it. To encourage personal interaction within the group, ask the participants share "their" jingle and explain why they remember or identify with that one most.

© The McGraw-Hill Companies, Inc.

2 to 4—Share Some More

Early in the session, pair up the participants in an activity designed to help them become acquainted with and feel comfortable about each other. Instruct them to interview each other using the following prompts as a guide:

- Tell two unusual things that have happened in their lives.
- Describe any special talents and hobbies they have.
- Tell what their most important job responsibility is.
- Tell who the person they most admire (or despise) in the world is and why.

After the pairs have shared, ask them to pair up with a different twosome and repeat the interviews. Then ask each member of the foursome to share one interesting thing they learned about a member of their small group.

Interview a Partner

Have participants pair up with someone they do not know and then ask one another the following questions:

- What is your full name, and what was your nickname growing up?
- What is your position at your school site, and what do you enjoy most about your job?
- How long have you been doing what you do?
- What are you most looking forward to at this presentation, professional development, or conference?
- What is your favorite hobby?
- What would be a dream vacation for you?
- If you could change one thing about the world, what would it be?
- Do you know any good (clean) jokes?
- What is one thing nobody in this room knows about you?
- What do you see yourself doing that will change the lives of kids?

Show and Tell

Before the day of the presentation, make sure the attendees are told to bring an object to the meeting that describes them or is important to them so that they can talk to the group about it. If they forget to bring something, they can use a personal item that they happen to have with them. This is a simple way to get to know a little something about one another quickly.

© The McGraw-Hill Companies, Inc.

Presentation Techniques and Practices

Planning a Professional Development that is both organized and creative can help its effectiveness and overall success. Presentation techniques and practices that you may find helpful follow.

Jigsaw Reading

Teams of people divide a reading into sections (perhaps based on subtitles) and each person reads a different section. Each person then shares a summary of what he or she has read. This breaks up the reading and increases comprehension, as readers have to summarize what they have read. A representative of each team might then share a summary of their complete reading with the entire group.

Question Parking Lot

It's not always easy to answer questions in the middle of delivering a presentation on a schedule. Having a place—a "question parking lot"— where participants can post their questions eliminates interruptions and ensures that everyone's questions will be addressed at a designated time. Having Post-it notes available for participants is an excellent way to handle this. Some of the posted questions might get answered in the course of the presentation itself; if not, they can be answered toward the end of the session.

List Goals or Objectives

Create a list of the goals or objectives and post them. Review the list with the whole group and check off items as they are covered. This keeps things organized and ensures that nothing is missed.

Question List

Start the session by asking, "What do you want to learn from this training?" Develop a list of questions from their responses. This tells you what your audience wants to know before you begin the main part of your presentation, and it also ensures that everyone's concerns are addressed.

KWL

Charting out what the participants *Know*, what they *Want* to know, and what they have *Learned* is a great way to organize the session. This gives you an idea about their backgrounds, good insight into what they want to know about, and even an evaluation of how you did when they share what they learned in the session.

© The McGraw-Hill Companies, Inc.

Showing Fingers

Showing the number of fingers to indicate how much time is left or having participants show you the number of minutes they still need to complete a task is a helpful (and quiet) way to handle time management for the group.

Numbering Off

Numbering off is a good way to divide up for discussions and activities, for example, "All the 4s can go to that table to discuss and then share back to the full group."

Charting

Asking small groups to chart their responses is a great way to share back to the group. This also gives you a good resource for typing up notes on the session and what was accomplished so that you have it to share later with the administrator or the participants.

Gallery Walk

A gallery walk involves walking from chart to chart and discussing what has been written. This is a good opportunity for dialogue, giving everyone a chance to share; it is also a time-saver if you don't have enough time at the end for each group to share individually.

Group Web

Creating a group web is a good way to share knowledge about a topic. Each participant can add to the web, writing down what stood out in a reading or what they have learned. Webs can then be discussed as a whole group.

© The McGraw-Hill Companies, Inc.

Speed Sharing

In this exercise, each participant shares an idea with a partner and switches to a different partner after a designated time—a minute or less. This helps the group focus on what is shared and it keeps things moving. Ideas shared can be specific thoughts about a reading, a reaction to something that was said, or even thoughts about the presentation as a whole.

Share and Listen

In a pair or small group, all but one person share findings or ideas, and the other person listens and takes notes. He or she does not interject ideas or thoughts. Once the conversation has finished, the silent participant comments. This technique focuses on the discussion, because the participants don't simultaneously interject or interrupt to add their own thoughts.

Table Kits

Have table kits available that include all the materials needed for activities during the session; this cuts down on interruptions and saves time that would have been spent passing the items out. It makes you appear more professional and prepared. It also allows participants to write, highlight, and post requests in a timely manner. Table kits could include Post-it notes, highlighters, small note pads, pencils, pens, markers for chart paper and illustrations, erasers, scissors and glue sticks if needed, and any other materials you think might be needed during the session.

© The McGraw-Hill Companies, Inc.

Professional Development Topics by Curricular and School-related Area

The following are ideas and brief descriptions for professional developments in representative curricular and school-related areas. Note that each description refers to related research on the topic, as well as possible videos or lesson ideas.

The Internet is a good resource for finding articles, books, and videos to use in leading professional developments. However, be aware that not everything found on the Internet is based on solid research; use good judgment when choosing which materials to use. The Education Resources Information Center (ERIC) is an excellent resource for locating research-based articles to support your training ideas. Dust off some of those teacher resource books you already have on your shelf, and share articles or teaching practices from those to validate your professional development planning. Talk to the support staff and faculty at your school site, as well as your principal, because they may have articles, videos, or websites to share. Remember, you work with people who are experts in their field. Ask them to join you as you plan and carry out a professional development that will be meaningful and useful to all the teachers and staff who attend.

A list of suggested topics is given for each area of professional development. It is important that the faculty have a say in what will be presented, as this increases their buy-in and therefore the ultimate success of your professional development. Use the list as a starting point.

Math

Math professional developments generally focus on the latest instructional strategies. Teachers will be introduced to new methodologies and research, have a chance to practice these methodologies, and be able to plan implementation and follow-through with their grade-level group. They should leave with a greater understanding of instructional delivery and facilitation. A Math PD can cover everything from hands-on activities using manipulatives to test-taking strategies.

- Math Learning Games
- Math Manipulatives
- Test-Taking Strategies
- Instructional Modifications
- Looking at State Standards for Grade Levels
- Establishing a Grade-Level Pacing Plan
- Hands-on Approach to Fractions: Adding, Subtracting, Multiplying, Dividing
- Sharing Best Teaching Practices Across Grade Levels

© The McGraw-Hill Companies, Inc.

Reading

Reading professional developments focus on reading skills, strategies, and literature. Teachers will be introduced to a research piece that supports the learning goal of the professional development and will have an opportunity to discuss it. This research material gives validity to the presentation itself. New strategies or methodologies are modeled and practiced. Teachers can discuss practical applications and set a timeline for implementation with their grade-level group. A Reading PD can include using literature across the curriculum, reading fluency, improving comprehension, and developing reading strategies.

- Reading Fluency
- Reading Comprehension
- Reading Strategies
- Test-Taking Strategies
- Literature Across the Curriculum
- Storytelling
- Creating Story Boards from District-Mandated Language Arts Reading Programs

Writing

Writing professional developments focus on writing and writing strategies. Teachers will be introduced to research, which is reviewed and discussed. New methodologies are practiced, applications are discussed at grade level, and an action plan is put into place. Writing PDs can include the writing process, a writer's workshop, pre-writing with graphic organizers, writing genres, journaling, writing strategies, and applications.

- Writers Workshop (the writing process supported by teacher and peers in the classroom)
- Writing Genres (narrative, expository, persuasive, friendly letter, poetry)
- State Writing Standards (what is expected at each grade level)
- The Writing Process
- Scoring Writing Using a Rubric (achieving consistency on grade level)
- Writing Strategies
- Best Writing Practices (shared by staff)
- Journaling
- Writing Across the Curriculum

87

© The McGraw-Hill Companies, Inc.

Science

Science professional developments can be fun hands-on experiences. One of the primary obstacles in science instruction is that teachers don't always feel comfortable teaching the subject matter. Science PDs can help teachers gain confidence in their instruction as well as knowledge in the subject area. Teachers are introduced to the latest research on science instruction, which is discussed and related to state standards. They learn about working with science at grade level by incorporating hands-on explorations that relate to these standards and by devising an action plan to teach science consistently across grade level. Science PDs can include the scientific method, integrating science and math, understanding the state standards for your grade level, and hands-on activities in life, physical, and earth sciences.

- Hands-on Science Lessons and Explorations That Meet Grade-level Standards
- Scientific Method and Ways to Use It at Each Grade Level
- Best Teaching Practices in Science (teachers sharing ideas)
- Science Curriculum (digging into adopted science programs)
- Exploring Life Science, Physical Science, and Earth Science at Each Grade Level
- Preparing Student Projects for the Annual Science Fair

Physical Education

Physical education professional developments help teach new games and strategies as well as refresh teachers on game play and common practices. Although physical education is often neglected, it is extremely important for our youth today: Fifth-graders are tested nationally on their fitness level. In a Physical Education PD, teachers are introduced to a research piece that can be read and discussed in small groups, especially with regard to how physical fitness plays a role in academic achievement. There is often an exploration component, such as exploring grade-level standards for physical education. Teachers might have an opportunity to practice methodologies or instructional delivery, and grade-level action plans and schedules might be developed. Physical Education PDs often cover age-appropriate skills and games, sports rules, and competitions.

- Use of Equipment
- Game Rotation (rotate through and actually play yard games)
- Select a Focus Sport (review rules and fair play)
- Age-appropriate Skills and Games (grade levels)
- Sports Day/Olympics
- Yoga and Stretching in the Classroom on Rainy Days
- Indoor Games

© The McGraw-Hill Companies, Inc.

The Arts

Arts professional developments can help train teachers in the arts and build their confidence in arts instruction. The arts include visual arts, performing arts/theatre, music, and dance. The arts are often neglected in today's classrooms, in part because teachers don't have time for them or aren't comfortable teaching them. In Arts PDs, teachers are introduced to research that demonstrates the importance of teaching the arts. They can discuss this research and share their experiences. Practical lessons in the selected arts can be introduced and practiced by the teachers, because the best way to learn the arts is to do the lesson yourself. You can usually find staff members who are strong in an area of the arts and who could be encouraged to share their expertise. An Arts PD can include actual arts lessons by professionals, group dancing, theatre arts games, singing, and playing musical instruments.

- Visual Arts (art lessons using different techniques, materials, or media)
- Dance (cultural and traditional dances)
- Theatre Arts (lessons incorporating literature units and other curricular areas)
- Music (using classroom instruments in simple lessons)
- Best Teaching Practices (sharing effective lessons across the Arts that support curricular areas)

Social Studies

Social studies professional developments can easily incorporate other curricular areas. By taking advantage of this cross-curricular instruction it is easy to create purposeful learning for students. Social studies includes curricular areas such as history and government. Art, writing, and math can be easily related to social studies units. In a Social Studies PD, teachers are introduced to current research on social studies instruction, which can be reviewed and discussed. Grade-level groups might meet to review their standards, pull resources together into units that support the standards, and create an action plan (for example, to create accountability and consistency on grade level). It is helpful to create a social studies continuum across grade levels to show staff their individual roles in teaching social studies. Social Studies PDs can include topics such as practical hands-on experiences and creating thematic grade-level units.

- Multi-cultural Studies
- Grade-level Standards-based Units
- Thematic Units Based Around Social Science Topics (cross-curricular studies)
- World Customs, Celebrations, and Holidays Throughout the Year
- Standards Connected to the Adopted Curriculum
- Grade-level Planning of Social Studies Throughout the Year

© The McGraw-Hill Companies, Inc.

Intervention

Intervention professional developments can help teachers meet the needs of those students who are performing below or far below grade level. If students don't improve, statistically there is a good chance they may never recover and graduate from high school. Knowing how to help those students while maintaining a classroom is one of the biggest challenges facing teachers today. Intervention PDs introduce teachers to statistics and research that show the need for interventions, focusing on what has worked. The best resource for such PDs is often the school's resource specialist or special education teachers, who have been extensively trained in intervention strategies and techniques, as well as in management of classroom interventions. An Intervention PD can present strategies that are demonstrated and modeled. Teachers can observe, dialogue, and ask questions, then meet in grade-level groups to discuss best practices and ways to incorporate the strategies into their instructional day. Intervention PDs may focus on one curricular area, such as math, or may be more specific, such as reading comprehension.

- Specific Strategies That Target Reading Comprehension
- Grade-level and Classroom Strategies
- Best Teaching Practices
- Referral Process
- Intervention Programs (School- or District-wide)

Health

Health professional developments can help teachers learn about adopted curriculums, collaborate on and plan lessons, share best practices, and plan their year incorporating health across the curriculum. Health education is an often-neglected curricular area that is important to address with today's generation: Eating and living in a healthful way often starts in the schools. In a Health PD, teachers are introduced to research on the health of children today, which can be reviewed and discussed. Teachers could work at grade level and plan the year based on an adopted curriculum aligned with grade-level standards. Health education could be woven throughout the curriculum. A Health PD could include healthful programs, classroom cooking, hygiene, nutrition, healthy choices for healthful living, anti-drug campaigns, and reading good labels.

- Nutrition
- Current Food Pyramid
- Hygiene
- Vegetable of the Month
- Fruit of the Month
- Standards for Health
- Share Best Teaching Practices
- First Aid
- Anti-drug, Anti-tobacco, and Anti-alcohol Education

90

© The McGraw-Hill Companies, Inc.

Technology

Technology professional developments can provide teachers with the technology background to use technology more extensively in the classroom. Technology is hardwired into this generation: Children today use cell phones, MP3 players, TiVo, and the Internet. In a Technology PD, teachers are introduced to research on technology in the classroom, which can then be reviewed and discussed to help teachers see the need for technology in the classroom. Teachers can participate in step-by-step instruction in the target area of a particular professional development. There should be follow-up, with built-in opportunities for teachers to use what they have learned. Teachers can discuss at grade level or as a whole and create an action plan for implementing technology in the classroom on a more consistent basis. Technology PDs may include computer basics, surfing the Web, and using programs like Word and PowerPoint; a computer lab (or laptops for each participant) is usually required.

- Training in Word
- Training in PowerPoint
- Using the Web
- Educational Websites
- Technology in the Classroom: Choosing Software
- Technology Standards for Grade Levels

Special Education

Special education professional developments help teachers better understand the special education program, their own role in mainstreaming students, and different physical and learning disabilities. While special education is more mainstream in the twenty-first century than it has ever been in years past, many teachers are unprepared to have children in their classrooms who have special needs and who require more intricate and specific planning. In Special Education PDs, teachers are introduced to research, which often includes videos on the topic, and then they review and discuss their experiences. Teachers can meet on grade level to share best practices and plan implementation, including support staff who work with these students. A school-wide action plan is important to keep things consistent and current. Special Education PDs can focus on differentiation of curriculum, awareness of student needs, and the responsibilities of teachers.

- Mainstreaming
- Meeting Specific Special Needs
- Referral Process
- Sensitivity Training
- Utilizing a Classroom Aide Effectively in Working with Students in Your Class Who have IEPs or 504 Plans
- Working Closely with Families Who Have Children with Special Needs

© The McGraw-Hill Companies, Inc.

Special Programs

Beyond set curriculums, schools often have special programs or adoptions (often mandated by the district or state), or grants that help in areas such as drop-out prevention or saying "no" to drugs. These programs usually have a coordinator who is appointed to oversee the project, attend the meetings, and facilitate any training. In a special program professional development, teachers are introduced to a research component that validates or supports the program. Participants can discuss and share their experiences, review program guidelines and expectations, and establish an action plan. Typically, with a district program, the training is set up and the staff needs to sign off after they have received it. A special program PD may include programs such as ESL for parents and students, bilingual support for a mandated curriculum, planning parenting workshops, and working with difficult parents.

• Program Orientation
• Program Training
• Program Implementation

© The McGraw-Hill Companies, Inc.

Professional Development Planner

Professional development name	
Date	Location
Presenter	
Description	
Goals	Research piece
Ice breaker	
Activity	
Materials	

© The McGraw-Hill Companies, Inc.

Sample Professional Development Plans

Incorporating Children's Literature Across the Curriculum

A professional development on how to choose rich literature to enhance curricula is a great way for reading teachers to offer advice to their colleagues in other subject areas (for example, science, social studies, math, and art). It would be good for teachers to work together to offer this professional development, because combining libraries will make it possible to offer a larger variety of book choices. It's even better to have a teacher from each grade level so that there are books available for each grade level.

On the day of the professional development, begin by breaking teachers into grade-level groups or curricular areas of interest. At each group table, books will be made available for teachers to peruse and discuss. Below is a checklist of things you want them to look for in each title, with your goal being to give them the building blocks so that they will develop the skills needed to select great books on their own.

• Is the text grade-level appropriate? What grade level might this title meet?

• Are the illustrations pleasing and engaging?

• How might I incorporate this book into my grade-level or subject area standards?

• How might I elicit dialogue with my students about the book?

• Should this book be used for read-alouds, shared reading, silent reading, or guided reading?

After each small group has worked with the materials at every table, have the whole group discuss what they learned, noticed, or would like to add. Allow them time to ask questions about using this approach in their own classroom.

94

© The McGraw-Hill Companies, Inc.

Sample Professional Development Planner

Professional development name
Incorporating Children's Literature Across the Curriculum

Date	Location
August 27, 2012	*Library*

Presenter
Michael Becker, 2nd Grade Teacher, and Sheri Thompson, Literacy Coach

Description
In order to enhance the district curriculum and pacing plans for the Reading and Language Arts program, we will be sharing best practices in incorporating children's literature into our daily planning. This will give teachers new and interesting ideas about choosing rich literature and exposing students to a wide variety of genres related to the Reading and Language Arts themes. Teachers will also consider additional titles to link the various curricular areas into their planning and instruction.

Goals	Research piece
• *Book selection* • *Sharing titles that incorporate curricular areas beyond Reading and Language Arts* • *Becoming more comfortable reading aloud and recommending books to students*	*Pantaleo, S. (2002). Children's Literature across the Curriculum: An Ontario Survey. Canadian Journal of Education, 27, 211–230.*

Ice breaker
Participants will choose the book that they feel best represents their personal interests from the twenty books displayed at their grade-level table. Each will share his or her choice with grade-level group members as a way to initiate a discussion of the books.

Activity
• *Ice breaker* • *Using district Reading/Language Arts Curriculum guides, grade-level groups will review each story in their current unit and locate any recommended children's books, trying to focus on a variety of curricular areas. Teachers will look for these titles in the school library and make a list of any missing titles that they would like to have available.* • *Once teachers have located recommended books, each teacher will choose one to read aloud to the group. The grade-level group will discuss whether the books that were shared will enhance the unit or theme.* • *As a follow-up activity, at staff professional development meetings throughout the year, teachers can review the next unit or theme for recommended books and review them, listing titles they would like to have available if they are not currently available in the school library.*

Materials
Grade-level tables with a variety of curriculum-related books

© The McGraw-Hill Companies, Inc.

Utilizing Math Manipulatives to Teach Basic Math Skills

For this agenda, break into grade-level groups and create manipulative tables that meet each of the different math strands (+, −, ×, ÷). One presenter should be at each table to show how to use these manipulatives (see Manipulatives Use Guide) for teaching particular math concepts. Ask teachers whether the items are grade-level appropriate, if the items are useful in teaching what was demonstrated for them, and if they can think of other ways to use them. After each group has visited each table, have teachers share their thoughts with the whole group.

• Are any of the manipulatives new to you and, if so, how might you use them in your own practice?

• Do you have other ideas about how to utilize any of the manipulatives presented?

• Are there any missing manipulatives that you think every teacher should have in his or her classroom?

• Are there any manipulatives that were presented that you need more clarification about?

© The McGraw-Hill Companies, Inc.

Sample Professional Development Planner

Professional development name
Utilizing Math Manipulatives to Teach Basic Math Skills

Date	Location
August 28, 2012	*Auditorium*

Presenter
Steve Springer, 6th Grade Teacher, and Jason Hornby, Math Coach

Description

As we all know, many of our students today learn best by manipulating objects to "show" a math skill. For example, when place value is taught, using place value blocks to show the number 22 (using two ten block sticks and two single unit cubes to display the number) makes the concept more concrete in the mind of the learner. There are many different types of manipulatives available today, but often teachers are uncomfortable using them appropriately or even at all. The goal of this professional development is to show the many uses of several types of math manipulatives to better serve the learning styles and ability levels of students in our classrooms.

Goals	Research piece
• *Review of uses of math manipulatives* • *Sharing grade-level appropriate manipulatives* • *Sharing best practices of teacher's current uses of manipulatives to meet basic math skills*	*Moch, P. (2001). Manipulatives Work! Educational Forum, 66, 81–87.*

Ice breaker

Bags of beans, bags of dice, bags of dominoes, and bags of crayons will be made available at each table. As a group, the teachers will need to come up with as many uses for the materials to teach math concepts as they can (in five minutes) and then make a list of them. These ideas will be shared with the whole group. The grade level with the most ideas will win a prize.

Activity

- *Ice breaker*
- *Share manipulatives ideas.*
- *The presenter will hand out geo-boards, tangrams, place-value blocks, and one other type of manipulative. He or she will lead the teachers through a variety of uses for these manipulatives and then ask for the teachers to add other ideas they might have for these tangible products.*
- *In grade-level groups, teachers will plan the next math unit and come up with a list of appropriate math manipulatives to use for teaching its concepts.*
- *Ask teachers to read the research article and share key ideas from the article with their grade-level group at the next meeting.*

Materials

Grade-level tables with a variety of math manipulatives (beans, dice, dominoes, crayons)
Pre-bagged math manipulatives (geo-boards, tangrams, place-value blocks, and one other)

© The McGraw-Hill Companies, Inc.

Using the Internet for Researching Papers and Reports

Teachers will meet in the computer lab for this presentation. The presenter will introduce them to many children's search portals and reference websites, show them quick ways to access data, and demonstrate how to use that data to organize a research paper for the children to write. After sharing several appropriate websites, the presenter should choose a sample science or social studies research topic from the grade-level standards and use it to demonstrate how a student could go about researching that topic.

Below you will find some suggestions for topics.

• Civil War Heroes

• State Reports

• Country Reports

• Science Fair Ideas

• The Lifecycle of the Butterfly

• Volcanoes

• Writing Effective Book Reports

• Martin Luther King, Jr., Rosa Parks, or César Chávez (influential people in history)

A list of representative search portals and research websites that are appropriate for children follows:

• http://ala.org

• http://www.ask.com

• http://www.askforkids.com

• http://cybersleuth-kids.com

• http://enviroliteracy.org

• http://www.google.com

• http://icdlbooks.org

• http://kids.yahoo.com

• http://www.kidsclick.org

• http://tumblebooks.com

98

© The McGraw-Hill Companies, Inc.

Sample Professional Development Planner

Professional development name *Using the Internet for Researching Papers and Reports*	

Date *August 29, 2012*	**Location** *Computer Lab*

Presenter

Brandy Alexander, 1st Grade Teacher, and Scott Karlman, Technology Facilitator

Description

Teachers must prepare students to use technology and the Internet, but it is even more important to teach them basic research skills so that they can prepare topic papers and research reports with all the tools at their disposal. In addition to hard copy resources such as newspapers, books, encyclopedias, and magazines, it is good for children to use the Internet to access online resource material. However, teachers do not necessarily know which websites are appropriate or what key words their students should be using in their Internet searches. This professional development will introduce teachers to appropriate websites and help them to think about the type of research and writing they want their students to do this year.

Goals	**Research piece**
• *Review appropriate websites* • *List research topics for the year* • *Review websites for grade-level appropriateness and usefulness*	*Franklin, L. (2006). Never Too Young to Learn: Web Site Evaluation Is Elementary! Library Media Connection, 24, 39–41.*

Ice breaker

Ask two teachers from different grade levels to review the website http://www.enchantedlearning .com together. Each teacher will choose a science topic for his or her grade level in advance. Then they will discuss the usefulness of this website and share their ideas with the whole group.

Activity

• *Ice breaker*
• *Share a list of generic research topics for the year (for example, president report, continent report, science fair project ideas).*
• *The presenter will ask the group to suggest a research topic, and on the wall-sized screen will lead teachers through the steps needed to locate information about that topic. He or she will visit at least three websites as demonstration.*
• *Teachers will be given a different topic to research using the websites. They will then meet in grade-level groups, share their findings, and discuss potential research topics for their students.*
• *Ask teachers to read the article and share key ideas at their next grade-level group meeting.*

Materials

List of websites and list of topic ideas
Computer lab that has at least one working computer for every two teachers

© The McGraw-Hill Companies, Inc.

Planning for an After-School Program

A professional development for an after-school program is meant to help teachers organize effective and well-planned after-school programs that will benefit the students at their school site. After-school programs are excellent opportunities for enrichment and intervention, especially for students who are deemed "at-risk" or who live in areas where few after-school opportunities are available in safe places. Schools are often able to offer these opportunities. With more children staying after school and parents working longer hours, an after-school program can offer great support for families.

There are many options for after-school programs. For any of them to be effective, they need to be well organized by teachers, support staff, and possibly an outside agency. No matter which after-school programs your school decides to pursue, it's important for like-minded people to get together in order to plan for the program.

© The McGraw-Hill Companies, Inc.

Sample Professional Development Planner

Professional development name	
Planning for an After-school Program	

Date	Location
August 29, 2012	*Auditorium*

Presenter
Kashala Alexander, 5th grade teacher, and Principal Cheryl Curtis

Description
Teachers will organize effective and well-planned after-school programs that will best meet students' needs and interests. Teachers will organize possible programs by category (for example, math intervention, reading intervention, computer lab, art). These groups will outline an after-school program plan and present it to the rest of the faculty and staff. Teachers will then decide which programs are most needed and most feasible for their school site, and when they ought to be offered. They will develop a team of teachers willing to lead the development of the program and select teachers and participants who are willing to lead the after-school program itself.

Goals	Research piece
• *Choose appropriate after-school programs* • *Outline programs* • *Organize development teams* • *Select leaders to run the programs*	*Viadero, D. (2007). High-Quality After-School Programs Tied to Test-Score Gains. Education Week, 7, 1.*

Ice breaker   *Four Corners Name Tag. Have white 8½" x 11" sheets of paper and colored pencils, crayons, or markers available. Ask participants to fold a sheet of paper into thirds to make a name tent, and then tell them to write their name in the center of one panel. Ask the participants to think of four after-school programs they have been a part of, would like to be a part of, or have seen work well in the past, and then to write the name of one of those four programs in each corner of their nametag. Once they have done this, ask them to introduce themselves through their nametag. This gives the participants an opportunity to know who is interested in what.*

Activity
• *Ice breaker*
• *Teachers meet in interest groups and fill out after-school program surveys.*
• *Teachers outline a potential after-school program on chart paper based on the discussion in their interest group.*
• *Each interest group displays its chart paper and shares ideas with the whole group.*
• *The whole group decides which programs are most realistic and feasible, based on the outlines.*
• *Teachers organize development teams to carry out planning for the after-school program.*
• *Teachers read the recommended resource piece to find out what other schools are doing.*

Materials
Grade-level tables based on interests and school needs
After-school program survey

© The McGraw-Hill Companies, Inc.

Creating Curricular Backpacks for Grade Levels

A professional development on creating curricular backpacks for grade levels leads teachers through a series of steps required to create curricular-area backpacks. These will include preparing lesson plans, exploring a variety of hands-on learning tools, choosing pictures to use for new vocabulary, and selecting fiction and non-fiction picture books to go with the lessons. The presenter will present a checklist of items that should go in each backpack, such as children's picture books, chapter books, or young adult novels; hands-on learning tools; lesson plans; and assessments (for example, quizzes, tests, or journal-writing prompts). After sharing one backpack for each curricular area at every grade level, ask teachers to divide into grade-level groups and develop ideas for creating backpacks that meet their grade-level standards for each subject area.

Backpack Elements to Review with the Whole Group

• Grade-level and subject area standards

• Lesson plan ideas

• Unit plan ideas

• Hands-on items

• Picture cards for new vocabulary

• Picture book or chapter book titles

• Assessment ideas

After you have shared the sample backpacks, ask teachers to rotate through subject area tables and analyze the materials in each backpack. Then ask teachers to meet in grade-level groups and develop a list of ideas for other curricular backpacks. Ask them to develop a list of ideas for each subject area. Afterward teachers will share their ideas with the whole group.

© The McGraw-Hill Companies, Inc.

Sample Professional Development Planner

Professional development name
Creating Curricular Backpacks for Grade Levels

Date	Location
August 30, 2012	*Room 35, Mrs. Persiani's Room*

Presenter
Kimberly Persiani, 4th Grade Teacher, and Damian Camacho, 3rd Grade Teacher

Description
Teachers will be led through a series of steps on creating curricular backpacks. These include steps on preparing lesson or unit plans, a variety of hands-on learning tools, pictures to use for new vocabulary, and fiction and non-fiction picture books to go with the lessons. A checklist of items that should go in backpacks, for example, children's picture books, chapter books, or young adult novels, hands-on learning tools, lesson plans, assessments (such as quizzes, tests, journal-writing prompts) will be included and discussed.

Goals	Research piece
• *Share sample backpacks* • *Review checklist of needed materials* • *Plan for backpacks at grade levels*	*Not applicable*

Ice breaker
In grade-level groups, teachers will explore the contents of their group's grade-level science backpack. Teachers will review the contents and discuss the possibilities for its use in the classroom. Each grade-level group will share their ideas about the backpack's strengths and weaknesses as they move to the next step of creating their own ideas.

Activity
• *Ice breaker* • *The presenter will share backpacks from other curricular areas.* • *The presenter will review the backpack checklist with the group and ask teachers for additional ideas.* • *Teachers will work in grade-level groups and will develop a suggestion for one curricular backpack for each subject area. This backpack suggestion should meet their grade-level standard, and it should be one that could feasibly be developed.* • *Teachers will share their ideas with the whole group.* • *As a follow-up activity, each teacher from each grade level will be in charge of creating a backpack to share with their grade level at the grade-level group meeting in October.*

Materials
Backpacks *Materials checklist* *Chart paper and pens*

© The McGraw-Hill Companies, Inc.

9

Mentoring New Teachers

Some school districts formally assign mentors; other districts ask veteran teachers to volunteer. In more formal arrangements, the mentor teacher is typically paid a small stipend for mentoring. Whether you have been asked formally or informally to mentor a new teacher (someone who has recently been hired or who is a first- or second-year teacher), it is good to come up with a long-range plan for the year. Review district requirements and plan your meetings around those. This will enable the new teacher to meet his or her district requirements without the mentor teacher imposing work beyond what is already mandated.

Setting Up an Agenda for Meetings

You will want to set up an agenda for meetings at the very beginning of the year. You might begin by discussing which days work best for both of you, what time of day those meetings should take place, and what you would plan to discuss at each meeting. If you can meet once every two weeks, your mentee will have plenty of time between meetings to try out any new techniques discussed, and then the two of you will be able to plan additional approaches and new ideas. You may want your mentee to keep a daily journal in which he or she can record thoughts and reactions related to the goal that was set at the previous meeting.

Quick Glance Tips

✔ Set up an agenda for the new teacher that includes the schedule of meetings and objectives for each one.

✔ Discuss different techniques and best practices.

✔ Together with the new teacher, develop a long-range plan for the year.

✔ Check district requirements for new teachers.

✔ Be supportive and caring.

© The McGraw-Hill Companies, Inc.

Mentor Teacher Checklist

☐ Fill out necessary paperwork for the district and ask if you will receive a stipend for your mentoring.

☐ Consult with other master teachers about best practices; ask how they are mentoring their new teachers. Find out what they established as goals and benchmarks for the year and how they determined what those would be.

☐ Identify the new teacher you will be mentoring, introduce yourself, and discuss an agenda for the year.

☐ Discuss goals and any district requirements with the new teacher.

☐ Together with the new teacher, develop an agenda for the year and discuss the details.

☐ Meet with and counsel the new teacher regularly, and provide any support needed. Remember, new teachers need to know that they will survive the first year!

☐ Ask the new teacher frequently what his or her needs are.

☐ Give feedback after every meeting or observation.

☐ Keep accurate records of all your meetings; districts that offer stipends typically want to see detailed documentation.

☐ Remember to bring the new teacher along slowly; provide a solid support system for his or her growth as a teacher. You will be looked to for guidance, for you are the master teacher.

© The McGraw-Hill Companies, Inc.

Planning Benchmarks and Goals

The following ideas may help you develop benchmarks or goals that the new teacher can focus on between scheduled meetings when the two of you discuss the outcomes. In addition, there may be district guidelines for establishing benchmarks, goals, or agenda items when meeting with the new teacher.

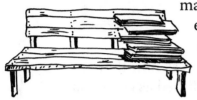

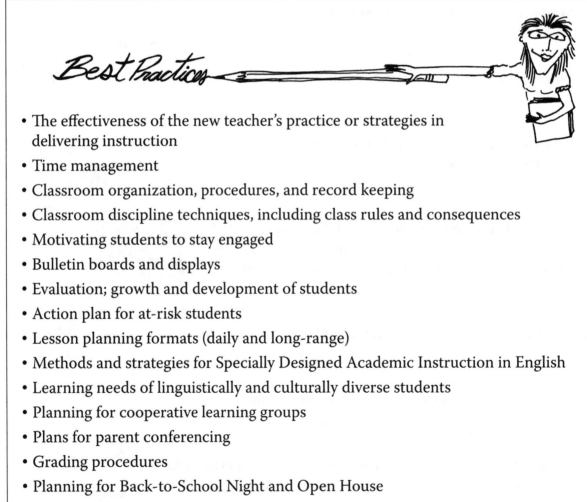

Best Practices

- The effectiveness of the new teacher's practice or strategies in delivering instruction
- Time management
- Classroom organization, procedures, and record keeping
- Classroom discipline techniques, including class rules and consequences
- Motivating students to stay engaged
- Bulletin boards and displays
- Evaluation; growth and development of students
- Action plan for at-risk students
- Lesson planning formats (daily and long-range)
- Methods and strategies for Specially Designed Academic Instruction in English
- Learning needs of linguistically and culturally diverse students
- Planning for cooperative learning groups
- Plans for parent conferencing
- Grading procedures
- Planning for Back-to-School Night and Open House
- Working with disruptive students
- Effective use of teacher aide

© The McGraw-Hill Companies, Inc.

Planning Formal and Informal Observations

Throughout the year, you may need to plan formal observations, especially if paperwork is required for the district office. However, if you are volunteering as a mentor for a new teacher, you may only be required to observe him or her informally, afterward providing feedback directly to the teacher and your principal. Multiple-subject teachers should observe their mentee in each curricular area; secondary teachers should observe their mentee during each class period. This will provide a well-rounded picture of the new teacher's practice and needs. Planning for and evaluation of the observations should be the focus of your scheduled meetings immediately prior to and following the observed class. Meetings at other times can focus on other topics.

- Remember to put your new teacher at ease during the observation, letting him or her know that it's informal.

- Provide feedback after each observation.

- Tell your new teacher five things he or she did well and one or two things to improve on.

- This is a new teacher, so be sympathetic!

- Be positive!

© The McGraw-Hill Companies, Inc.

Counseling Strategies

In your regularly scheduled meetings with the new teacher, keep in mind the following suggestions for counseling strategies that will support the new teacher.

- Plan meeting topics in advance, and have all pertinent information available at the meeting. Be prepared to provide specific and tangible suggestions.

- Create a supportive atmosphere, and conduct the conference where you will have full privacy and no interruptions.

- Keep an open mind as you review the teacher's performance, concerns described in his or her daily reflection journal, or matters that come up in discussion.

- Focus on a collaborative approach to analyzing the teacher's performance against the benchmarks set, and determine any changes to be made.

- Limit the conference to a discussion of one or two important items.

- Conclude each conference with tangible plans for the week(s) before the next scheduled meeting.

- Listen attentively. Give realistic and supportive feedback; don't focus on the negative.

Quick Tips

✔ Leave positive notes. ✔ Try to hit benchmarks. ✔ Be realistic with goals.

© The McGraw-Hill Companies, Inc.

Meeting Agenda (New Teacher–Mentor Teacher)

Mentor teacher		Date of meeting
New teacher	Room number	Time

Agenda items

What to bring

Goals to be discussed	Notes

© The McGraw-Hill Companies, Inc.

Feedback and Needs Assessment Worksheet (New Teacher)

Name	Date

Things I'm doing well

Areas where I have questions or needs

Three goals for this term

1.

2.

3.

© The McGraw-Hill Companies, Inc.

Observation Feedback Form
(Mentor Teacher)

New teacher	Date
Mentor teacher	Time
Lesson observed	Curricular area

Order of events in lesson

Five things you did well!

1.

2.

3.

4.

5.

One or two areas to improve on

1.

2.

Rank these areas of performance

Time management	Posture and positive attitude
Needs improvement Excellent	Needs improvement Excellent
1 2 3 4 5 6 7 8 9 10	1 2 3 4 5 6 7 8 9 10

© The McGraw-Hill Companies, Inc.

Supporting a Student Teacher

How Do You Know If You Are Ready to Support a Student Teacher?

If you would like to take mentoring to a higher level, you may be ready to invite a student teacher to complete his or her teaching preparedness in your class. This will take time and energy, but it can be very rewarding and meaningful for you and your students. Student teachers are typically assigned to a school-based cooperating teacher—a master teacher like you—and a supervisor from their university program.

The responsibility of a cooperating teacher is to supervise, model, guide, and assess the student teacher in order to further the development of the student teacher's teaching practice. With that in mind, the cooperating teacher should make the student teacher feel welcome and comfortable in the classroom. A master teacher who is supervising a student teacher will need to make sure that the classroom environment is open to new people and is supportive for the student teacher's learning.

The student teaching experience is essential for the development of teaching skills required for certification and the development of the student teacher's own teaching practice. It is an excellent opportunity to learn from an experienced master teacher. The master teacher who takes on this role provides a great service to the student teacher, and the student teacher will also be of immeasurable help to the master teacher and the students in the class.

© The McGraw-Hill Companies, Inc.

Important Characteristics of a Cooperating Teacher

The effective cooperating teacher has good relationships with the administration, colleagues, parents, and children. In addition, the cooperating teacher continues to build his or her professional portfolio by keeping up-to-date on new techniques and procedures both in the specific subject area and in the study of teaching itself, and then uses this information in actual classroom work with children. It is also important that the cooperating teacher have experience working with new teachers and in supervising teaching techniques; he or she must be flexible, consistent, and patient.

In today's world, it is critical that the cooperating teacher have training in the multicultural and global aspects of delivering the curriculum. It's not only important to be a highly qualified and experienced teacher; it's also important to be experienced in working with diverse populations, ages, cultural and linguistic backgrounds, and ability levels in a respectful, caring, and supportive way.

As a master teacher, when you invite a student teacher into your classroom, you are making a significant commitment, a large part of which is the responsibility for setting the tone so that the student teacher feels a part of the class and a part of the school as a whole. At the classroom level, you must be willing to share classroom and school materials, including teacher manuals, manipulatives, and classroom supplies. On a more philosophical level, your attitude toward the teaching profession, as well as toward your job position, students, and colleagues, should be positive in order to be a good model for the student teacher.

© The McGraw-Hill Companies, Inc.

How Shall I Prepare for a Student Teacher?

The time that you spend preparing for the student teacher's arrival will pay great dividends in providing a positive learning environment for the student teacher, and it will make the transition for the student teacher and the children that much easier.

Prior to the student teacher's presence in the classroom for the first time, cooperating teachers should consider the following:

✔ Prepare the children for the arrival of the student teacher, emphasizing that he or she is a *teacher*.

✔ Let parents know that you will be having a student teacher in your class. Include the start and end dates of the student teacher's time with the class, and invite the parents to come to meet him or her. It is important for you to help the parents understand how much this experience will enhance their child's learning and how valuable a role the student teacher will play in the class.

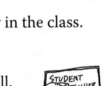

✔ Be sure that your administrator knows the start and end dates as well, so that the administrator can introduce himself or herself to the student teacher on the first day.

✔ Obtain copies of materials that will be helpful for the student teacher, such as extra teacher manuals, current school newsletters or classroom handouts, and any new teacher orientation materials.

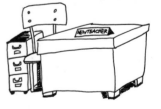

✔ Provide dedicated space for the student teacher, such as a desk, table, adult-sized chair, file cabinet drawer, and cupboard, so that the student teacher can organize his or her materials and supplies.

✔ Prepare a draft of your daily schedule—from your arrival time to your departure time—so that the student teacher knows when to be available for planning, when staff development meetings are, and what your contract times are.

© The McGraw-Hill Companies, Inc.

What Do I Do When My Student Teacher Arrives?

Orient Your Student Teacher to the School Campus

✓ Share important information about the school and community, and familiarize the student teacher with the campus on a short tour.

✓ Introduce the student teacher to faculty, staff, resource personnel, principal, vice-principal, counselors, office staff, custodians, nurse, aides, cafeteria workers, bus drivers, and others.

✓ Provide a general introduction to the building plan of the school, including the location of offices, cafeteria, lounge, adult restrooms, and copying facilities.

✓ Provide the student teacher with schedules for both the school and the class that he or she will be teaching.

✓ Discuss the importance of developing good relationships with teachers and other personnel.

✓ Discuss the philosophy of the school.

✓ Acquaint the student teacher with the library, audiovisual aids, computers and computer lab, and the location of supplies and materials.

✓ Familiarize the student teacher with co-curricular and extracurricular activities (for example, tutoring before school and any after-school programs).

✓ Make your student teacher feel at home in your school environment.

✓ Be kind. Remember that this may be a student teacher's first experience in a profession that you love. You have the power to make it a great one!

✓ In most cases, student teachers adhere to the contractual obligations of their cooperating teacher, so it is important for the student teacher to be provided with the district requirements concerning the cooperating teacher's daily responsibilities.

© The McGraw-Hill Companies, Inc.

Orient Your Student Teacher to Your Classroom and Students

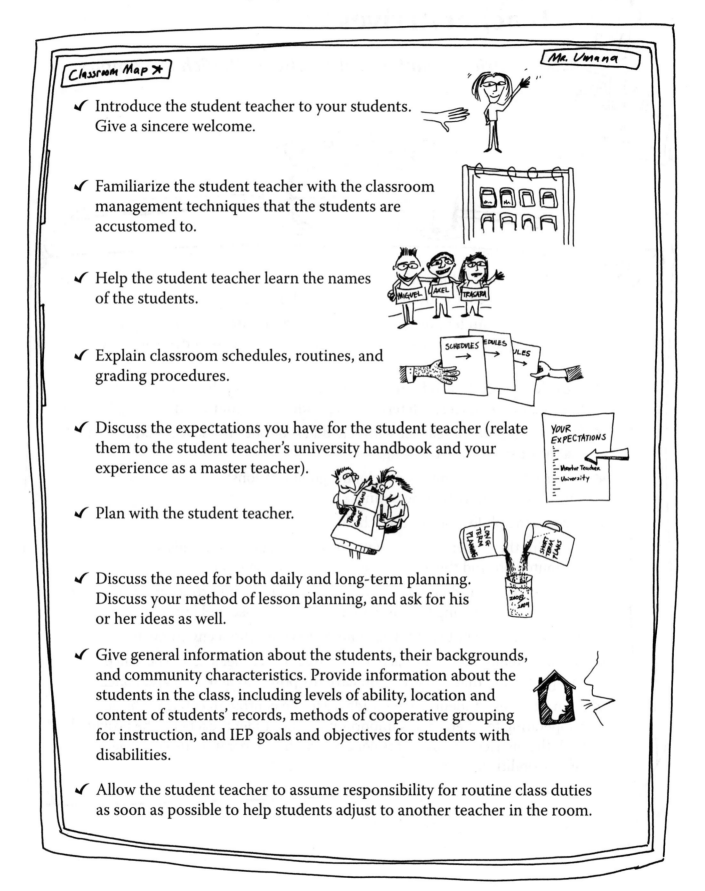

Classroom Map

Mr. Umana

✓ Introduce the student teacher to your students. Give a sincere welcome.

✓ Familiarize the student teacher with the classroom management techniques that the students are accustomed to.

✓ Help the student teacher learn the names of the students.

✓ Explain classroom schedules, routines, and grading procedures.

✓ Discuss the expectations you have for the student teacher (relate them to the student teacher's university handbook and your experience as a master teacher).

✓ Plan with the student teacher.

✓ Discuss the need for both daily and long-term planning. Discuss your method of lesson planning, and ask for his or her ideas as well.

✓ Give general information about the students, their backgrounds, and community characteristics. Provide information about the students in the class, including levels of ability, location and content of students' records, methods of cooperative grouping for instruction, and IEP goals and objectives for students with disabilities.

✓ Allow the student teacher to assume responsibility for routine class duties as soon as possible to help students adjust to another teacher in the room.

© The McGraw-Hill Companies, Inc.

Informing the Student Teacher About School Policy: A Checklist

☐ Discuss a teacher's responsibilities for attending meetings, including PTA meetings, staff meetings, parent conferences, Individualized Education Program (IEP) meetings, and Student Success Team (SST) meetings.

☐ Provide information about school policies regarding curriculum and instruction, discipline procedures, attendance policy (including absentee and tardy management), safety drill exercises, special schedules, handling of substance or parental abuse, and the proper methods of procuring needed equipment, materials, and supplies. This information may be available in the faculty handbook.

☐ Discuss the chain of command for resolution of problems.

☐ Discuss standards of dress for both students and teachers.

☐ Brief the student teacher on any unwritten school policies.

☐ Discuss emergency plans for earthquake and fire drills.

117

© The McGraw-Hill Companies, Inc.

Student Teacher Responsibilities

The level of teaching responsibility given to a student teacher should increase as the cooperating teacher feels that the student teacher is ready. As you work together, talk with your student teacher about his or her fears and strengths. This will help you to know when the student teacher is ready to take responsibility for certain curricular areas or tasks. Remember that some student teachers are brand new to teaching, while others may have had previous experience as a teacher aide, a classroom teacher, or a substitute teacher in another setting. Some student teachers will be ready to take over instruction early in their placement with you, while others may need a little more hand-holding.

A recommended timetable for gradually increasing the student teacher's responsibilities may be provided by the student teacher's university program, with guidelines that would depend on whether the student teacher is in an elementary, secondary, or special education program. The master teacher should develop a draft of a timetable for each student teacher at the beginning of the placement, with the student teacher having input as well. You should decide on the responsibilities you feel comfortable handing over. Begin with the following suggestions for listing responsibilities, and add to them as you see fit.

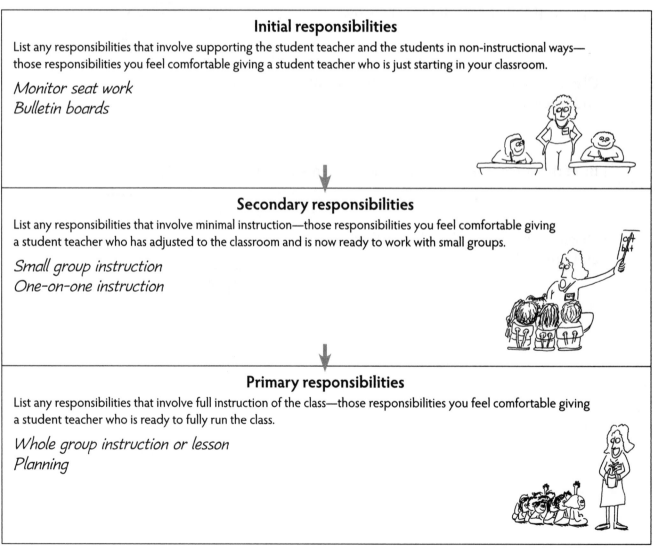

Initial responsibilities

List any responsibilities that involve supporting the student teacher and the students in non-instructional ways—those responsibilities you feel comfortable giving a student teacher who is just starting in your classroom.

Monitor seat work
Bulletin boards

Secondary responsibilities

List any responsibilities that involve minimal instruction—those responsibilities you feel comfortable giving a student teacher who has adjusted to the classroom and is now ready to work with small groups.

Small group instruction
One-on-one instruction

Primary responsibilities

List any responsibilities that involve full instruction of the class—those responsibilities you feel comfortable giving a student teacher who is ready to fully run the class.

Whole group instruction or lesson
Planning

118

© The McGraw-Hill Companies, Inc.

Cooperating Teacher Responsibilities

A cooperating teacher guides the student teacher in developing his or her own teaching practice and skills. While the master teacher is in charge of daily supervision, student teachers are also supervised by their university program. This supervision usually takes the form of scheduled formal lessons that are focused on a particular subject. All student teachers are different; some may need more support than others. However, all can benefit from your experience when creating their lessons for observation by their university supervisor.

It is important to remember that different university programs focus on different aspects of teaching, and many programs look for different things at different times in the placement. Some programs require two semesters of student teaching, while others require an entire year at two hours per day. Other programs specify that a full-time assignment covers a certain period of time (such as 10 weeks, or one quarter). During each placement period, university supervisors will evaluate student teachers on various aspects of their teaching. The master teacher supports the student teacher throughout this process, however it is defined.

In addition to supporting student teachers as they move through their university programs, the cooperating teachers themselves are usually asked to provide feedback and to evaluate student teachers on their progress. This feedback might be a

conversation with a university professor, or it might be provided on standardized forms, open-ended questionnaires, or Scantron forms provided to the cooperating teacher by the university program. These are important evaluations, and they may ultimately determine the student teacher's future. They are official and legal documents, so be honest in your evaluation, and be as clear and concise as possible. Be sure to ask for clarification if you need it when filling out the required paperwork.

Some university programs require extensive paperwork in the form of observations or reports. Universities can provide you with information about these responsibilities and requirements, so you will know what is expected of you before making a commitment.

Whether it is formally required or not, it is a good idea to make observations and provide feedback. Write down your thoughts, along with any suggestions you have, so that you are prepared to hold an effective conference with your student teacher.

© The McGraw-Hill Companies, Inc.

Role in Supervising

The cooperating teacher provides the most significant supervision for the student teacher, simply because he or she spends more time with the student teacher than does any other assigned supervisor. The cooperating teacher will use both formal and informal supervision techniques that involve observing and recording the student teacher's performance over time. In discussions intended to enhance growth in the student teacher's teaching skills, the cooperating teacher will provide detailed and helpful feedback. Keeping a journal on the student teacher's performance will facilitate this.

Ideas for Developing Rapport

It is important that the cooperating teacher engage his or her student teacher in candid and meaningful communication. Below are some suggestions for doing so.

✔ Be clear about the nature and frequency of pre-observation conferences, observations, and feedback conferences. It is important to make your expectations known at the very beginning of the placement; unclear expectations lead to frustrations for both parties.

✔ Treat the student teacher as a co-teacher rather than as "just a student teacher." Do not make suggestions or correct the student teacher in front of the class or within earshot of students, unless the destruction of property or safety is involved.

✔ To encourage the students to treat the student teacher as an authority figure, redirect the students to the student teacher if they come to you for assistance when the student teacher is in charge of the class.

✔ If the student teacher is struggling, make every effort to support and guide him or her; however, if problems increase and there is no evidence of improvement, make time to meet with the university supervisor.

✔ Try to remember what it was like to be a student teacher, and try to demonstrate sensitivity to the needs of the student teacher during stressful periods. What has become a simple task for you is bound to be much more difficult the first time it is attempted.

✔ If the student teacher is expressing concerns about his or her performance after having observed you several times, you may want to encourage the student teacher to visit other classes at the same grade level to observe alternative practices for the same curriculum.

✔ Offer honest and constructive encouragement.

✔ Offer positive feedback as well as suggestions for improvement on a daily basis.

✔ Provide prompt feedback via written anecdotal notes, verbal comment, or other observational data. Engage in constructive conversation based on observations and routinely ask the student teacher to reflect on his or her lessons.

© The McGraw-Hill Companies, Inc.

Initial Days: Observation

Most of the student teacher's activities during the first day or two will consist of observation—to learn about the master teacher's teaching style, the daily routine, the students in the class. This should be a period in which the student teacher has an opportunity to see the master teacher and his or her students during a typical day.

Every teacher is different, and real life exposure to a teacher's particular style is important. Student teachers will be observing how you interact with your students. They will get a sense of how you differentiate your instruction to meet the needs of a diverse group of learners and how your room environment supports this. This will be a powerful experience for them, one they may very well model in their own classroom. It is important to show them your best. Use this as an opportunity to be on top of your game—a motivation to demonstrate your best teaching and organization.

Plan a meeting at the end of each day of the first week to review the student teacher's notes and to clarify any questions or concerns he or she may have at that time. Consider the following questions as a way of structuring observations of the master teacher's classroom.

Classroom Observation Questions

- How does the daily agenda or schedule compare to the one posted?
- What routine for class procedures has been established?
- What strategies are used to motivate students when new lessons are introduced?
- What provisions have been made for individual differences?
- What classroom management techniques are being used that might be helpful to the student teacher?
- What instructional techniques and activities are being used to develop a classroom environment that enhances learning?
- What activities are being used to enhance higher-level thinking skills in students?
- How are transitions managed?
- What is the homework policy?
- How does one plan for a classroom aide or parent volunteers?

© The McGraw-Hill Companies, Inc.

Conferencing

Cooperating teachers should plan to conference with student teachers and provide oral or written feedback daily. Conference topics will depend on both the needs of the student teacher and the classroom situation.

Conference Discussion Topics

- Daily schedule and time allotments
- Classroom organization and procedures, including record keeping and seating arrangements
- Classroom management techniques, alternatives, and teaching strategies
- Motivating students to learn and stay engaged
- Questioning techniques and activities to enhance higher-level thinking by the students
- Procedures for dealing with emergencies
- Bulletin boards and displays
- Arranging for field trips using available resources
- Evaluation of students
- Growth and development of students
- Action plan for at-risk students
- Professional ethics
- Prioritizing areas for the student teacher's professional growth (for example, helping the student teacher establish realistic goals, develop strategies for instruction, and use assessments for lesson planning)

Other Important Ideas for Discussion

- Cumulative files and IEP and SST paperwork
- General day-to-day record keeping
- Lesson planning formats (daily and long-range)
- Special education placement and procedures
- Effective questioning skills for all students
- Methods and strategies for Specially Designed Academic Instruction in English
- Learning needs of linguistically and culturally diverse students
- Planning for the first day and first week of school, as well as the final week; preparing cumulative files
- Cooperative learning groups
- Parent conferencing and parent communication protocol
- Grading procedures
- Building an effective classroom climate
- Planning for a substitute
- District, county, and community family and educational resources
- Back-to-School Night and Open House preparation ideas
- Working with disruptive students
- Effective use of classroom aides and parent volunteers

© The McGraw-Hill Companies, Inc.

Effective Conferences

Suggestions for Meaningful Conferences with the Student Teacher

The cooperating teacher and the student teacher should have regularly scheduled conferences. Conference topics might include lesson planning, discussions about particular students, or ideas for teacher-led activities. A conference should always be held after the student teacher has been observed delivering a formal lesson. Listed below are suggestions for conducting effective conferences to support the student teacher's instructional improvement.

✔ Be prepared for conferences by knowing what you would like to discuss. Have notes, observation materials, samples of students' work, records, and other pertinent information available for your meeting. Be prepared to provide specific and tangible suggestions for improvement.

✔ Create a supportive atmosphere and conduct the conference where you have full privacy and time without interruptions.

✔ Review the student teacher's performance by looking for strengths as well as areas for improvement.

✔ Focus on a collaborative approach to analyzing the student teacher's performance and determining changes to be made.

✔ Limit the conference to a discussion of one or two important items. Do not overwhelm the student teacher.

✔ Conclude each conference with plans for showing improvement on a timeline.

✔ Focus attention on the objective teaching-learning situation rather than on the student teacher.

Student Teacher Conference Checklist

☐ Schedule (private, no interruptions)

☐ Prepare (know what you want to say, have any supporting documentation)

☐ Focus (focus on one or two areas or items)

☐ Plan (have plans to improve)

☐ Goals (set goals with student teacher)

☐ Positive (always try to find at least one positive thing to discuss and encourage)

☐ Document (keep records of all conferences)

© The McGraw-Hill Companies, Inc.

Professional Issues

There are some issues you should consider discussing with your student teacher so that he or she is aware that dealing with such issues is also part of a teacher's professional life. Keep in mind that the student teacher's university will likely have much of this covered, but it's good for the two of you to have these conversations as well. The following are some topics you may choose to discuss with your student teacher.

Reporting Child Abuse

The student teacher should report any suspicions of child abuse to the cooperating teacher so that he or she can follow procedure. It is then up to the school to contact the appropriate authorities if warranted.

Dress Code

Student teachers should dress professionally. Some schools have a relaxed dress code; however, student teachers need to be aware that how they dress affects the way students respond to them in the classroom.

Use of Electronic Devices During the Day

Student teachers should not use pagers, cell phones, or other electronic devices during instructional time. Emergency telephone calls should be directed to the school office. In addition, checking e-mail on the classroom computers during instructional time is not acceptable. If the student teacher abuses any of these guidelines, consider notifying the university supervisor.

Curriculum

Ensure that instructional content, as determined by state standards and district mandates, is being planned for and taught. It is not appropriate for student teachers to revise curriculum or change the classroom management plan. Student teachers should be mirroring what you already have in place while trying out a few techniques of their own.

Grades

Establish a very clear understanding about how grading is to be handled. Make sure that the student teacher realizes that the cooperating teacher is, as the teacher of record, ultimately responsible.

Parent Conferences

It is important for the student teacher to have experience working with parents. It is advised, however, that the student teacher only observe conferences and meetings between the master teacher and the parent (and optionally the administrator or support personnel—school psychologist, nurse, resource teacher), participating only if invited to do so by the master teacher.

© The McGraw-Hill Companies, Inc.

Self-reflection (Cooperating Teacher)

Below is a list of questions designed to encourage reflection on the part of the cooperating teacher. It is important to ask yourself these questions during the first week of the student teacher's placement with you, and again midway through the term. It also serves as a teaching tool as you model reflection on your own practice for the student teacher.

Check off those items that you feel you have covered. Add comments to the written reflection portion.

At the End of the First Week

☐ 1. Have I done what I can to see that pupils will accept my student teacher favorably?

    ☐ Did I let them know in advance of his or her arrival?

    ☐ Did I explain the student teacher's role?

    ☐ Did I act pleased to have a student teacher?

    ☐ Did I let the student teacher introduce himself or herself to the students?

☐ 2. Have I become acquainted with the student teacher?

    ☐ Did I use the information furnished by the university?

    ☐ Did we discuss his or her personal and academic background?

    ☐ Did I encourage the student teacher to express his or her ambitions, concerns, and expectations?

    ☐ Have I provided a good model for presenting lessons?

☐ 3. Have I helped the student teacher identify the following teaching components?

    ☐ Motivational strategies

    ☐ Methods of discipline

    ☐ Objectives of the lesson with assessment to evaluate instructional effectiveness

    ☐ Hands-on activities to correlate with the lesson

    ☐ Curriculum materials used

    ☐ Active participation strategies

    ☐ Instructional equipment used

☐ 4. Did I brief the student teacher on the following school procedures?

    ☐ Fire or earthquake drills

    ☐ Playground and school rules

    ☐ Reporting of child injury or illness

    ☐ Releasing students during school hours

    ☐ Checking the weekly bulletin

    ☐ Ordering supplies

    ☐ Using the library, library books, and instructional materials

    ☐ Selecting district-approved booklists and support materials

    ☐ Utilizing support services—for example, nurse, counselor specialists, coaches

    ☐ Cumulative records and tests

© The McGraw-Hill Companies, Inc.

At the End of the First Week (cont'd)

- ☐ 5. Did I brief the student teacher on the following classroom procedures for instruction?
  - ☐ Differentiated instruction
  - ☐ Types of instructional materials such as manipulatives and teacher guides
  - ☐ Roles of paid aides and parent or community volunteers
  - ☐ Recording student progress
- ☐ 6. Have I oriented the student teacher to school equipment (for example, copy machines, computers, audiovisual)?

At Midterm

- ☐ 1. Have I done the following to assist the student teacher in developing lesson plans?
  - ☐ Provide district-designed lesson plan forms or select a lesson plan form from the student teaching handbook.
  - ☐ Examine lesson plans prior to their being used by the student teacher and making appropriate suggestions.
  - ☐ Explain, assist, and monitor the development of daily, unit, and long-range lesson planning.
- ☐ 2. Have I developed and maintained a positive relationship with the student teacher?
- ☐ 3. Have I provided opportunities for the student teacher to work on bulletin boards and displays?
- ☐ 4. Have I modeled and encouraged a variety of instructional methods?

- ☐ 5. Have I modeled and discussed a variety of ways to evaluate student progress in order to maximize instructional time and student progress?
- ☐ 6. Have I successfully modeled appropriate strategies for working with English Language Learners? Did my student teacher have opportunities to practice these techniques?
- ☐ 7. Have I successfully modeled appropriate strategies for working with children with special needs and disabilities? Did my student teacher have opportunities to practice these techniques?
- ☐ 8. Have I successfully modeled appropriate strategies for working with students who demonstrate higher levels of ability? Did my student teacher have opportunities to practice these techniques?
- ☐ 9. Has my student teacher observed me working with parents, colleagues, and administrators in productive ways?

© The McGraw-Hill Companies, Inc.

After the Student Teacher Completes the Placement

1. What will I do differently with my next student teacher?

2. What were my strengths as a cooperating teacher with this student teacher? List three.

3. In what areas do I feel that I could improve as a cooperating teacher?

4. What questions or concerns do I have for the student teacher's university supervisor or program?

5. Other

© The McGraw-Hill Companies, Inc.

Student Teaching Forms and Resource Documents

Student Teaching Meeting Agenda

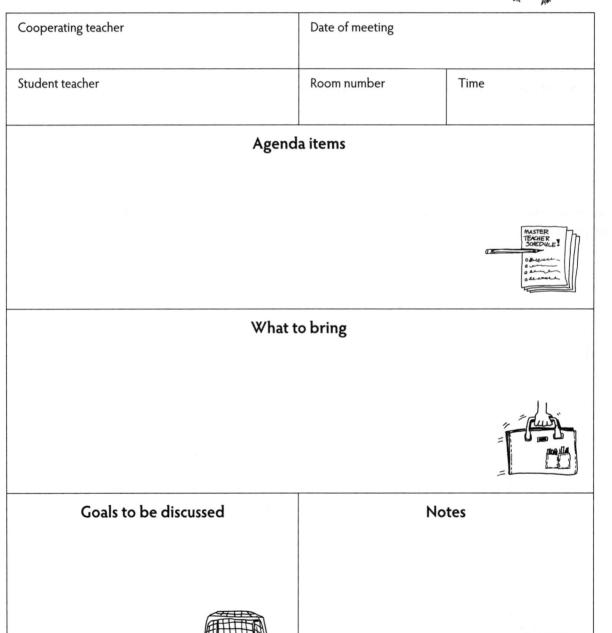

Cooperating teacher	Date of meeting	
Student teacher	Room number	Time

Agenda items

What to bring

Goals to be discussed	Notes

© The McGraw-Hill Companies, Inc.

Classroom Observations (Student Teacher)

Record your observations of the cooperating teacher's classroom. Add any additional observations or questions. If more space is needed, continue on the back. Save this page for future reference.

What does the daily agenda or schedule look like compared to the one posted?
What routine has been established for classroom procedures?
What strategies are used to motivate students when new lessons are introduced?
What provisions are made for individual differences?
What classroom management techniques are used that might be helpful to a student teacher?
What instructional techniques and activities are used to develop a classroom environment that enhances learning?
What activities are used to enhance higher-level thinking skills in students?
How are transitions managed?
What is the homework policy?
How are plans made for the classroom aide or parent volunteers?
Other observations

© The McGraw-Hill Companies, Inc.

Observation Feedback Form (Cooperating Teacher)

Student teacher	Date
Cooperating teacher	Time
Lesson observed	Curricular area

Order of events in lesson

Five things you did well!

1.

2.

3.

4.

5.

One or two areas to improve on

1.

2.

Rank these areas of performance

Time management	Posture and positive attitude
Needs improvement Excellent	Needs improvement Excellent
1 2 3 4 5 6 7 8 9 10	1 2 3 4 5 6 7 8 9 10

© The McGraw-Hill Companies, Inc.

Reflective Journal (Student Teacher)

Record your reflections on a specific lesson, on your observations, on your thoughts in general about a day in the classroom. Keeping a journal is an excellent way to process your experience. Some suggestions to guide your reflections follow.

Date
What did I observe or do?
How do I feel about it? How did it go?
What would I change about it?
What were my strengths?
What can I improve?
What did I learn?

© The McGraw-Hill Companies, Inc.

Self-reflection (Student Teacher)

Name	Date

Things I'm doing well

Areas where I have questions or needs

Three goals for this term

1.

2.

3.

© The McGraw-Hill Companies, Inc.

Student Teaching Timetable

Project when the student teacher will take on certain events and responsibilities over the course of this teaching experience. Indicate which are initial, secondary, or primary responsibilities. Note all lesson observations and meetings. The cooperating teacher and the student teacher should develop the timetable together.

Cooperating teacher	Student teacher
Month	
Week 1	
Week 2	
Week 3	
Week 4	
Week 5	
Month	
Week 1	
Week 2	
Week 3	
Week 4	
Week 5	
Month	
Week 1	
Week 2	
Week 3	
Week 4	
Week 5	

© The McGraw-Hill Companies, Inc.

Student Teaching Weekly Planner

Student teacher		Year

Cooperating teacher

Ideas/Goals/Meetings

Week 1	Week 2	Week 3	Week 4	Week 5

Week 6	Week 7	Week 8	Week 9	Week 10

Notes

NOTES

© The McGraw-Hill Companies, Inc.

Observation Log (Cooperating Teacher)

Student teacher	Cooperating teacher

Notes

Theme or subject taught	Date	Time	Observation/Meeting

University/College requirements

135

© The McGraw-Hill Companies, Inc.

Conference Log (Cooperating Teacher)

Record thoughts and observations in this log. Keep for documentation records.

Cooperating teacher	Date
Student teacher	Week

1 to 3 items to discuss (Be sure to include the positive!)

Plan of action

Goals

Timeline

© The McGraw-Hill Companies, Inc.

Informal Observations (Cooperating Teacher)

Record informal observations of an activity or lesson. (This is not formal documentation).
Keep a copy for reference when filling out formal university evaluation forms.

Cooperating teacher	Student teacher

Observation (Activity/Lesson) ☐ Whole class ☐ Small group ☐ One-on-one	Date

Goal/Objectives   ☐ Clear   ☐ Unclear

Brief overview or summary of activity/lesson

☐ Introduction   ☐ Independent practice
☐ Lesson   ☐ Follow-up
☐ Guided practice   ☐ Modifications
☐ Questions   ☐ Assessment

Standards met

Strengths	Areas to improve

Questions

Notes

© The McGraw-Hill Companies, Inc.

Reflective Journal (Cooperating Teacher)

Record reflections about your student teacher. It may be helpful to refer to it when you fill out an evaluation or are asked about the student teacher. Some suggestions for your reflective journal follow.

Date
Is the student teacher engaged in the classroom?
Is the student teacher growing professionally?
Is the student teacher organized and in control?
Is the student teacher professional?

© The McGraw-Hill Companies, Inc.

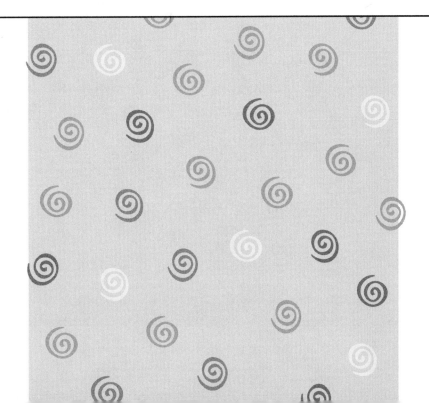

III
Leadership Outside the Regular Classroom

12 Planning, Organizing, and Leading After-school Programs 141

13 After-school Program Ideas 159

14 Getting Parents Involved 166

15 Incentive Programs 190

16 Fund-raising 212

17 Grant Writing 235

18 Preparing for a Formal Evaluation 259

12

Planning, Organizing, and Leading After-school Programs

After-school programs are an excellent opportunity for enrichment and intervention. Because more children are staying after school and parents are working longer hours, an after-school program can offer significant support for students and their families. There are many options for after-school programs, but for any of them to be effective, they need to be well organized. This chapter will assist you in choosing and organizing an after-school program.

If you are considering leading an after-school program, you have only to look around you to find teachers who could potentially staff it—your colleagues. If funding is in place for their services, it will be easier to persuade them to get involved. Without a source of funding, you might need to investigate applying for a grant in order to fund an after-school program for the students at your school. Once you have secured the funding, materials can be purchased, teachers can be hired and paid, and students will begin to benefit from the enrichment programs and academic support.

You'll find a list of after-school program ideas in Chapter 13, but you may be able to come up with ideas yourself that suit the needs of *your* students at *your* school. Network—ask other teachers and visit other schools for ideas about after-school programs. If you find out about an after-school program that works for another school, start there. Another program's structure and implementation may serve as a good model even it is aligned with different goals. An existing program can be adjusted to fit your school's needs.

In determining whether to offer an after-school program and, if so, which one it should be, each school should consider the questions on the following page.

© The McGraw-Hill Companies, Inc.

Where have we been?

School-wide reflection on after-school programs

> What worked?

> What didn't work?

↓

Where are we now?

School-wide inventory of needs

> Test scores

> Target areas

> State/District mandates

> Gifted and Talented Education (GATE) program requirements

> Federal requirements

> Parent and community needs

> Grant proposal for implementation

↓

Where are we going?

School-wide goals for after-school program

> Alignment to standards

> Hours of service

> Community resources

> Outside providers

After-school program

> Schedule: days of week, times, total hours of service

> Targeted grade levels/classrooms

> Teachers

> Materials and supplies (such as vehicle, books, activity sheets)

> Qualifications for students

> Parent letter

> Permission or waiver

> Class attendance sheet

> Teacher sign-in sheet for office

> Documentation

> Pre- and post-assessment

> Snacks

142

© The McGraw-Hill Companies, Inc.

After-school Program Survey

Survey results will guide preparation of the After-school Program Planner.

What is the primary need for our student population?

Why?

What funding source is available?

☐ Program _____ ☐ School funds _____

☐ Grant _____ ☐ Other _____

Who are the targeted students?

☐ Primary (K, 1, 2)　　☐ High-achieving students　　☐ Special needs students

☐ Upper (3, 4, 5, 6, 7, 8)　　☐ Low-achieving students　　☐ _____

☐ After-school population　　☐ ESL students

What would be used for instruction?

Curriculum

Materials

Resources

Where would the program or classes be located?

☐ Classrooms _____　　☐ Library　　☐ Music room

☐ Auditorium　　☐ Computer lab　　☐ Play area

☐ Cafeteria　　☐ Art room

Who will facilitate the program?

☐ Program coordinator _____　　☐ Community volunteers

☐ Teachers _____　　☐ Parents

☐ School aides/Assistants

When will the program take place? For how long?

	Monday	Tuesday	Wednesday	Thursday	Friday	Saturday
A.M.	_____	_____	_____	_____	_____	_____
P.M.	_____	_____	_____	_____	_____	_____

From _____ to _____　　Duration _____

143

© The McGraw-Hill Companies, Inc.

After-school Program Academic Needs Review

List the top three grade-level or target population academic needs at your school

1.

2.

3.

List test or assessment scores for these academic areas

Test/Assessment   Date   Scores

List curriculum and other resources

Federal/State/District

Community/Parent

Grant

Number of hours required for program: _____ per week _____ total

Days of the week available for program: M T W Th F Sa

Target standards to be addressed

Number of students to be targeted

Grade level(s) of focus

Class size

Classrooms available (both total number of rooms and volunteered rooms)

Available/Interested teachers

© The McGraw-Hill Companies, Inc.

After-school Program Planner

Program name	Academic	Enrichment

Program goals (at least three)

Standards and learning goals aligned to program (at least three)

Targeted student population	Sponsor/Funding	Curriculum/Resources
Coordinator	Facilitators	Location

Program overview (What will the program look like? What is the daily schedule or routine?)

Schedule

	Monday	Tuesday	Wednesday	Thursday	Friday	Saturday
A.M.	_____	_____	_____	_____	_____	_____
P.M.	_____	_____	_____	_____	_____	_____

Timeline

Start date _____ End date _____ Total days per week _____ Total hours per day _____

145

© The McGraw-Hill Companies, Inc.

Sample After-school Program Planner

This sample planner is based on the Reading Tutoring after-school program in Chapter 13.

Program name *Reading Tutoring*	(Academic) Enrichment

Program goals (at least three)
- *To improve word attack skills (sounding out, phonics skills)*
- *To improve fluency*
- *To improve comprehension*

Standards and learning goals aligned to program (at least three)

- *Decoding and word recognition:*
    Decode two-syllable nonsense words and regular multi-syllable words
    Read aloud fluently and accurately and with appropriate intonation and expression
- *Comprehension and analysis of grade-level-appropriate text:*
    Restate facts and details in the text to clarify and organize ideas

Targeted student population	**Sponsor/Funding**	**Curriculum/Resources**
Students who are designated "at-risk" or "below basic" in Reading.	*District-approved; facilitators will be paid through district funds.*	• *Hooked on Phonics* • *tumblebooks.com* • *Phonics-based worksheets*
Coordinator	**Facilitators**	**Location**
Mr. Springer, 6th grade teacher	*Mr. Alexander and Mrs. Monaghan*	• *Room 4, Monday and Wednesday* • *Computer Lab, Friday*

Program overview (What will the program look like? What is the daily schedule or routine?)

- *3 days per week: Monday, Wednesday, Friday*
- *Monday and Wednesday will include Blending of new Vocabulary, Read Aloud a new story, Retelling the story in sequence using Story Boards, and Phonics practice worksheets.*
- *Friday will consist of Storytelling, then tumblebooks.com in the Computer Lab to practice fluency and play comprehension games on the computer.*

Schedule

	Monday	Tuesday	Wednesday	Thursday	Friday	Saturday
A.M.						
P.M.	*X*		*X*		*X*	

Timeline

Start date *10/4/2012*   End date *12/17/2012*   Total days per week *3*   Total hours per day *90*

© The McGraw-Hill Companies, Inc.

After-school Program Home Letter

A letter explaining the proposed program and how the program will benefit its participants should be sent home to parents. As with all communications home, it must first be approved by the school administrator or district. This letter should outline the program, including its schedule and procedures; it must have a place for the parent to sign and date it. The letters must be saved in a safe place, because they are documentation of parental permission.

Home Letter for After-school Program: Checklist

- ☐ On school letterhead (recommended for any home communication)
- ☐ States purpose or goals (What is the specific goal or purpose of the program?)
- ☐ Lists criteria for invitation (Why was my son or daughter chosen to participate?)
- ☐ Outlines program (What will be covered? Include overview of schedule.)
- ☐ Gives logistics (room, instructors, back-up plan if instructor is absent, pick-up location, times)
- ☐ Has blank for parent signature and date (blanks for both printing name and signature)
- ☐ Has space for contact information (cell phone number, alternate number, emergency contact)

After-school Program Permissions and Waivers

A student must have parental or legal guardian permission in order to participate in any after-school function. Legal waivers may also be needed, depending on the program. Schools usually have district forms for both permissions and waivers; if your school doesn't have district-approved forms, your administrator will need to approve them. Below is a checklist that includes the minimum information that is required.

Permission or Waiver for After-school Program: Checklist

- ☐ All the dates of the program sessions, classes, or meetings
- ☐ Logistics (teacher, room number, start and end times, back-up plan, dismissal location)
- ☐ Parent/Guardian information (name, address, phone, alternate phone, emergency contact with phone number)
- ☐ Signature and date lines (location where parent or guardian signs and dates form)

© The McGraw-Hill Companies, Inc.

After-school Program Daily Routine Planner

Plan activities in chunks—15- to 20-minute activity blocks (somewhat longer for older students)—to keep students alert and attentive. Establish a daily routine that accomplishes program goals and meets the needs of your students.

Daily business (_____ minutes)
Warm-up activity (_____ minutes)
Directed lesson (_____ minutes) **Goal/Standard** **Lesson overview**
Follow-up activity (_____ minutes)
Extension activity (_____ minutes)
Wrap-up (_____ minutes)
Teacher notes

© The McGraw-Hill Companies, Inc.

Sample After-school Program Daily Routine Planner

Below is a sample daily routine for the Reading Tutoring after-school program.
Note the fast-paced agenda.

Daily business (__10__ minutes)

attendance
snacks/refreshments

Warm-up activity (__15__ minutes)

Daily Oral Language: List 3–5 sentences on the board. Leave out all capitalizations, punctuation, and include a few spelling errors. Students will need to re-write these sentences correctly. Share corrections as a whole group.

Directed lesson (__30__ minutes)

Goal/Standard

Students will engage in a daily written activity in order to develop their vocabulary, decoding, punctuation, spelling, and grammar skills.

Lesson overview
- *Introduce new vocabulary words with matching picture cards and child-friendly definitions.*
- *Lead students through blending exercise using words with two syllables from the new story.*
- *Preview new story, then read aloud.*
- *As a whole group, sequence the story using a storyboard.*
- *Review the story one more time.*

Follow-up activity (__15__ minutes)

Hand out a worksheet listing ten multi-syllable words, and have students draw a slash at the appropriate spot in the word to show where the syllables divide the word. Share answers as a whole group.

Extension activity (__10__ minutes)

In writing journals, students will write a one-paragraph overview of the story read aloud that day, using the sequenced story board to help them. Students will then illustrate their favorite scene.

Wrap-up (__10__ minutes)

Student volunteers will share their illustrations and a summary of the story.

Teacher notes

On Wednesday, after reviewing vocabulary and introducing new two-syllable words through blending, students will listen to the story again, following along with the CD as it is read to them in the listening center. On their own, they will fill in a storyboard to sequence the events in the story, followed by a new practice worksheet to show where two-syllable words split.

© The McGraw-Hill Companies, Inc.

After-school Program Attendance Sheet

Program name	Program dates
Instructor	Program hours

Student name	Dates of attendance													

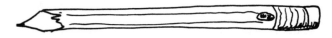

150

© The McGraw-Hill Companies, Inc.

After-school Program Roster

Program name	Program dates
Instructor	Program hours

Student name	Assessment scores		Contact number
	Pre	Post	

© The McGraw-Hill Companies, Inc.

After-school Program Teacher Sign-In Sheet

Program										
Week of										

Name	Monday		Tuesday		Wednesday		Thursday		Friday	
	In	Out	In	Out	In	Out	In	Out	In	Out
1.										
2.										
3.										
4.										
5.										
6.										
7.										
8.										
9.										
10.										
11.										
12.										
13.										

152

© The McGraw-Hill Companies, Inc.

After-school Program Cancellation Notification

If the after-school program has to be cancelled for one day, giving advance notice is key in avoiding potential issues. Send a notification home in advance if you know prior to any such cancellation. Have students' phone numbers on file so that you can notify guardians of late changes in the schedule.

Use a notification form modeled on the one below in the event of a cancellation.

After-school Program Cancellation Notice

The after-school program will be cancelled on _____.

After-school Program Cancellation Notice

The after-school program will be cancelled on _____.

After-school Program Cancellation Notice

The after-school program will be cancelled on _____.

After-school Program Cancellation Notice

The after-school program will be cancelled on _____.

© The McGraw-Hill Companies, Inc.

After-school Program Assessments

Monitoring the gains of an after-school program, especially a mandated or grant-sponsored program, is very important. Funding is often based on measurable results. Good pre- and post-assessment procedures should be put in place for any academic or intervention program. These assessments must be administered consistently by the program instructors as each student enters and exits the program.

Check the guidelines for each program when you're deciding which assessment to use. Assessments might be found in the adopted curriculum or in an assessment provider's resources. Alternatively, they could be created by the after-school program coordinator and instructors. It is important to be consistent in both the assessment and the scoring. You may want to discuss and even practice assessments in a pre-program training session.

Pre-assessment

The Pre-assessment needs to be easy to administer. Since it is hard to assess a student when you're in the middle of an active group, teachers may wish to partner for the assessments.

The assessment should target the specific skills and standards that are the focus of the program.

Keeping the assessment instrument on one page makes it easy to manage and keeps paperwork to a minimum.

If the assessment is a writing sample, teachers should agree on the scoring rubric for consistency.

Keep assessments and samples of each student's work in intervention folders. These folders provide documentation for what has been covered. Such folders may be required, especially for state- or district-mandated programs. They may also be stored in the student's cumulative records.

Post-assessment

The Post-assessment should be similar to, but not exactly the same as, the Pre-assessment. It will test students for gains made. It needs to be easy to administer.

It should target the skills and standards that the after-school program is focused on.

Post-assessments are compared to pre-assessments in order to measure gains.

© The McGraw-Hill Companies, Inc.

After-school Program Progress Report

Record your observations, including specific learning demonstrated, areas of improvement, and areas that need more work.

Student name	Grade/Homeroom
Intervention	Instructor

Program assessment scores: Pre _____ Post _____

Observations

Student name	Grade/Homeroom
Intervention	Instructor

Program assessment scores: Pre _____ Post _____

Observations

© The McGraw-Hill Companies, Inc.

After-school Program Evaluation (Teachers)

Name	Program

1. What program elements created the most improvement in students' academic, emotional, or social development?

2. What elements of the program created the least improvement in students' academic, emotional, or social development?

3. What elements of the program did students respond to most positively?

4. What elements of the program did students respond to with the least enthusiasm?

5. What elements were missing from the program that might have helped the students' success?

6. How can this program be improved for next time?

7. For future program planning, what advice do you have for other facilitators or coordinators?

© The McGraw-Hill Companies, Inc.

After-school Program Evaluation (Students)

Evaluation Form for Elementary Students

Name	Program

Please circle the face that matches how you liked this after-school program.

Did you like the after-school program? ☺ ☹

Did you learn something new? ☺ ☹

Did it help you? ☺ ☹

Would you like to participate in another after-school program? ☺ ☹

My favorite part was _____ .

Evaluation Form for Upper-level Students

Name	Program

Please evaluate the after-school program that you participated in.

What was your favorite part of this after-school program? Why?

What part of this after-school program was your least favorite? Why?

List three things you learned from this after-school program.

Would you participate in this or a similar after-school program again? ☐ Yes ☐ No

Why? (Write your answer on the back.)

© The McGraw-Hill Companies, Inc.

After-school Program Checklist

Organize all the components of your after-school program. Add any components to the list that may be specific to your program. Highlight all the components you need to successfully implement your program.

Program Name _____ Dates _____

- ☐ Program funding
- ☐ Test/Assessment scores (if applicable for an academic-based program)
- ☐ Program start date _____
- ☐ Program end date _____
- ☐ Program meeting times
- ☐ Program goals
- ☐ Aligned standards
- ☐ Program training
- ☐ Program resources/curriculum/equipment
- ☐ Program coordinator
- ☐ Program facilitators/instructors
- ☐ Teacher sign-in (for timesheet)
- ☐ Program location/classrooms
- ☐ Targeted student population
- ☐ Permission/Waiver/Letter home
- ☐ Daily schedule/routine
- ☐ Student roster (3 copies: Instructor, Coordinator, Office)
- ☐ Student attendance sheet (for taking attendance)
- ☐ Pre- and post- assessments
- ☐ Program student progress report
- ☐ Program evaluations
  - ☐ Instructor
  - ☐ Student

Coordinator/Facilitator name
Teacher/Instructor names
1.
2.
3.
4.
5.
6.
7.
8.
9.
10.
11.
12.

© The McGraw-Hill Companies, Inc.

13

After-school Program Ideas

There are many options for after-school programs. Take time to determine which program best meets the needs of your school. You might decide on a program mandated by the state or district, a program funded by a grant, or even a program funded by the school or a parent organization. Whatever the source of funding, it is important that teachers and staff have buy-in, as the after-school program's success ultimately depends on them. Below are a few program suggestions.

- Reading Fundamentals (phonics, fluency, comprehension)
- Reading Circles (literature circles, discussion circles)
- Math Fundamentals (number sense, operations, algebra, geometry, measurement)
- Math Games (hands-on experiences, manipulatives)
- Writing (grammar, mechanics)
- Writing (school newspaper)
- Creative Writing (stories, poetry)
- Science (experiments, projects)
- Social Studies (projects, plays)
- Art Club (fine arts)
- Dance Club
- Theatre Club
- Music Club
- Band
- Chorus
- Film Club
- Technology Club
- Chess Club or Game Club (higher-level thinking skills)
- Sports Club
- Homework Club
- Environment Club (recycling, environmental awareness, specific causes)
- Community Service (community projects, school beautification)

In this chapter we have chosen a sampling of academic and enrichment after-school programs to serve as models. We have also included numerous forms and checklists for planning and implementing a successful after-school program.

© The McGraw-Hill Companies, Inc.

Reading Tutoring After-school Program

Target group

Students who are designated "at risk," "below basic," or "far below basic" in Reading

Goals

1. To improve word attack skills (sounding out and phonics skills)
2. To improve fluency and comprehension

Notes

An after-school program such as this one in Reading gives teachers a chance to develop curriculum that focuses directly on specific students' needs and skills. It provides a way to give one-on-one or small group instruction that the regular school day does not always allow. Pre- and post-assessments from an after-school program give additional information to the teacher of record about the child's performance in relation to the class or grade level. Teachers in the lower grades, where the basic reading techniques and strategies are essential, are often the ones who participate in such programs, so check with them first. At the secondary level, check with teachers who work with students that struggle with reading and writing; these teachers spend a lot of time planning this type of instruction. Secondary-level teachers may not be interested in participating as after-school teachers, but they may be willing to share materials with those teachers who are.

Use the following checklist, along with the After-school Program Planner, to plan your school's Reading Tutoring after-school program.

Reading Tutoring After-school Program Checklist

☐ Targeted student list (students "at risk," "below basic," and "far below basic")

☐ Curriculum and materials to be used

☐ Teachers and rooms secured

☐ Letters home to parents, permission slips

☐ Groups formed and notified of room assignments

☐ Class or group rosters formed (with contact number for student's guardian)

☐ Office notified of assignments and rosters (teachers, students, room numbers)

☐ Teacher sign-in established (payroll report in office)

☐ Pre- and post-assessments established

© The McGraw-Hill Companies, Inc.

Math Tutoring After-school Program

Target group

Students who are designated "at risk," "below basic," or "far below basic" in Math

Goals

1. To improve mathematical operations
2. To improve number sense

Notes

An after-school program in Math such as this one allows the teacher to practice basic math facts with the students. These students may be in the lower grades and need help with addition, subtraction, multiplication, or division; or they may be in the upper grades and need help with pre-algebra, geometry, and algebra. This is also an excellent opportunity for students to develop their critical thinking by working with word and story problems that require problem-solving abilities.

Teachers in the lower grades, where the basic math facts are introduced and taught, are often the ones who participate in such programs, so check with them first. At the secondary level, check with teachers who work with students that struggle with math; these teachers spend a lot of time planning this type of instruction. Secondary-level teachers may not be interested in participating as after-school teachers, but they may be willing to share materials with those teachers who are.

Use the following checklist, along with the After-school Program Planner, to plan your school's Math Tutoring after-school program.

Math Tutoring After-school Program Checklist

☐ Targeted student list (students "at risk," "below basic," and "far below basic")

☐ Curriculum and materials to be used

☐ Manipulatives

☐ Teachers and rooms secured

☐ Letters home to parents, permission slips

☐ Groups formed and notified of room assignments

☐ Class or group rosters formed (with contact number for student's guardian)

☐ Office notified of assignments and rosters (teachers, students, room numbers)

☐ Teacher sign-in established (payroll report in office)

☐ Pre- and post-assessments established

© The McGraw-Hill Companies, Inc.

Computer Lab After-school Program

Target group

Students selected on basis of interest, academic performance, or targeted grade level

Goals

1. To improve technology skills
2. To improve skills with a specific program or application focus

Notes

An after-school computer lab program such as this one offers students an opportunity to sharpen technology skills, work on research reports, play interactive and academic games, or simply practice using a computer. It greatly benefits students who don't get computer time in class (sometimes because they simply take more time than others to complete assignments).

Even students who are able to use computers during the day will find an after-school computer experience helpful in researching assignments and writing papers. Others may want to participate in an after-school computer lab program simply because the use of technology is what interests them most. You may want to check with the computer lab teacher to see if he or she would be willing to run a Computer Lab after-school program.

Computer Lab After-school Program Checklist

- ☐ Targeted student list (chosen on basis of grades, interests, grade level)
- ☐ Computer program or software (selected for instruction or project)
- ☐ Teachers and room or computer lab secured
- ☐ Letters home to parents, permission slips
- ☐ Groups formed and notified of room assignments
- ☐ Class or group rosters formed (with contact number for student's guardian)
- ☐ Office notified of assignments and rosters (teachers, students, room numbers)
- ☐ Teacher sign-in established (payroll report in office)
- ☐ Pre- and post-assessments established (final project)

© The McGraw-Hill Companies, Inc.

After-school Chess or Game Club

Target group
Students selected based on interest or participation in gifted program

Goals
1. To improve critical thinking
2. To learn sportsmanship

Notes
An after-school chess club is a place where chess skills can be taught systematically, and teams or partners can practice and play the game. While an after-school math club might also offer a time period for playing and practicing chess or other games, the focus of an after-school chess or game club is somewhat different—specific math skills are secondary to the focus on critical thinking and sportsmanship. If you are interested in a broader focus for an after-school game club, you might consider establishing a club where students can play other games that develop the brain much like chess does. All of these games are meant to challenge students and develop the logical and mathematical part of the brain.

Suggested alternative games

Abalone	Checkers
Backgammon	Connect Four
Blokus	Pente
Cathedral	Trigon

After-school Chess or Game Club Checklist

☐ Interested students, selected high-achieving students

☐ Chess sets or games to be used

☐ Teachers and rooms secured

☐ Letters home to parents, permission slips

☐ Groups formed and notified of room assignments

☐ Class or group rosters formed (with contact number for student's guardian)

☐ Office notified of assignments and rosters (teachers, students, room numbers)

☐ Teacher sign-in established (payroll report in office)

© The McGraw-Hill Companies, Inc.

Art After-school Program

Target group

Selected students, interested students

Goals

1. To expose students to various art media
2. To emphasize the principles of design and the elements of art

Notes

An after-school program in art could include several options, depending on your school's funding. Art activities such as clay, photography, drawing, painting, and origami are just a few ideas for this type of after-school program. During this time of "high stakes testing" and with a push for math and science, art is often neglected in the regular school day for grades K–12. An after-school program where students can develop their artistic abilities is relatively simple and fun to establish. Teachers who are gifted in the arts might alternate weeks, teaching on a rotating basis. This will give the children in the after-school art program many opportunities to try out a variety of mediums. Check with teachers and other artistically talented people in the community who might be willing to help facilitate an Art after-school program.

Art After-school Program Checklist

☐ Interested or selected students

☐ Curriculum, materials, and supplies to be used

☐ Teachers and rooms secured

☐ Letters home to parents, permission slips

☐ Groups formed and notified of room assignments

☐ Class or group rosters formed (with contact number for student's guardian)

☐ Office notified of assignments and rosters (teachers, students, room numbers)

☐ Teacher sign-in established (payroll report in office)

☐ Planned art show (to showcase work)

© The McGraw-Hill Companies, Inc.

After-school Homework Club

Target group
Students who are designated "at risk," "below basic," or "far below basic" in any or all subject areas; interested students

Goals
1. To assist with homework
2. To improve study habits
3. To improve organizational skills

Notes
In many areas of the country, students are in after-school programs primarily because their parents work and the parents prefer that their children stay at school rather than be at home alone. After-school homework clubs offer a safe haven for many students. They also offer a time for students to complete their assignments before going home, where chores, dinner, showers, and time with family await them. In addition, teachers—and older students—can offer homework assistance in these after-school clubs that parents may not be able to give. A homework club is an after-school program that can benefit any student who needs a place to complete his or her assigned work. You will most likely be able to find teachers who are interested in spending  an hour or so after school to work with students as they complete their assigned homework. Remember, too, to check with school aides or parents. For the elementary grades, high school students are a good option, especially if working in the program can serve as part-time employment for them.

After-school Homework Club Checklist

☐ Targeted student list (students "at risk," "below basic," and "far below basic"

☐ Supplies and materials to be used

☐ Teachers and rooms secured

☐ Letters home to parents, permission slips

☐ Groups formed and notified of room assignments

☐ Class or group rosters formed (with contact number for student's guardian)

☐ Office notified of assignments and rosters (teachers, students, room numbers)

☐ Teacher sign-in established (payroll report in office)

© The McGraw-Hill Companies, Inc.

14

Getting Parents Involved

The involvement of parents and families in a child's school life is critical to the child's success in school. When families understand what you are trying to achieve, they can provide valuable support and assistance. Helping to develop and implement behavior management plans can go a long way. Parents can participate as classroom volunteers. They can make classroom management easier by assisting you with time-consuming but easy tasks, such as changing out bulletin boards, sorting papers into portfolios, working with small groups, or organizing the classroom library.

Back-to-School Night is an excellent time to ask parents about getting involved in the classroom. Have all parents sign in, and provide a place on the sign-in sheet for them to tell you how they would like to help in the classroom. A parent who can draw may be able to help at home by drawing picture cue cards to use for new vocabulary. A parent who can sew might be asked to sew costumes for the school play. Parents who read to their child each night might be willing to come in and read aloud to the class on occasion. Other parents may be interested in being involved in activities that are related to sports, coordinating food drives, or field trips. Parents can help in the upper grades or secondary level, too. You just need to know what they are interested in helping with.

Some teachers may feel a reluctance to bring students' families into the classroom, because it does take extra time and energy to prepare for their time in the classroom. Parents may also be reluctant to be there. Many parents today have to work two jobs to make ends meet; they don't have time to come to school. Others may not be comfortable because of language issues. Parents may believe that schooling should be left to the professionals and that parents shouldn't interfere. And some parents simply don't feel comfortable on a school campus because of their own experiences with education. Yet the benefits for the child of seeing his or her parent involved in the classroom (and taking school seriously) outweigh many of the daily challenges that parents deal with. If parents aren't able to help out in class, they might be able to help out at home (for example, cutting out materials sent home with the student, sewing felt storyboard characters, or writing vocabulary words onto index cards for a new unit), or perhaps they can help the school during non-school hours. There are many ways parents can contribute.

© The McGraw-Hill Companies, Inc.

In order to ensure that parents understand their role in the classroom, the teacher should make a list of possible activities for the parent volunteers to work with. It is the teacher's responsibility, too, to explain to parents what behavior they are to reinforce when working with students, and the parents should be willing to comply. This should prevent a situation where parents intervene when they shouldn't or offer instruction in ways that contradict what the teacher has done. In addition, the teacher must let parents know that if they are uncomfortable helping with certain tasks in the classroom, they can help in a different way.

Parents often don't get involved in the classroom at the secondary level as much as they did when their children were in elementary school. Instead, they often spend more time in volunteer services for the school. However, because secondary teachers still like to update bulletin boards and put together long-range projects for their students, they might still want parents to help with these things.

Parents can take on many of the minor tasks that take up a great deal of time at the beginning of the day (taking chairs down, handing out books, handing out papers, sharpening pencils); at the end of the day (putting up chairs, handing out homework, grading papers, changing out bulletin boards); and during the day (cutting out materials, preparing manipulatives for a science or math lesson, working with small groups, grading papers). Let them help.

Many ways for parents to help out in the classroom, at the school site, or at home are described later in this chapter.

Parent Involvement Checklist

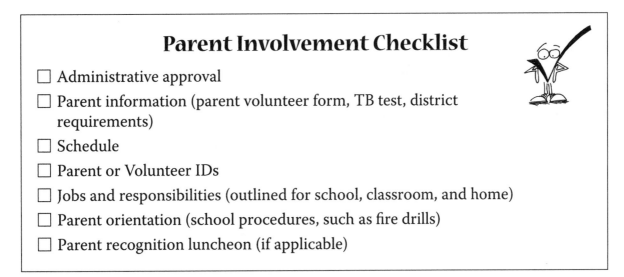

☐ Administrative approval

☐ Parent information (parent volunteer form, TB test, district requirements)

☐ Schedule

☐ Parent or Volunteer IDs

☐ Jobs and responsibilities (outlined for school, classroom, and home)

☐ Parent orientation (school procedures, such as fire drills)

☐ Parent recognition luncheon (if applicable)

© The McGraw-Hill Companies, Inc.

Ways to Communicate

Good communication with parents is important on many levels. Good communication with parents about a child's academic progress and behavior is paramount. Information about opportunities to volunteer in the classroom or at the school must also be communicated; many times parents aren't aware that they can volunteer, or are not sure how to do so.

Keeping parents up-to-date is important, and it goes a long way when you need their support or have an issue with a particular student. A professional relationship with the parent or guardian is easy. Even a simple note or a five-minute conversation after school will make the teacher-parent relationship stronger.

Below is a list of suggested ways to communicate with parents and guardians. Use these suggestions, and add your own to the list. Be sure to communicate with parents—at a minimum—on the first day of school, at open house, at back-to-school night, and at parent-teacher conferences.

• Weekly, monthly, or quarterly newsletter

• Phone tree—you or a parent volunteer call or e-mail the rest of the parents to remind them of upcoming events, such as field trips and picture day

• Report cards

• Progress reports

• Memos

• E-mail messages

• Phone calls

© The McGraw-Hill Companies, Inc.

Parent Letters

Some suggestions for communicating with your students' families follow. Everything that goes home should be approved by the administrator.

Invitation Letters

Parents need to know well in advance about events or volunteer opportunities in your classroom and at school. A list of what such an invitation letter might include appears below.

- Introduction
- Brief explanation of the opportunity or event
- Brief explanation of how a parent can participate
- Specifics (time, date, location)
- Thank you

Thank-you Letters

Following through with a simple thank-you letter is important. It demonstrates recognition for the parent's time and effort. Here is a list of items that could be included.

- Introduction
- Thank you for participation
- Give example of how the parent participated
- State how their participation helped
- Close with a thank-you

Tear-off Section for Response

Having a tear-off section included on your letter gives parents a way to respond to you or to the school. It could include the following items.

- Please complete and return
- Name
- Child's name, room, teacher
- Contact information (phone number, e-mail)
- Confirmation (Yes, I can … / No, I will be unable …)

© The McGraw-Hill Companies, Inc.

Sample Parent Newsletter

Room 35 · Mr. Becker's 3rd Grade

Getting in Touch with Mr. Becker

You can e-mail me anytime at becker@ yourschool.com. Also, I am usually at school by about **6:45** but always by **7:00**. You can also reach me right after school between **2:40** and **3:00**. Otherwise, you can leave a message for me in the office and I will return your call just as soon as I receive it.

Homework

This week, your child will have the regular homework of **Spelling**, **Math**, and **Health**. In addition, your child will begin reading a chapter a night from a chosen book at your child's instructional reading level. Following the reading of each chapter, your child will have a role or job to write about. Please see

Literacy Circles below for more instruction on how to help your child.

Literacy Circles

I have purchased the following titles for Literacy Circles: *My Name Is Maria Isabel, The Stories Julian Tells,* and *The Mouse and the Motorcycle.* Students will read a chapter a night of their assigned book and complete a given role for that night. It is imperative that your child complete his or her role in order for the rest of the book group to able to function appropriately. The roles include Discussion Director, Wild and Crazy Word Finder, Art Director, Connector Director, and Summary Director. Every child will have his or her turn at each of the roles but is only to do one per night in the order in which they are organized in the Literacy Circle Folder.

I ask you to please make sure your child carefully handles his or her book. I will send them home in Ziploc bags to help in this process, but since I am buying the books, I would like to make them last as long as possible. Your help with this will be greatly appreciated.

P.E. and Nutrition

As you know, I often take the children to P.E. as is dictated by the state Content Standards. 3rd Grade requires 100 minutes per week. Now that the school year has gotten off to a good start, I will be spending those 100 minutes teaching P.E. skills and will occasionally offer the children choice in their activities.

In the meantime, I am also arranging for a weekly nutrition lesson so **please let me know if your child**

© The McGraw-Hill Companies, Inc.

Room 35 · Mr. Becker's 3rd Grade

is allergic to any foods. This will help in the planning. Last week we made fruit juice soda with orange juice, grape juice, and cranberry juice that we mixed with carbonated water. We compared the nutrition labels with soda pop to show how tasty this juice and soda water combination can be as opposed to its sugary counterpart. In the meantime, I have included two websites which offer you short readings on the connection between nutrition and physical activity on academic achievement.

www.delicioustreats.com
www.snacksareawesome.com

Also, please remember that my wife, Mrs. Becker, teaches a nutrition lesson each week and uses real food to do so. ***If your child is allergic to any foods, please let me know immediately.***

Online Websites for Practice and Homework Help

Here are a few websites to visit in helping your child with homework or practice in areas they are struggling with:

www.somewebsite.com: This is a new website that …

www.anotherwebsite.com: A great website for researching and finding answers …

www.goodreadingwebsite.com: Use this website to get help in reading.

Reading

I am including a list of suggested chapter books to read. Visit the library, check out a book, and READ! This week's selections are all by author Beverly Cleary.

Chapter Books
Henry Huggins
Muggie Maggie
Runaway Ralph
Strider

Have a fabulous week. Thanks to those of you who came to Back-To-School Night!

© The McGraw-Hill Companies, Inc.

Parents at Home

Involvement of the parents at home is critical for a child's success in school. Parents can serve as an extension to what is being learned in the classroom. There are many simple strategies that parents can implement at home with their children. A list of some strategies that parents can use at home is easy to compile and is very beneficial for your students. Teachers could meet on grade level to develop this list. Holding parent workshops to review and practice strategies will  familiarize parents with the skills and increase the chance that those skills will be used at home.

We have included some ideas below that are good learning strategies for parents to use. You may add to the list as teachers share their ideas across grade levels. For example, first grade teachers are strong in phonics and can remind us of powerful reading strategies that a fifth grade teacher might be able to use with a student who is struggling with reading.

Home Strategies for Parents

✔ Encourage parents to take their child to the library to check out books that pertain to the current unit or theme. This is also a good time for the child to work on the library computer to complete research assignments using books and the Internet.

✔ Ask parents to review their child's homework on a daily or weekly basis and to sign it.

✔ Ask parents to read aloud to their child, whether in English or in their native language.

✔ Encourage parents to start a double-entry writing journal: The parents ask the child to respond to a prompt and, after the child writes about it, the parent writes about it as well.

✔ Ask the parents to prepare classroom materials at home, such as cutting out materials, sewing costumes, or drawing picture cards to go with new vocabulary.

✔ Send a list home of "G" rated films that you think they might enjoy seeing as a family. They can then write about the movie—for example, summarize the movie, write about their favorite part, or write about a character.

✔ Encourage parents to meet their child's basic needs at home so that their child can be ready to learn each day (for example, healthy diet, getting enough sleep, and having a bath and clean clothes). Parents can be given encouragement to support school learning and appropriate behavior.

© The McGraw-Hill Companies, Inc.

Parents at School

The presence of parents at the school site is very important. Parents can accomplish a great deal for the school if the school is willing to work with them. Parent buy-in leads to a sense of community at the school. Parent volunteers can help the school in its day-to-day operations, such as helping with supervision of the students. Parent groups, such as the PTA or Booster Club, can raise funds for the school and organize community events. All of these things contribute to the success of the school and its students.

The following is a list of suggestions for parent involvement at the school site. Discuss these ideas; choose the activities that will work best for your school, its staff, and its students—and that would be likely to get administrator approval. Your district has almost certainly established guidelines for volunteer involvement.

School Site Jobs for Parent Volunteers

- Academic workshops (for example, attend Family Literacy Night, Math Night, Science Fair Night)
- English Language Learning classes
- Translators (for teachers and the administration during conferences or parent nights)
- Lunch duty, recess duty
- Office assistant (make copies, distribute supplies)
- Organize or assist with fund-raiser
- Participate in PTA or Booster Club
- Participate in school functions (attend student performances, athletic events, or other programs)
- Proctor assistant (for testing sessions)
- Tutor in the after-school program

School Site Parent Volunteer Checklist

- ☐ School or administrative approval
- ☐ School volunteer form (designated by the school)
- ☐ Volunteer badge or sign-in (organized and in office)
- ☐ TB Test, other district-required documentation (check with district)
- ☐ Volunteer orientation (if applicable)
- ☐ Job and responsibilities (clear expectations)
- ☐ Schedule (organized with volunteer)

© The McGraw-Hill Companies, Inc.

Parents in the Classroom

Parents are a great resource in the classroom itself. In addition to providing a very much needed helping hand, they can bring rich life experiences to your classroom. Being organized is the best way to ensure that your parent volunteers are utilized to their fullest potential. Having jobs and responsibilities clearly spelled out, students needing extra support selected ahead of time, and even an organized management system in place will all maximize your use of parent volunteers.

What are some things parent volunteers can do? Below are some suggested ways to make use of parent volunteers in your classroom. Use these ideas and add to the list. Ask other teachers how they utilize their parent volunteers. Do what works for you and what you are comfortable with.

Classroom Jobs for Parent Volunteers

✔ Invite parents to the classroom to tell their family stories— for example, immigration stories, the story of how their child got his or her name, career information.

✔ Invite parents to chaperone field trips.

✔ Invite parents to Back-to-School Night, Open House, and conferences.

✔ Ask parents to donate supplies and materials for the class (for example, Kleenex, pencils, snacks).

✔ Ask parents to volunteer to take down chairs and sharpen pencils before school starts, to help in a subject area of their choice, to put up bulletin boards, to make copies, or to work with small groups.

✔ Ask parents to organize class parties.

✔ Ask parents to help with an end-of-the-month family class social with doughnuts and juice in the morning before school.

✔ Ask parents to volunteer to tutor children before or after school in your classroom.

✔ Ask parents to help with a school or class play: to plan it, prepare students, and hold rehearsals.

✔ Invite parents to come in and read stories aloud to the class.

Classroom Parent Volunteer Checklist

☐ School or administrative approval

☐ School volunteer form (designated by the school)

☐ Volunteer badge or sign-in (organized and in office)

☐ TB Test, other district-required documentation (check with district)

☐ Volunteer orientation (if applicable)

☐ Classroom job and responsibilities (clear expectations)

☐ Schedule (organized with volunteer)

© The McGraw-Hill Companies, Inc.

Parent Volunteer Considerations

Parent Orientation: The Orientation Packet

Creating a parent orientation packet is a way to inform parents of general school or classroom procedures and regulations. Though the packet could be handed out at Back-to-School Night, it would be more effective if you and the principal (or you and another teacher) could plan and present an orientation meeting at the beginning of the year for parents who are interested in volunteering at the school. At a meeting, you would have time to review the packet and ask parent volunteers to complete parent volunteer surveys relevant to your school site. In any case, parents should sign an acknowledgment that they have reviewed the packet and are aware of school and classroom policies and procedures. The following is a list of policies, procedures, and other areas needing attention that could be included in your presentation.

- School bell schedules
- Staff directory, positions, and room numbers
- Emergency drill procedures
- Lock-down procedures
- Reporting child abuse
- First aid policies
- Accident or incident report
- General conduct, appropriate behavior
- General overview of classroom schedules
- Ideas for volunteering as they complete their surveys
- Use of cell phones in the classroom
- Maintaining objectivity when volunteering in a child's classroom

General Considerations

Many parents work, and the combination of work and family responsibilities will limit parents' time and availability. Show consideration by being organized and prepared for your parent volunteer.

You must maintain a professional relationship with the parent volunteer and clearly establish roles and responsibilities. If a parent becomes too comfortable in the classroom and begins to act independently of your plans, he or she should be tactfully reminded of the appropriate role of volunteers in the classroom.

Ensure that no favoritism is shown. Parents who volunteer in their own child's classroom must understand that they are there to serve the whole class, not just their own child. If there is a problem with favoritism, it may be that this parent should volunteer in another classroom, and you will need to be prepared to handle the situation.

A parent volunteer needs to be focused and on task. This is not a time for play or disruption. The classroom teacher sets the tone. If you maintain a very professional environment, this should not be a problem.

So how do you get parent volunteers? Begin by using the forms that follow, many of which are designed to be filled out and shared with other teachers.

© The McGraw-Hill Companies, Inc.

Parent Volunteer Form

Please fill out this form completely. Thank you for volunteering!

Name	Date
Student(s) (if applicable)	

Phone (home)	Phone (cell)
Emergency contact Phone	Emergency contact Phone

Availability (please enter times)	Monday	Tuesday	Wednesday	Thursday	Friday
Early A.M.					
Late A.M.					
Lunch					
Early P.M.					
Late P.M.					

Special skills, interests, and experience (sewing, organization, etc.)

_____
Print name

_____   _____
Signature   Date

OFFICE USE ONLY

☐ TB test: Date _____ Expires _____

Other forms or requirements

© The McGraw-Hill Companies, Inc.

Parent Volunteer Planner (Volunteer)

Please use this form to track your work in our classroom. Thank you for your support! Your help is greatly appreciated.

Volunteer		Classroom	Grade	Teacher
Student(s) Time	Date			
	Goal I			
	Goal II			
	Goal III			
Student(s) Time	Date			
	Goal I			
	Goal II			
	Goal III			
	Date			
	Job/Task			
	Job/Task			
	Job/Task			

Notes or reminders from the teacher

177

© The McGraw-Hill Companies, Inc.

Parent Volunteer Sign-In Sheet

Thank you for participating at our school!

Please sign in and complete the information.

Name	Phone number	E-mail address	Skills, donations, experiences, interests
1.			
2.			
3.			
4.			
5.			
6.			
7.			
8.			
9.			
10.			
11.			
12.			
13.			
14.			
15.			

© The McGraw-Hill Companies, Inc.

Parent Volunteer
Certificate of Recognition

_____
Volunteer Name

has supported us with

_____
Classroom/School Responsibilities

during the _____ school year.
Date

We proudly recognize and appreciate
your support at our school.

Your participation makes a difference.

Thanks from all of us at _____.
Name of School

_____   _____
Administrator's Signature   Coordinator's/Teacher's Signature

© The McGraw-Hill Companies, Inc.

Parent Nights

Schools are often required to present parent nights during the school year. Asking parents to help with the planning and implementing of parent night workshops for literacy, math, science, and other curricular areas is a great way to get parents more involved at the school. It also gives them ideas that will support their child's schoolwork at home.

To have a successful parent night, regardless of its focus or emphasis, the event needs to be well thought-out and organized. Teachers, perhaps in grade-level groups, should decide what activities for the chosen subject area would be most appropriate and aligned to the learning standards. The teachers would lead the workshops on the selected activities on a voluntary basis. A calendar date must be set in order to reserve the facility during off-hours. Typically a custodial staff member needs to be present to assist in opening and closing the school, and this should be arranged well in advance. Teacher volunteers would then gather materials and organize grade-level or grouped presentations. An invitation letter would be sent home to explain the evening's purpose and to give times, locations, and names of workshops that will be available. It helps to have a tear-off portion at the bottom of the letter that can be signed and returned if parents plan to attend. This will provide an estimate of attendance for planning purposes.

Once you have made the facility arrangements, decided on the presentations, and estimated the attendance, you can purchase refreshments and make copies of handouts. It is important to prepare a sign-in sheet for the evening, not only for documentation purposes, but also as a way of getting contact information from parents who attend. In addition, this is a good way to track which students attend with their parents; many teachers hand out homework passes to the children who come.

On Parent Night, welcome all parents before they break out into workshop sessions. These workshops should be 20 to 30 minutes long—enough time to introduce, demonstrate, and practice the concept. Five to ten minutes needs to be factored in for rotations. It is good to offer parents choices: If they can attend three sessions, offer four to choose from. This gives parents ownership in the learning, which makes for a more powerful experience. After the rotations are complete, parents can reassemble to debrief in the auditorium; refreshments can be offered. This is an excellent time to get to know parents and to recruit for school involvement. Try to keep any discussion of student behavior and academic progress to a minimum. This is not a conference, and those discussions would distract from the purpose of the evening.

Parent Night Workshop Checklist

☐ Administrative approval

☐ Location approval (auditorium, individual classrooms)

☐ Invitation letter with tear-off confirmation

☐ Agenda, sign-ins

☐ Rotation and schedule

☐ Activities (20–30 minutes)

☐ Handouts

☐ Materials and equipment

☐ Snacks and refreshments

© The McGraw-Hill Companies, Inc.

Parent Night Workshop Planner

Workshop title		Date

Purpose

Agenda general outline (welcome, Session I, etc.)		Presenter	Room	Activity
Time	**Activity**			

Welcome notes

Session I	Session II
Purpose	Purpose
Activity	Activity
Standards	Standards

Session III	Session IV
Purpose	Purpose
Activity	Activity
Standards	Standards

Debriefing notes

© The McGraw-Hill Companies, Inc.

Parent Night Workshop Agenda

Having an organized agenda will help your workshops run smoothly. Remember that parent night involves a significant commitment of the parents' valuable time, so you want it to be as effective as possible.

Teachers presenting workshops should plan together so that there is consistency in their delivery. Each teacher will deliver his or her particular workshop the same number of times, once in each rotation. (Always keep a sample of handouts and activities for future workshops.)

Agendas will vary depending on the number of rotations you have planned and the time available for each one. You can use your own experiences from attending or presenting at workshops to help develop an agenda that best suits you. Below is a sample agenda for an event with three rotations.

Sample Parent Night Workshop Agenda

1 · Welcome/Introduction (15–20 minutes)

Parents arrive and (optionally) have refreshments. (This is a great opportunity for the PTA or Parent Booster Club to raise money by selling refreshments.) School business or plans might be briefly mentioned, but it is important to honor the parents' time and move right into the workshops.

2 · Transition (5–10 minutes)

3 · Rotation I (15–30 minutes)

First activity or workshop. Present concept, relate it to standards, demonstrate, and practice. The activity needs to be short and focused. It should target one specific concept if possible; too much can be overwhelming and hard to grasp in such a short period of time. Keep it simple! You will be delivering this presentation as many times as there are rotations, so clean-up and set-up need to be simple and quick.

4 · Transition (5–10 minutes)

5 · Rotation II (15–30 minutes)

Second activity or workshop. Present concept, relate it to standards, demonstrate, and practice. The activity needs to be short and focused. It should target one specific concept if possible; too much can be overwhelming and hard to grasp in such a short period of time.

6 · Transition (5–10 minutes)

7 · Rotation III (15–30 minutes)

Third activity or workshop. Present concept, relate it to standards, demonstrate, and practice. The activity needs to be short and focused. It should target one specific concept if possible; too much can be overwhelming and hard to grasp in such a short period of time.

8 · Debriefing (15–20 minutes)

Parents come together for refreshments and mingling. A brief thank-you and wrap-up can be made. Teachers have an opportunity to get to know parents at this time, and it is an excellent time for volunteer recruitment.

A Couple of Reminders

✔ Practice first! Have teachers run through their presentations, practicing for each other. This will identify any problems, and other teachers can offer input.

✔ Always have a back-up activity in case someone cannot present. Be ready to step in.

✔ Read your audience. If they are ready to move on, move on. If they seem to be asking several clarification questions, slow down and review with them what you have done so far.

✔ Relax and enjoy! Let the presentation flow. Every group is different. Don't take anything personally!

© The McGraw-Hill Companies, Inc.

Parent Night Workshop Sign-Up Sheet

Please sign up for the workshops you would like to attend.

Workshop title		Location
Parent name	**Student name**	**Student's room number**
1.		
2.		
3.		
4.		
5.		
6.		
7.		
8.		
9.		
10.		
11.		
12.		
13.		
14.		
15.		
16.		
17.		
18.		
19.		
20.		

© The McGraw-Hill Companies, Inc.

Parent Night Workshop Tickets

Tickets such as the ticket sample shown below can be used by parents to attend workshops. Customize your tickets with the specific workshop information for your school's Parent Night.

Admit One

_____
Workshop

_____
Location

_____
Time

Admit One

_____
Workshop

_____
Location

_____
Time

Admit One

_____
Workshop

_____
Location

_____
Time

Admit One

_____
Workshop

_____
Location

_____
Time

Admit One

_____
Workshop

_____
Location

_____
Time

Admit One

_____
Workshop

_____
Location

_____
Time

© The McGraw-Hill Companies, Inc.

Parent Night Themes

Literacy Night

Literacy is extremely important, and yet many parents don't know how to support their children in this area. Teachers take for granted all the tricks and strategies they know and use—from phonics to reading comprehension. Simply instilling a love for reading is important. A parent workshop with this focus can be a powerful experience for parents.

A literacy workshop can focus on the wonders of reading and comprehension or on the mechanics of reading (phonics, decoding, fluency), or even on a combination of the two. It is best, however, to keep it simple and as focused as possible. For example, if you focus on comprehension, you could offer workshops on the techniques for improved comprehension. This won't overwhelm the parent and can be more effective. Match the workshop to one of the school's learning goals aligned to the standards.

It is a good idea to have all participants gather for an introduction and to cover the workshop's agenda. Use tickets or a sign-up sheet to ensure that each rotation workshop has participants.

Individual workshops should be focused, easy to follow, and practical. You want parents to be able to take what they've learned and use it at home with their children. Make sure that the explanation and practice in the workshops prepares them to do that.

The following are a few ideas for workshops. You may add to this list as you come across new strategies and ideas when you network with other teachers, attend conferences, or take classes.

Ideas and Suggestions for Literacy Night

- Book-making: simple-to-make books at home
- Phonics games: matching sounds to pictures, letter cards for spelling, etc.
- Storytelling: strategies for reading a story or telling one orally
- Library visit: what to see, what to look for
- Reading comprehension: create bookmarks and teach comprehension strategies to parents
- Book reports: ideas for what to write about after reading (main character, plot, etc.); a list of 25 book report ideas
- Art: word collages from magazines
- Newspaper activities: word search, vowel pattern search, etc.

Literacy Night Checklist

- ☐ Administrative approval
- ☐ Location approval (auditorium, individual classrooms)
- ☐ Teacher workshop leaders or coordinators
- ☐ Invitation letter with tear-off confirmation
- ☐ Agenda and sign-ins
- ☐ Rotation or schedule

- ☐ Activities (20–30 minutes each)
- ☐ Handouts (for individual sessions)
- ☐ Materials and equipment (for each session; for example, scissors, glue, overhead)
- ☐ Snacks or refreshments (possibly sold by the PTA or Booster Club)

© The McGraw-Hill Companies, Inc.

Math Night

Math is an excellent subject area for parent workshops. There is a great deal that can be done at home to support students in this curricular area, because math is all around us in our daily lives. Teachers know many strategies and practices that can be shared with parents. They can be simple, like making flashcards, or more advanced, like teaching strategies for finding common denominators or adding fractions. Being able to use strategies relevant to everyday life helps people form connections that can lead to stronger learning.

It is a good idea to cover just one of the major standard strands of math (for example, number sense) rather than to cover many different things at once, which can be overwhelming. Selecting which math concept to focus on is important. A math night that concentrates on fractions, for example, might have activities that cover fractions standards across the grade levels. Kindergarten might learn about cutting things in half, and the fifth grade might focus on how to determine fractional parts of a whole with a bag of M&Ms.

The set-up and sign-ups for rotations are the same for a math night as for a literacy night. Practice your presentation. Have a meeting with the other presenters and run through the presentations. Is the timing right? Is it easy to follow? Do you have the necessary supplies?

The following are just a few ideas for workshops. You may add to this list as you discover new strategies and ideas when you network with other teachers, attend conferences, or take classes.

Ideas and Suggestions for Math Night

- Creating flash cards
- Deck of cards (math operations, positive and negative numbers, greater than, less than)
- Manipulatives—beans, buttons, coins (count, sort, use with operations)
- Dice (math operations, probability)
- Price tag (add with decimals, estimating)
- Money (operations, value, sorting, counting)
- Telling time (use a clock with hands)
- Measuring (use a tape measure, ruler, yard stick to measure length; use a cup, pint jar, etc. to measure volume)
- Creating story problems (real life scenarios and situations to solve)

Math Night Checklist

☐ Administrative approval

☐ Location approval (auditorium, individual classrooms)

☐ Teacher workshop leaders or coordinators

☐ Invitation letter with tear-off confirmation

☐ Agenda and sign-ins

☐ Rotation or schedule

☐ Activities (20–30 minutes each, aligned to math goal, standard strand)

☐ Handouts (for individual sessions)

☐ Materials and equipment (for each session; for example, scissors, glue, overhead)

☐ Snacks and refreshments (possibly sold by the PTA or Booster Club)

© The McGraw-Hill Companies, Inc.

Science Night

A science night offers many opportunities for great hands-on experiences and is a chance for parents to work on a project with their child. Students love to explore and discover, but parents don't always have the resource knowledge in science to assist their child. A science night can provide them with the basic information they need to assist their child at home. This is especially important toward the end of the year, when students plan and prepare their science fair projects to be shared with other students in their class, grade level, and school.

You can find many suggestions for running a science night in books. For example, most adopted science series have labs and suggested experiments that are grade specific and align to the standards. Another great resource is the Internet: Some websites have information about great hands-on projects and experiments that are easy for parents to do with their child. These ideas and projects can be gathered, aligned to grade level standards, and presented in a way that can be done at home.

Planning for science night can be fun! When you invite families to come and explore science, you help motivate parents to encourage science learning at home. They'll be able to see how much fun they can have with it as they move through the rotation, where each workshop is geared toward a different hands-on science project. Prepare a handout listing resources that includes stores, books, websites, and museums so they can find out about more fun science activities to experience outside of school.

Science can also be combined with other curricular areas, such as writing and math. You may want to plan a combination math-and-science night where all workshops focus on both curricular areas.

Ideas and Suggestions for Science Night

- Planning for the year-end science fair
- Hands-on science experiments
- Math-and-science night: cooking, temperature, measurement, etc.
- Outside learning environments: teaching science to your child by visiting the beach or taking a walk in your neighborhood
- Visiting the library, choosing science-related books, what to do with them

---

Science Night Checklist

- ☐ Administrative approval
- ☐ Location approval (auditorium, individual classrooms)
- ☐ Teacher workshop leaders or coordinators
- ☐ Invitation letter with tear-off confirmation
- ☐ Agenda and sign-ins
- ☐ Rotation or schedule

- ☐ Activities (20–30 minutes each, aligned to science goal, standard strand)
- ☐ Handouts (for individual sessions)
- ☐ Materials and equipment (for each session; for example, scissors, glue, overhead)
- ☐ Snacks and refreshments (possibly sold by the PTA or Booster Club)

© The McGraw-Hill Companies, Inc.

Multicultural Night

A multicultural night is a wonderful chance to build community. Because today's classrooms are so diverse in student population backgrounds, giving families a chance to share their culture is an excellent opportunity to increase understanding and respect. Families can bring in items to share that represent their culture and background, for example, articles of clothing and traditional handicrafts. Each item tells a story.

In addition, workshops can encourage parents and guardians to read grade-level-appropriate multicultural children's picture books or excerpts from young adult multicultural fiction to their children, followed by discussion about them. A workshop is a chance to model how to read stories aloud, and the reading can be followed with a dialogue about the book to see how the child connects with the characters and content. A workshop might also include oral storytelling facilitated by the parents themselves—not just the teachers. Classroom workshops might include a variety of cultural art activities, cultural artifact displays, and musical instrument, dance, or song sessions.

A teacher might act as a facilitator rather than as a presenter at a workshop such as this. It is a good idea to meet prior to the event with any parents who are presenting workshops in order to run through the presentation of what they are sharing. For example, if a parent is going to read a story, you may want to discuss and share tips on reading aloud to a group.

Students who attend can write summaries of the presentations, stories about the culture, or thank-you letters. You may find that parents would be willing to share their presentations with the whole class during the school day.

Below is a list of some activities that could be included in a multicultural night.

Ideas and Suggestions for Multicultural Night

- Share foods from the cultures (potluck, international food celebration)
- Teach cultural dances
- Share cultural artifacts
- Play traditional games
- Sing traditional songs
- Create traditional art

Multicultural Night Checklist

- ☐ Administrative approval
- ☐ Location approval (auditorium, individual classrooms)
- ☐ Teacher coordinators
- ☐ Invitation letter with tear-off confirmation
- ☐ Agenda and sign-ins
- ☐ Rotation or schedule

- ☐ Activities (20–30 minutes)
- ☐ Handouts (for individual workshops, if applicable)
- ☐ Materials and equipment (for each session)
- ☐ Snacks and refreshments (possibly sold by the PTA or Booster Club)

© The McGraw-Hill Companies, Inc.

Homework Passes

Homework passes can be issued to the students whose parents attended the workshop night at school. Confirm attendance from the sign-in sheet. You can use the sample Homework Pass below as the basis for creating one for your school.

Homework Pass

This pass can be exchanged for one FREE homework night!

_____
Date used

_____
Teacher's initials

Homework Pass

This pass can be exchanged for one FREE homework night!

_____
Date used

_____
Teacher's initials

Homework Pass

This pass can be exchanged for one FREE homework night!

_____
Date used

_____
Teacher's initials

Homework Pass

This pass can be exchanged for one FREE homework night!

_____
Date used

_____
Teacher's initials

Homework Pass

This pass can be exchanged for one FREE homework night!

_____
Date used

_____
Teacher's initials

Homework Pass

This pass can be exchanged for one FREE homework night!

_____
Date used

_____
Teacher's initials

© The McGraw-Hill Companies, Inc.

15

Incentive Programs

An incentive program is any program that involves a rewards system or recognition. Setting goals and expectations supported by a consistent system of rewards is important in a school setting.

Children should be rewarded for doing a good job at school. While grades reflect their hard work in class and at home, it's also nice to show them that their efforts—whether those efforts result in high grades or not—are noticed, taken seriously, and rewarded.

If your school does not yet have anything in place to recognize the children who go above and beyond in their personal behavior and in their academics, you may want to consider investigating and establishing an incentive plan at your school. Establishing an effective incentive plan requires buy-in from the teachers and volunteers who will be implementing it, as well as buy-in from the students themselves. Consistency in the program and its implementation is necessary in order to build trust and to make it ultimately successful. Starting the program but not following through or skipping days here and there will make the program ineffective; it will lose student buy-in.

The incentive program must be well thought-out. There are many important aspects of a successful incentive program. What is the specific behavior that is being rewarded? When is it being rewarded? How often? Who gets rewarded? What are the rewards? How are the students recognized school wide? What happens if the schedule is changed—will the program continue? How long will the program continue? Have students and parents been notified of the program and its guidelines?

This chapter will help you to develop and implement an incentive program that will work for your school. Your experience, in coordination with that of other teachers who incorporate a strong discipline plan in their own classrooms, will support this school-wide effort and help more students make a serious effort to improve their behavior, in terms of both conduct and academics.

© The McGraw-Hill Companies, Inc.

Any incentive program is dependent on student buy-in. At first, rewards should come quickly; this will increase student buy-in and build trust. Over time, a set schedule can be established for rewards.

We highlight a few sample incentive programs in this chapter to give you suggestions for developing an incentive program. Checklists and forms are provided to help you plan and implement an incentive program at your school. Many of these documents are designed to be filled out and shared with other teachers.

Incentive Program Checklist

☐ Administrative approval

☐ Staff buy-in (program presented, input received)

☐ Presented to school (for example, at an assembly)

☐ Letter home (explains guidelines of incentive program) or contract (signed commitment)

☐ Awards and incentives (purchased and ready to distribute)

☐ Staff training (review guidelines for staff who will implement the program; answer questions)

☐ Establish timeline (start and end dates, special assemblies, daily schedule or routine)

☐ Execute and maintain program (daily implementation)

© The McGraw-Hill Companies, Inc.

Incentive Program Survey

Complete the survey below and share it with the group. Group discussion will help determine what incentive program will work best at your school. Use this information to plan your program using the Incentive Program Planner.

Name	Group or grade level

What school-wide incentive programs have worked at our school? Do you know of school-wide incentive programs that are successful at other schools? Why are they successful?

Incentive program name	Reason for success (briefly explain)

What small group or classroom incentive programs have worked in your classroom? Do you know of classroom incentive programs that are successful at other schools? Why are they successful?

Incentive program name	Reason for success (briefly explain)

List three aspects of an incentive program that make it successful (school wide or in the classroom). Briefly explain.

1.

2.

3.

What school-wide incentive program would you like to see used at this school and why?

What classroom incentive program would you like to see used in classrooms at this school and why?

© The McGraw-Hill Companies, Inc.

Incentive Program Planner

Incentive program name	☐ School wide ☐ Grade level ☐ Classroom

Incentive goals (List at least three goals or behavior modifications.)

Targeted student population

Rewards and positive reinforcements

Leader or coordinator

Facilitators

Location

Program overview (What will the program look like? What is the daily schedule or routine? What behavior is being rewarded? What is the reward?)

Introduced (check all that apply)

☐ Letter home   ☐ Parent meeting   ☐ Weekly bulletin   ☐ Monthly bulletin   ☐ Classroom presentation
☐ Assembly   ☐ Other _____

Timeline

Start date _____   End date _____   Total days _____   Total hours _____

Days ☐ M   ☐ T   ☐ W   ☐ Th   ☐ F   ☐ Sa   Time _____

© The McGraw-Hill Companies, Inc.

Sample Incentive Program Planner

Incentive program name *Perfect Attendance*	☒ School wide ☒ Grade level ☐ Classroom

Incentive goals (List at least three goals or behavior modifications.)

- *Students will arrive on time but preferably 15 minutes prior to the bell ringing. Teachers will consistently promote this in their classroom.*
- *At the beginning of the next month, teachers will send a newsletter home to inform parents and guardians of the grade-level and school-wide contest and the importance of attendance for their child's academic success at school.*
- *Teachers will have their students come up with a class motto expressing why attendance is important to them that will be placed on the office bulletin board along with the mottos of all the other classes.*

Targeted student population	**Rewards and positive reinforcements**
All students	• *The grade level with the fewest absences will get one funded field trip of their choice.* • *The top classes at each grade level will have popcorn and a movie on the first Friday of the next month.*

Leader or coordinator	**Location**
Mrs. Johnson, 3rd Grade, Room 4	*Morning intake on the school yard*
Facilitators	*Auditorium*
Grade-level team leader Student Council president *Classroom teachers Lead parent of the PTA*	*Classroom*

Program overview (What will the program look like? What is the daily schedule or routine? What behavior is being rewarded? What is the reward?)

- *On a daily basis, classroom teachers and the lead parent of the PTA will document the number of students who are absent that day. In the classroom, teachers will track this in their own attendance book as well as keeping track on a classroom chart that they post next to the class attendance motto.*
- *On the last day of the month, the lead parent of the PTA and the grade-level team leaders, along with the Student Council president, will check attendance numbers and report the winners over the school loudspeaker.*
- *On the first Friday of the next month, a movie will be chosen to show to the top classes of each grade level. This will be shown in the auditorium, and popcorn will be served. The classroom teachers of the winning classrooms will have that time as a prep period for their reward.*

Introduced (check all that apply)

☒ Letter home   ☐ Parent meeting   ☒ Weekly bulletin   ☐ Monthly bulletin   ☐ Classroom presentation
☒ Assembly   ☐ Other _____

Timeline

Start date ___*March 1*___   End date ___*March 31*___   Total days ___*approx. 23*___   Total hours ___*N.A.*___

Days ☒ M ☒ T ☒ W ☒ Th ☒ F ☐ Sa   Time ___*a.m.–p.m.*___

© The McGraw-Hill Companies, Inc.

Behaviors and Rewards

Clear expectations and follow-through are the keys to a successful incentive program. All behaviors should be stated in a positive way. The following is a list of desired behaviors and rewards. These are only suggestions; space has been left for you to add more that are specific to your school. Be realistic about both the behaviors and their rewards. If students can't realistically meet the standards, or if you can't fulfill the promise of a reward, it is not worth it.

Positive Behaviors

School wide

- Fair play
- Play area clean-up
- Academic achievement and growth
- Lunch clean-up
- Citizenship
- Following morning intake procedures
- Assembly behavior
- Breakfast and lunch etiquette
- Emergency procedure behavior

Classroom

- Raises hand
- Completes homework
- Cleans up
- Stays on task
- Shares materials
- Follows directions
- Helps others

Positive Rewards

School wide

- Banner to display in classroom
- Trophy to display in classroom
- Attendance awards
- Student of the Week or Month
  - Pencils
  - Folders
  - Backpacks
  - Books
  - Healthy snack
  - Lunch with the principal
  - Academic certificates or awards
- Citizenship certificates or awards
- School jobs or responsibilities
- Ice cream party
- Pizza party
- Field trip
- Movie

Classroom

- Classroom jobs or responsibilities
- Popcorn party
- Ice cream party
- Free time
- Computer time
- Center activities
- Movie

© The McGraw-Hill Companies, Inc.

Rewards and Incentives

Incentives that are tangible—things that students can hold and actually see accumulating—are very powerful motivators. It's easy to create incentive tickets to use in your program. You can buy tickets in rolls, create them on the computer, or use the set provided in this chapter. You may want to laminate a master set so that it can be used several times. Do make sure that individual tickets have been marked or personalized in some way so that each one is unique.

There are many options for rewards and many ways to implement the program. It is important for the staff to decide what works best for them. As with any incentive program, follow-through is crucial! Consistency and follow-through create buy-in with students so that they trust that their behavior will be recognized and rewarded. This cannot be stressed enough. For example, imagine that you were a student who had been told that you would be given a $100 gift certificate if you had perfect attendance for the semester. If you achieved perfect attendance, you would expect your reward. Now imagine that the administrator said, "Sorry, we can't give you the certificate, but 'Good job!'" You would be upset, and you would also not be motivated to be part of the program again. You would likely not buy into the next proposed incentive program. An incentive program requires follow-through and consistency! Kids are savvy, and they see what's going on.

Administering an incentive program can be a very simple process. Students are handed incentive tickets by teachers, staff, the principal, or any other district employee when they are "caught" doing something good. These tickets may be kept by students for individual rewards, or they may be given to the teacher so that at the end of the week or month, several tickets can be drawn for class or school-wide rewards.

What you use for rewards is limited only by your imagination: Rewards can be purchased items if funds are available, donated items solicited from the community, or a popcorn or ice cream party (entrance might require five tickets). It can be quite effective if students take part in deciding what the reward will be.

Suggestions for Rewards

- School supplies (pencils, erasers, notebooks)
- Popsicle party (for several or all students in the class, depending on what was promised)
- Lunch with the teacher or principal
- A book from the Scholastic Book Club or the current Scholastic Book Fair
- Computer time in the class or in the computer lab
- Free time at activity centers

© The McGraw-Hill Companies, Inc.

Incentive Tickets

Use incentive tickets to reward good behavior. A specific number of these tickets will be redeemable for an activity ticket. Students should write their name on each ticket and save them until they have enough to redeem. They can be saved in a resealable storage bag or kept together with a paper clip or rubber band. The sample tickets below can be used as a basis for creating incentive tickets for your school.

Sample Incentive Tickets

Good Job Ticket *Keep it up!* _____	**Good Job Ticket** *Keep it up!* _____	**Good Job Ticket** *Keep it up!* _____
Good Job Ticket *Keep it up!* _____	**Good Job Ticket** *Keep it up!* _____	**Good Job Ticket** *Keep it up!* _____

Sample Incentive Program Activity Tickets

Admit One

Good for one admission to our
PIZZA PARTY

This ticket has been awarded to _____.

Admit One

Good for one admission to our
ICE CREAM PARTY

This ticket has been awarded to _____.

197

© The McGraw-Hill Companies, Inc.

Student Recognition (Student of the Week)

Recognizing students within the student body as "Student of the Week," for example, is an excellent way of motivating students to improve behavior as well as academics. While certain students are obvious choices for this recognition, it is important to try to select those who aren't so obvious whenever possible. Some recognition for what is good, even something small, can go a long way. Try to spread the recognition across your class if at all possible. It is important to see the good in all students, even those who are a little more challenging.

Your school may decide to do this on a weekly, monthly, semester, or even yearly basis. It is important to decide on a schedule that the whole school—especially the staff—buys into in order to get good participation. Awards can be given at assemblies, broadcast over the public announcements system, or written about in a newsletter. Recognition is more effective if done in a public manner.

With this type of incentive, each teacher nominates one or two students. The award can be based on academics, citizenship, attendance, or a combination of these areas.

If the award is presented at an assembly, parents can be notified in advance and invited to attend. Trophies and certificates might be awarded. Pictures could be taken of students, parents, and the administrator, and displayed in the office each month. The picture could then be presented to the student at the end of the time period.

At the end of the year, academics, citizenship, and perfect attendance for the year could be recognized with a trophy or certificate. This is also a good opportunity to recognize students who might otherwise not get an award, but who could benefit greatly by receiving one. Examples for these awards might be the most improved, hardest working, or most helpful student.

A school might choose to recognize students on a classroom basis. Students in each class can vote to choose the classmate who best meets the criteria for the program if it is behavior-based. For academic awards, teachers obviously determine who receives the award. At the end of the time period, awards are announced and presented according to the program guidelines. Having an administrator present the awards adds to the recognition.

© The McGraw-Hill Companies, Inc.

Suggested Criteria for Student Recognition

• Show respect to his or her classmates

• Turn in all homework

• Perfect attendance

• Good academic work

• Complete all classroom assignments

Student Recognition Incentive Checklist

☐ Administrative approval

☐ Staff buy-in (staff collectively deciding on and implementing the incentive program)

☐ School plan for implementation (award schedule, awards and certificates, recognition)

☐ Home letter (outline program) or contract (signed commitment)

☐ Coordinator or facilitator

☐ Teachers (teacher selection)

☐ Certificates (trophies)

☐ School-wide recognition (school assembly or presentation, announcements, newsletter)

© The McGraw-Hill Companies, Inc.

Movie Day

Showing a movie can be an excellent, inexpensive, and easy way to reward students. You may want to reward students who have achieved a targeted behavior, had perfect attendance, or met an academic goal (for example, knowing multiplication tables or reading a certain number of books). This incentive program can be school wide (rewarding individual students or whole classes), or it can involve a single classroom.

Any movie shown at the school must be a district- or school-approved movie. It is more motivating for students if they are allowed to vote on the movie they want to watch. This gives students a sense of ownership and increases buy-in to the program.

Movie Day is not limited to a movie; cartoons or shorter videos can also be used. The video could even be related to a unit of study. The important thing is for these students to receive a reward for their good behavior. A small treat can be offered (one with minimum clean-up).

It could be organized as a lunchtime event, where students have lunch and watch the videos in the auditorium. A special ticket or pass can be issued for admission. Teachers can track students for this reward on a roster tracking sheet or students can receive individual tickets and turn them in for the special admission ticket when they have accumulated the appropriate number of tickets.

A teacher (or group of teachers) would need to supervise the event. If this is to be a regular event, a rotation could be set up so that teachers take turns supervising. Clearing the event with the lead custodian or plant manager is important if the auditorium is to be used to show the movie.

The event could also be organized on grade level: The participating students would gather for the movie in one grade-level classroom; students who aren't participating would do school work in a different grade-level classroom.

200

© The McGraw-Hill Companies, Inc.

Movie Incentive Checklist

☐ Administrative approval

☐ Lead custodian or plant manager clearance

☐ Staff buy-in (staff collectively decides on and implements the incentive program)

☐ Behaviors and rewards

☐ School plan for implementation (daily routine, award schedule, recognition)

☐ Home letter (outline program) or contract (signed commitment)

☐ Coordinator or facilitator

☐ Teachers (teacher supervisors, rotation schedule)

☐ Tickets (special movie admission ticket)

☐ Movie Day (set date)

☐ School-wide recognition (school assembly, public announcements, newsletter)

© The McGraw-Hill Companies, Inc.

Sports Day or Activity Day

An incentive program that can be a school-wide event is a sports day or activity day. On a designated afternoon, teachers and staff members handle group sessions—for example, a sport, a yard game, art, or cooking. Teachers sign up to conduct a session on whatever they are comfortable teaching, and students can sign up for a session that involves something they are interested in learning. These activities can be aligned to standards across the curriculum, including physical education. Participation in this event rewards students who have shown good behavior or good academic performance, as outlined in the incentive program guidelines.

Any student who has demonstrated poor behavior or academic performance according to those guidelines would not be eligible to participate in the event. This needs to be spelled out in a letter home so that if a student has to miss the event, the parents understand the reason why. The library and cafeteria are likely places to gather these students during the sports day or activity day event. If the incentive program is based on academic work, the nonparticipating students would report to a designated room or study hall to work on academic assignments. If the incentive program is based on behavior, the nonparticipating students might be required to write a letter to the teacher or principal explaining the poor behavior and how they will avoid it in the future. Teachers could also require that these students do additional school work during this time. Students usually only have to miss one of these special sports days or activity days. After they see their friends have fun and they hear all about it, students won't want to miss the next one.

Students who struggle with academic performance and behavior need to, if at all possible, participate in the first sports day or activity day. This will help motivate them to qualify to participate in future events. Behavior from student to student varies, and what is "good" for one student may not be "good" for another. Take into account that some students need more patience, but be careful to avoid showing favoritism.

© The McGraw-Hill Companies, Inc.

This day needs to be well planned. Teachers should create the list of possible activities together, and then teachers and staff will sign up for what they want to teach. Once the list of activities is finalized, students will choose and sign up for activities. Rosters can then be provided to the teachers.

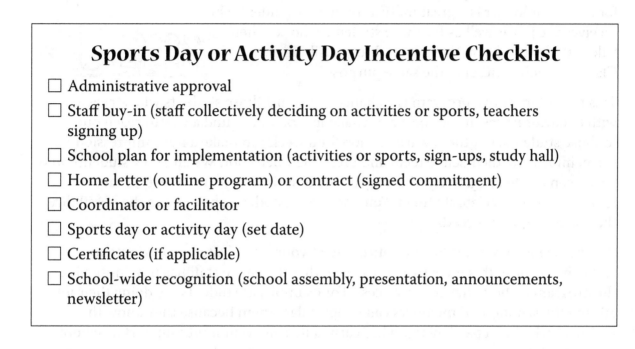

Sports Day or Activity Day Incentive Checklist

☐ Administrative approval

☐ Staff buy-in (staff collectively deciding on activities or sports, teachers signing up)

☐ School plan for implementation (activities or sports, sign-ups, study hall)

☐ Home letter (outline program) or contract (signed commitment)

☐ Coordinator or facilitator

☐ Sports day or activity day (set date)

☐ Certificates (if applicable)

☐ School-wide recognition (school assembly, presentation, announcements, newsletter)

© The McGraw-Hill Companies, Inc.

Jobs and Responsibilities

The assignment of jobs and responsibilities to students is a great incentive for encouraging positive behavior around the school and in your classroom. At the school level, the staff should first decide which jobs can be assigned to students whose behavior has met the guidelines established in your school-wide incentive program. The added responsibility of a job for a week or longer is a great motivation for the student who receives the job as well as for those students who see their fellow students take on these special responsibilities. Classroom jobs can serve the same purpose.

This type of incentive program is a chance to reward those students who struggle with behavior issues. It may be a real challenge for you to find a way to reach out to those students, but the reward of a job for a week can make a huge impression on them, improving their self-esteem and often their behavior. We all know students who have been labeled negatively; this may be the first time in years (or ever) that someone found a reason to celebrate them. You know your students; be open to the possibility that each one can succeed.

It is especially important for the entire staff at your school site to contribute to and help establish this incentive program so that the entire staff has buy-in—giving the program its best chance for success. For example, as students are doing their jobs around the school, staff members can congratulate them because they know that a student who has a particular job has earned it. This community support at school makes the jobs even more special and makes the incentive that much more important.

Jobs and responsibilities around the school could include the following.

School-wide Jobs

- Flag salute leader—public announcements, morning assembly
- Raising the flag at school
- Monitoring lunch clean-up
- Being a play leader in a lower grade class
- Assistant in lower grade classroom
- Office monitor for the day or week
- Library assistant
- Nurse monitor

© The McGraw-Hill Companies, Inc.

Classroom Jobs

- Board monitor
- Flag salute leader
- Pencil sharpener
- Physical education equipment assistant
- Line leader
- Hall, office, nurse, or restroom monitor
- Teacher's assistant
- Clean-up monitor

Jobs and Responsibilities Incentive Checklist

☐ Administrative approval

☐ Staff buy-in (staff collectively decides on and implements the incentive program)

☐ School plan for implementation (jobs and job schedule, certificates, recognition)

☐ Home letter (outline program) or contract (signed commitment)

☐ Coordinator or facilitator

☐ Classroom implementation

☐ Certificates (if applicable)

☐ School-wide recognition (school assembly, presentation, announcements, newsletter)

© The McGraw-Hill Companies, Inc.

Incentive Program Notification

Family support for an incentive program helps make it successful. A letter home outlining the program offers parents a chance to get involved. This letter can have a tear-off portion to be signed by both the parent or guardian and the student before being returned to the teacher. This serves as a contract and offers accountability.

A commitment tear-off form is a way for both students and parents to show that they not only read about and understand the incentive program, but that they will support it. Keep the language on this form general; focus on their having read through the guidelines and their willingness to support it. A sample commitment tear-off form appears below. Create one that is tailored to your program.

Parents or guardians should be invited to any recognition assembly that their child may be attending. This is a chance to publicly recognize not only the child, but also the parents and family. Certificates and prizes can be awarded by the administrator or principal. It is also a chance to take pictures, which can be displayed in the office for all to see.

Incentive Program Notification Letter

- Briefly outline program
- Describe desired behavior
- Describe the reward
- Thank parents for their support
- On school letterhead
- Approved and signed by administrator

Recognition Invitation Letter

- Briefly outline program
- Why student was selected (for academics, citizenship, behavior)
- Logistics of assembly (time and place)
- Thank parents for their support
- On school letterhead
- Approved and signed by administrator

Sample Commitment Tear-off Form

I have read and reviewed the new incentive program guidelines with my child. My child is aware of the expected behavior and the rewards for that behavior. I will support my child as he/she participates in this program.

_____   _____
Parent name   Student name

_____   _____
Parent signature   Student signature

© The McGraw-Hill Companies, Inc.

Incentive Program Roster

Incentive program		

Coordinator	Date

Highlight all that apply and check off on the day of the presentation.

☐ Student names submitted   ☐ Assembly set-up   ☐ Approved DVD

☐ Certificates and awards   ☐ Photographer   ☐ Equipment

☐ Date selected   ☐ Recognition bulletin board   ☐ Other _____

☐ Invitation letters   ☐ Snack purchased   ☐ Other _____

Student name	Grade	Room	Student name	Grade	Room
1.			16.		
2.			17.		
3.			18.		
4.			19.		
5.			20.		
6.			21.		
7.			22.		
8.			23.		
9.			24.		
10.			25.		
11.			26.		
12.			27.		
13.			28.		
14.			29.		
15.			30.		

© The McGraw-Hill Companies, Inc.

Incentive Program Student Tracker

Important: Recognize the good in every student at some point, in some way, during the year.

		Class or group						School year		
		List name of incentive program or any awards or jobs students have earned. Enter a check mark in each column for recognized students.								
Student name	**Room**									
1.										
2.										
3.										
4.										
5.										
6.										
7.										
8.										
9.										
10.										
11.										
12.										
13.										
14.										
15.										
16.										

© The McGraw-Hill Companies, Inc.

Certificate of Recognition

_____
Name of Participant

has been recognized in our

_____
Incentive Program

at _____
Name of School

on _____.
Date

We proudly recognize your outstanding example in school. You set an excellent example for your fellow students.

We appreciate you. Keep up the great work!

_____   _____
Administrator's Signature   Coordinator's Signature

© The McGraw-Hill Companies, Inc.

Sports Day/Activity Day Instructor Sign-Up Sheet

Please sign up to be an instructor or facilitator for one of the designated sports or activities. Thanks for making this a successful event!

Sports Day/Activity Day coordinator		Date	
Sport or activity	**Instructor**	**Location**	**Equipment and materials**
1.			
2.			
3.			
4.			
5.			
6.			
7.			

© The McGraw-Hill Companies, Inc.

Sports Day/Activity Day
Student Sign-Up Sheet

Sign up for the sport or activity listed below. You will stay in this sport or activity until the end of the rotation.

Sport/Activity			Instructor(s)		
Location 1			Location 2		
Equipment					

Student name	Grade	Room	Student name	Grade	Room
1.			16.		
2.			17.		
3.			18.		
4.			19.		
5.			20.		
6.			21.		
7.			22.		
8.			23.		
9.			24.		
10.			25.		
11.			26.		
12.			27.		
13.			28.		
14.			29.		
15.			30.		

© The McGraw-Hill Companies, Inc.

16

Fund-raising

Planning for fund-raising—whether school-wide, grade-level, or departmental—is not necessarily easy, but fund-raising can be a great experience for students and is definitely helpful to the school. Consider the following questions:

- Has this fund-raising project been done before?
- What fund-raising projects has the school done?
- Which ones were successful? Why?
- Which ones were not successful? Why?

When you have a fund-raising idea that you think may be a good fit for your school, take it to your administrator or principal for consideration. Once you have approval for a project, there are many things to consider, such as a timeline to plan and follow, school and district requirements, willing participants, and availability of the product.

Many companies are in the business of fund-raising. Schools get catalogs and flyers promoting these companies and their products; ask your office manager to save them for you. When you network with teachers from other schools, ask if their school has fund-raisers and get contact information. Find out if the school was happy with the project and if it was successful.

Ideas for Fund-raisers

- Sale of products
- Flea market
- Walk-a-thon or run
- Performance
- Talent show
- Pancake breakfast
- Sock hop
- Silent auction or eBay auction
- Carnival

Fund-raiser Elements

Why	Why is a fund-raiser needed? How much money is needed or proposed to be raised? What is it for?
Who	Who is involved? (students that benefit, teacher buy-in, parent support)
What	Project or activity
How	Process of notification, introduction, materials distribution, execution, collection
When	Strategic calendar date
Where	School or community
Permission	Administrator approval, district guidelines

© The McGraw-Hill Companies, Inc.

Fund-raising Survey

Please complete the survey on fund-raising. It is designed to help choose the best fund-raiser to meet specified needs.

Name	Date

What are some needs (grade-level, department, or school-wide) that would require additional funds?

Academic (materials, supplies)	Extracurricular (field trips, events)	School facility (murals, furniture)	Equipment (physical education, technology)

What fund-raising activities have you participated in or heard about from other schools?

Project	Participants	Goal

Which of these fund-raising activities have been successful? Why?

After considering various fund-raisers, what fund-raiser would you like to participate in? Why?

Who would participate in this fund-raiser?

Where would the fund-raising take place?

Who would supervise the fund-raiser?

© The McGraw-Hill Companies, Inc.

Fund-raising Checklist

Use the following fund-raising checklist to prepare and carry out your fund-raiser. Highlight applicable items, write their proposed date, and then check items off as completed.

☐ Need

☐ Approval (Date _____)

☐ District or school paperwork

☐ Established timeline

☐ Teacher buy-in (faculty meeting, survey) (Date _____)

☐ Parent support (letter, parent meeting) (Date _____)

☐ Student participants (returned parental permissions)

   (Date _____)

☐ Facilitator (Name _____)

☐ Home notifications (Date _____)

☐ Home permission (Date _____)

☐ Permissions collections (Date _____)

☐ Introduction, kick-off (Date _____)

☐ Distribution of materials (Date _____)

☐ Daily collections (Location _____)

☐ Updates and notifications (newsletter, public announcements)

☐ Final collection (Date _____)

☐ Awards distribution (Date _____)

☐ Accounting

☐ Allocation or budget

☐ Purchase order

☐ Published update (Date _____)

☐ Thank-you notes (Date _____)

© The McGraw-Hill Companies, Inc.

Advertising Your Fund-raiser

Promoting your fund-raiser is important! Eye-catching posters and flyers remind people of the event and encourage people to participate. Students can help create these materials while learning the basics of advertising. The following are suggestions for promoting your fund-raising event.

Flyer

A flyer is an easy way to promote your fund-raiser. A computer-generated flyer can be effective, but student work can often be more powerful. If you decide to ask students to submit flyers in a school-wide contest, distribute the fund-raiser information and the guidelines for the contest. The winning entry would then be used for the fund-raiser. A flyer should include the following information.

- Large easy-to-read fund-raiser name
- Times and dates
- Catch phrases and slogans
- School name
- School contact information (phone, website)

Poster

Posters can be student generated. Provide students with fund-raiser information and the guidelines for creating a promotional poster. It is important to give them guidance in this process to help them see what a good poster should look like and what it should include. Can you read it from a distance? What catches your eye on the poster? Are the illustrations relevant? Posters should include the following information.

- Large easy-to-read fund-raiser name
- Times and dates
- Catch phrases and slogans
- School name
- School contact information (phone, website)

Media

- Newspaper—Local newspapers often have community calendar sections that post local events; flea markets can be listed in the classified section for a nominal fee. Be sure to arrange this well in advance.

- Radio—Radio stations are also an option. Some stations have community announcements and are glad to promote school events.

- Television news—Local news stations usually have a local events segment or announcements. Call your local station and ask about their procedures.

© The McGraw-Hill Companies, Inc.

School Fund-raiser Planner

Group	Date
Project or activity	
Goal	
Coordinator or facilitator	
Participants	

Materials and facilities	Supplier
	Contact
	Phone
	Fax

Kick-off date and time
Sale procedures
Collection procedures

Collection location or drop-off	Collection schedule

Updates and notifications (communications, letters, announcements)

End date	Awards
Award presentations	

216

© The McGraw-Hill Companies, Inc.

Sample School Fund-raiser Planner

Group	PTA		Date	Saturday, May 12, 2012

Project or activity *Flea Market*

Goal *To earn money for the end-of-the-year field trips; to be equally disbursed to all teachers*

Coordinator or facilitator *Mrs. Jackson, PTA President, and Mr. Joseph, 5th grade lead parent*

Participants *Teachers, staff, parents, students, school site neighborhood and community members*

Materials and facilities *Auditorium reserved for Saturday, May 12, 2012; price tags and raffle tickets; cash register; receipt book; long tables to showcase goods; tablecloths or butcher paper to cover tables; trashcans; snack table for bake sale; three gift cards from local restaurant to be raffled off*	**Supplier** *Donations from teachers, staff, faculty, parents, students, school site neighborhood and community members* **Contact** *Mrs. Jackson* **Phone** *213-555-5555* **Fax** *213-555-5555*

Kick-off date and time *Sat., 5/12/12 at 9:00 a.m.*

Sale procedures

As shoppers enter the auditorium, they will be asked to purchase raffle tickets at a dollar apiece to earn a chance to win one of three gift certificates to a local restaurant.

Goods will already be price-tagged and displayed on relevant tables (for example, kitchen supplies together, bedding together, clothes together, furniture together).

Shoppers will bring their items to the cash register to pay. They can pay by cash or check and there will be no haggling. A phone number must be written on checks.

Items sold will be placed in plastic bags for the shopper to take home.

Collection procedures

Two weeks prior to the Flea Market, teachers, staff, parents, students, school site neighborhood and community members will drop off donated goods.

Upon arrival, PTA members will sort through items and put price tags on those goods able to be sold in good condition. The rest will be donated to the local thrift store. Tagged goods will be held in the auditorium until the morning of Saturday, May 12, 2012, when they will then be organized on tables to be sold.

Collection location or drop-off *School auditorium*	**Collection schedule** *Mon–Fri 7:30 a.m.–2:30 p.m.*

Updates and notifications (communications, letters, announcements)

Solicitation letters will be sent home with every child, approximately three weeks prior to the Flea Market date (April 22, 2012)

Solicitation letters will be distributed throughout the community beginning approximately three weeks prior to the Flea Market date (April 20–April 30, 2012)

End date *May 12, 2012*	**Awards** *Raffle will be done on the day of the flea market at 12:00 p.m. in the school auditorium.*
Award presentations *Three gift cards to a local restaurant will be raffled off.*	

© The McGraw-Hill Companies, Inc.

Sale of Products

Selling products is one of the most popular and easiest ways to have a fund-raiser. It is best to use an established fund-raising company. Their experience can help tremendously and make things run more smoothly. Your district may have a list of recommended companies.

Selling sweets can be a very effective fund-raiser. Although selling sweets is not encouraged as the only type of fund-raiser, these fund-raisers are easy to manage and very popular. There are several major companies that have organized fund-raising programs. See's Candies, based in California, is one such company. See's provides consumers with high quality chocolate and candy treats and has been running its fund-raising program for many years. Through Red Apple, your school can sell cookies by Otis Spunkmeyer, as well as other high quality and flavorful items.

Other companies offer similar service and dependability. Search online and check with your office manager—many of these companies send out flyers and magazines promoting their programs. Check, too, with other schools and teachers to find out what has worked for them.

Another popular fund-raiser is the sale of wrapping paper and holiday gifts around the winter holidays. Companies provide a catalog filled with small gifts, sweets, and wrapping paper; orders can be placed and delivered in time for the holidays.

Other fund-raising suggestions include a holiday boutique where students can purchase gifts, Valentine candygrams, spring pictures of students, Scholastic Book Fairs (which can be done several times throughout the year), and school pride T-shirts. Booster organizations like the PTA often put on bake sales or pizza-by-the-slice sales during the week of parent conferences, Back-to-School Night, Open House, Science Fair, or parent workshops. It is important to note, however, that many schools do not promote bake sales or the sale of any food item that is not pre-packaged. Check with your school for district policies.

Sale of Products Checklist

- ☐ Approved by administrator or district (necessary paperwork submitted)
- ☐ Staff presentation
- ☐ Approval partner company selected, contract signed
- ☐ Site coordinator selected
- ☐ School-wide presentations (parents, students, community)
- ☐ Timeline established (start date, collections, distributions, end date, awards)
- ☐ Communications, permissions, parent letters ready
- ☐ Logistics established (product storage, money, bags for distribution)

© The McGraw-Hill Companies, Inc.

Flea Market

A flea market is an excellent way to raise money for the school, and it could be scheduled as a monthly or seasonal event. Parents and students donate used items in good condition over a period of three to four weeks. After everything has been sorted and price-tagged, the school holds a Saturday flea market where the community can purchase these items and the money can be donated for school needs.

It is critical to have strong parent support when considering this type of event, because although teachers may help on a voluntary basis, they are not obligated to work beyond their contracted hours. Creating a fun day with refreshments provided can make it more appealing. Teacher buy-in increases teacher participation. It is also a great chance for teachers to clean out their rooms and homes—and we all know how much stuff teachers can accumulate. A flea market also builds community as everyone spends the day together and works together. It is important to start early, so be organized the night before so that set-up will be an easy job early in the morning. Many flea market buyers start at the crack of dawn.

After items are collected, they can be sorted for sale. Separating items into categories such as clothes, household items, tools, art, jewelry, sports equipment, and furniture can make the sale easier to manage. Pricing items ahead of time helps things go more smoothly on the day of the event. This event can simply be a sale of items or, as you gain experience, you may add a food or bake sale, or even a silent auction. Always check the district or school policy on the sale of food, however, because policies sometimes allow only pre-packaged food items to be sold.

For a silent auction, classrooms can solicit donations from local merchants or students can contribute items, which can then be put into themed baskets. Themed baskets could include things like bath and beauty items, sports-themed items, food, or pet supplies. Baskets can be decorated, wrapped, and finally displayed for bidding. Teachers can participate in the silent auction even if they can't come to the flea market itself.

Flea Market Checklist

☐ Approved by administrator or district (necessary paperwork submitted)
☐ Staff presentation (faculty meeting)
☐ Site coordinator and team selected
☐ School-wide presentations (parents, students, community)
☐ Timeline established (advertising, collections, sorting, pricing, worker sign-up)
☐ Communications, parent letters ready
☐ Logistics established (storage)
☐ Advertising (radio, newspaper, flyer, posters)
☐ Set-up (tables, chairs, food, coffee, water, goods to be sold)
☐ Clean-up

© The McGraw-Hill Companies, Inc.

Walk-a-thon

A walk-a-thon is a popular way to raise money and promote a healthy lifestyle. It can bring the whole community together. Community merchants and healthcare practitioners can be invited, and this event can grow over the years into a community walk-a-thon and healthful living fair. For the real adventurers, it can even be incorporated into a 5K run. To make the day successful, many volunteers will be needed for tasks like registering participants, collecting donations, serving refreshments, and cleaning up.

Over a period of two to three weeks before the scheduled date for the walk-a-thon, students and their parents will collect promised donations from friends and family. A specified amount is donated for every unit of distance walked by the participant (for example, $5 per mile). The walk-a-thon can be held on a Saturday, and a pre-designated and measured route can be used. This route needs to be approved by the city or county where it is to be held. Often the police department can stop traffic where needed, and they can also serve as general support. Because this is an event requiring physical exertion, it is recommended that a handout showing the location of all emergency facilities be prepared. For an activity such as this, parental consent is required for student participation.

Participant packets must be created and assembled. Each participant will receive a packet to use for soliciting and tracking donations. Usually there is an entrance fee for the participant to help cover the cost of staging the event, such as refreshments or a deposit for the location. Sometimes T-shirts can be printed and awarded to each participant when they register that day. It's especially fun if the T-shirt design is selected from student work. Have a T-shirt design contest!

If the event develops into a healthful living fair, it is important to have enough tables, chairs, and even shade (for example, tents). This is an excellent opportunity for local merchants to make donations as a means of outreach to their community.

© The McGraw-Hill Companies, Inc.

If the walk-a-thon grows into a 5K-run event, it might be professionally facilitated, which will make it easier for you. Runners will be grouped and timed. Trophies and awards will need to be purchased so that awards can be given to top runners in each age category. Establishing a sanctioned 5K run can create an annual draw for runners. It can be advertised in running publications and grow over time. For help with establishing a 5K run in your community, check with runners in your area to find out who facilitates other 5K runs so that you can talk with their organizers.

Walk-a-thon Checklist

- ☐ Approved by administrator or district (necessary paperwork submitted)
- ☐ Event coordinator and team established
- ☐ Community police and parking reinforcement notified
- ☐ Route secured
- ☐ Parent and community volunteers
- ☐ School-wide presentations (parents, students, community)
- ☐ Timeline established (donation packets, T-shirts, donation collection, set-up, run, clean-up)
- ☐ Orders (T-shirts and trophies)
- ☐ Communications, permissions, parent letters, donation packet ready
- ☐ Logistics established (location, route, tables, chairs)

© The McGraw-Hill Companies, Inc.

Performance

Most schools have performances, and these offer a great opportunity for fund-raising. It is important to make it very clear why there is a small charge for admission to these performances. Students can invite parents and relatives to these special fund-raising performances, and attendees can be given a flyer stating exactly what their donations will be used for.

Students practice hard for these performances, and parents and relatives love to watch their children perform. Schools often schedule performances based on holidays, such as a winter holidays performance in December, an African-American celebration performance in February, or a Latino heritage performance in May or September. Depending on your school's demographics, you may celebrate other cultural holidays. In secondary schools, performances might be organized by the drama or choir departments.

Another performance fund-raising opportunity is to have a talent show. It's fun for everyone: Students, teachers, staff, and administrators can all participate. Tickets can be sold in advance or at the door. This is an excellent way to bring a school community together. It showcases all the talent within the school's community.

A talent show must be very well organized. A faculty member or parent should be in charge to organize try-outs, rehearsals, and the final show. A well-organized show will be a successful event. Communication and advertising is important: A letter home, posters, and flyers are great ways to get the word out and help draw a bigger audience. If the show is to be judged, a panel of judges must be selected and awards and prizes purchased. Last, every participant should receive a certificate of participation.

If the district and school permit it, food can be sold on the night of the show.

Performance Checklist

- ☐ Approved by administrator, district (necessary paperwork submitted)
- ☐ School head custodian consulted
- ☐ Staff presentation and input (faculty meeting)
- ☐ Site coordinator and team selected
- ☐ School-wide presentations (parents, students, community)
- ☐ Timeline established (advertising, try-outs, rehearsals)
- ☐ Communications, parent letters ready
- ☐ Logistics established (use of auditorium and equipment such as sound system, lights)
- ☐ Advertising (radio, newspaper, flyer, posters)
- ☐ Awards, prizes, and certificates of participation
- ☐ Set-up (stage, judges, food tables, chairs, trash)
- ☐ Clean-up

© The McGraw-Hill Companies, Inc.

Pancake Breakfast

A popular community event that is also a great fund-raiser is a pancake breakfast, which can be held on a Saturday morning. It is a great time to welcome the community into the school and a chance to socialize with parents and other staff members. Strong participation from both parents and teachers is very important in the organization and implementation of this fund-raiser.

Check district policies to make sure that non-prepackaged food is allowed; find out if any permissions are needed. If everything is approved at the district level, then logistics at the school site can be worked out. It is important to discuss the event with the plant manager or head custodian, the cafeteria manager, and the cafeteria staff. They are ultimately responsible for the facilities management and clean-up, and they are the ones most impacted by such an event.

Once use of the school site and cafeteria has been secured, planning can begin. Many volunteers are needed, tickets must be sold, supplies must be purchased, and cookware must be arranged for. Prior to the event itself, jobs and responsibilities must be assigned. A school site sign-up sheet should be made available. In addition, letters home should include a sign-up sheet with space for the participant's name, contact phone number, and job choices they are interested in (list three choices). Parents need to sign an official permission form if their son or daughter will be selling tickets. Tickets can be sent home in sets of ten. Daily collection of money must be organized. Once information has been collected, it needs to be organized on a master list that can be used on the day of the breakfast. This will help keep things running smoothly. A work schedule should be posted so that everyone will know what they are doing and when.

Perhaps the most important way to ensure this event's success and continuation is to have an effective and organized clean-up. The less the plant and cafeteria managers feel impacted, the more willing they will be to assist future events. Always think about how any event will affect other staff at the school. Everyone's buy-in is important to the success of the event.

Pancake Breakfast Checklist

- ☐ Approved by administrator, district (necessary paperwork submitted)
- ☐ Staff presentation, input (faculty meeting)
- ☐ Site coordinator and team selected
- ☐ School head custodian and cafeteria manager consulted
- ☐ School-wide presentations (parents, students, community)
- ☐ Timeline established (tickets sold, sign-ups, organization, breakfast, clean-up)
- ☐ Communications, parent letters ready
- ☐ Logistics established (use of auditorium and equipment such as sound system, lights)
- ☐ Advertising (radio, newspaper, flyer, posters)
- ☐ Awards and prizes, certificates of participation
- ☐ Set-up (food tables, chairs, trash)
- ☐ Clean-up

© The McGraw-Hill Companies, Inc.

Sock Hop

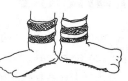

A fun way to raise funds is to have a sock hop. Students can bring in 50 cents and dance for the last 15 to 20 minutes of the lunch period. They enjoy the free time, and it is easy to manage. If a sock hop is coordinated with a project such as holiday baskets (baskets for the needy donated in the school's neighboring community), a can drive can be incorporated into the event, with the funds and canned good items used to prepare food baskets. If refreshments are part of the event, select snacks that involve minimal clean-up and are healthful (for example, fruit roll-ups).

An expanded version of the sock hop would involve scheduling an after-school sock hop or dance. This requires a little more organization, but it can be a great student activity and fund-raiser. Tickets can be priced a little higher and refreshments can be included in the ticket price. Again, keep in mind that refreshments should involve minimal clean-up. Clearance with both your school administrator and your plant manager or head custodian is needed. Keeping all of the affected staff in the loop is very important.

This fund-raiser can be a great project for the student council or student body government. Students can organize and run the dance—a great opportunity for them to learn organizational, decision-making, and leadership skills. They can enjoy organizing, assembling the music playlists (with school-appropriate lyrics), and decorating. Photographs can be taken and sold as an additional fund-raiser. It is also fun to award simple prizes for dance contests, participation, and music games. (Such activities are also helpful in getting students to dance.)

As with any fund-raiser that involves students, adult supervision is necessary. Any potential problem areas in the facility where students cannot be supervised (for example, storage closets) should be closed. Each student should have a signed permission slip or waiver to participate.

Sock Hop Checklist

- ☐ Approved by administrator, district (necessary paperwork submitted)
- ☐ School head custodian consulted
- ☐ Staff presentation, input (faculty meeting)
- ☐ Site coordinator and chaperones
- ☐ School-wide presentations and announcements (parents, students, community)
- ☐ Timeline established (letter, permissions, tickets sold, set-up)
- ☐ Communications, parent letters ready
- ☐ Logistics established (use of auditorium and equipment such as sound system, lights)
- ☐ Refreshments and prizes
- ☐ Set-up (decorations, food tables, trash, sound system, music)
- ☐ Clean-up

© The McGraw-Hill Companies, Inc.

Collection Drive

School-wide collections can be an effective way to raise funds and teach students the importance of giving. Suggestions for school-wide collections that work well include collecting recycling to sell, product labels to redeem, and pennies or loose change—all of these projects are easy, and the funds can add up!

Collection drives can be turned into classroom competitions. This builds classroom spirit and increases the funds raised. Prizes such as a grade-level ice cream party or pizza party for the winning classroom serve as great motivation. A school chart showing all the participating classrooms can be displayed so that students can track the collection competition. A daily collection should be a part of the school day for a specified period of time.

A school-wide recycling project is a fund-raising idea that not only provides money for a variety of programs, materials, and field trips, but also addresses the social reality of our desperate need to recycle. Individual teachers, teams of teachers, school aides, parents, and designated students or classes can be in charge of organizing and implementing the collection of cans and plastic to be delivered to a local recycling center in exchange for cash.

As with any school-wide solicitation, be sure to check into district policies on how money is to be handled. Having students count and roll coins is a terrific way to have them practice their counting skills, especially in the lower grades. Another option is for the collected change to be sorted and weighed at the bank to determine its value. Collecting only pennies makes it easier in some ways (everyone has pennies to get rid of), and that allows the collection drive to be accessible to all students, whatever their economic background.

As with all other fund-raising ideas, organization is the key. A designated coordinator or facilitator is very important. This person makes sure that everyone is informed and that the project runs smoothly. The facilitator can arrange for storage and collection times throughout the school day so that class schedules are not disrupted.

Collection Drive Checklist

- ☐ Approved by administrator or district (necessary paperwork submitted)
- ☐ Staff presentation, input (faculty meeting)
- ☐ Site coordinator or facilitator
- ☐ School-wide presentations, announcements (parents, students, community)
- ☐ Timeline established (letter, collection, start and end dates, report)
- ☐ Communications, parent letters ready
- ☐ Logistics established (daily collections, locations, bank and recycling center)

© The McGraw-Hill Companies, Inc.

Fund-raising Solicitation Letter

Local merchants and businesses can be major supporters of fund-raising efforts for a school, and a fund-raising solicitation letter is a powerful tool for requesting their support. It is a way to get the school's community involved. Businesses may participate in many different kinds of fund-raisers: They can sponsor students for the walk-a-thon, donate time and goods to a pancake breakfast or flea market, and buy tickets to performances. In most cases, all you need to do is ask. Many companies or merchants make donations as part of their business practice. Some even adopt a school to support and help with community events. Supporting school fund-raisers can be a powerful form of advertising as well as a tax deduction for them.

A friendly letter inviting local merchants and businesses to take part in school fund-raising projects will very likely get a positive response. Having the students write letters is the most effective way to get results. Not only do the students get practice writing letters (both friendly and persuasive), but the letters will also have a greater influence with these merchants and businesses. It makes the process more personal and attaches real people to the solicitation. A donation form should be enclosed with the letter. The district or school may have a standard form for use as a donation form or receipt.

Suggestions of Merchants or Businesses to Consider

- Supermarkets
- Restaurants
- Retail stores
- Real estate offices
- Banks
- Hair salons
- Bookstores
- Parents who have a business or who work for a business that would contribute

Information to Include in a Solicitation Letter

- Introduction—who you are and what school is involved (school letterhead)
- Proposed fund-raiser
- Purpose of fund-raiser
- Explanation of how and why their donation will make a difference
- An advance thank-you for considering the donation
- Attach administrator's business card (optional)

Donation Form

- Should accompany the solicitation letter
- Include Tax ID number of school (cleared with administrator) so the business can claim a tax deduction
- Information section: Name, address, phone number
- Place for item name, description, value

226

© The McGraw-Hill Companies, Inc.

Fund-raising Resource Documents

On the pages that follow, you will find templates that can be used with the various fund-raisers covered in this chapter. You may choose to use them as is, filling in your own school information, or you may choose to use them as a guide for creating your own forms, customized for your event.

Donation Receipt *page 228*

Check first with your district or school, because many of them already have a standard form to be used with any donations. If not, this form can be used, but only with your administrator's approval. The school tax identification number may be needed for tax deduction purposes for a business donation; this also needs your administrator's approval. Date and initial all receipts.

Volunteer Sign-Up Sheet *page 229*

Volunteers need to provide their name, preferred phone number (home, work, or cell), and e-mail address. This is important in case you need to contact them about any changes in the event. Under availability, write either the specific times (for example, 8:00–9:00 A.M.) or time frames (for example, morning) that they can sign up for.

Silent Auction Bid Sheet *page 230*

This sheet can be placed in front of an item to be auctioned. Individuals who want to bid on an item write their name and list the amount of their bid. Individuals then outbid each other by signing on the next line with a new, higher amount. Sometimes bidding increments are established (for example, $5 increments), and sometimes there is a specific starting bid amount (for example, $25) that the first bidder must meet or exceed.

Tickets *page 231*

This ticket template can be used for many different kinds of fund-raisers, including pancake breakfasts, talent shows, performances, and sock hops. You may also decide to buy tickets. Make sure tickets are not easy to duplicate. Stamp them with a unique stamp—perhaps a school stamp—to eliminate any forgery.

Volunteer Job Schedule *page 232*

A volunteer job schedule should be filled out and posted the day of the event. You could also make copies and distribute them to volunteers before the event. While it is important to have contact information in case there are any schedule changes, it should be optional on any form that is to be distributed or posted.

Certificate of Participation *page 233*

Recognition of participants is important. This certificate template can be used for both volunteers and participants. There are also many computer programs that can be used to create your own certificates.

Pledge Form *page 234*

This pledge form can organize your sponsors and pledges for events such as walk-a-thons. Check out other walk-a-thons for their pledge forms and procedures. "Other Information" could include T-shirt size if T-shirts are being presented to participants.

© The McGraw-Hill Companies, Inc.

Donation Receipt

Donation Receipt

School name				Phone
School address				School tax ID

Item	Number	Value	Description

Date received	Initials

Donation Receipt

School name				Phone
School address				School tax ID

Item	Number	Value	Description

Date received	Initials

© The McGraw-Hill Companies, Inc.

Volunteer Sign-Up Sheet

Please sign up. Thank you in advance for all your help and support with this event. You make it successful!

Event	Date

Name	Contact (preferred phone number and e-mail address)	Availability (select a time slot)

© The McGraw-Hill Companies, Inc.

Silent Auction Bid Sheet

Please write your name and bid in the appropriate column. Note the starting bid and the bid increment amount, if applicable. Good luck!

Event			Date	

Item description				

Starting bid			Bid increment	
Name	**Amount**	**Name**		**Amount**
1.		16.		
2.		17.		
3.		18.		
4.		19.		
5.		20.		
6.		21.		
7.		22.		
8.		23.		
9.		24.		
10.		25.		
11.		26.		
12.		27.		
13.		28.		
14.		29.		
15.		30.		

© The McGraw-Hill Companies, Inc.

Tickets

Ticket
This ticket is good for
admission to or the purchase of
_____

School_____

Date _____

Value _____

Ticket
This ticket is good for
admission to or the purchase of
_____

School_____

Date _____

Value _____

Ticket
This ticket is good for
admission to or the purchase of
_____

School_____

Date _____

Value _____

Ticket
This ticket is good for
admission to or the purchase of
_____

School_____

Date _____

Value _____

Ticket
This ticket is good for
admission to or the purchase of
_____

School_____

Date _____

Value _____

Ticket
This ticket is good for
admission to or the purchase of
_____

School_____

Date _____

Value _____

© The McGraw-Hill Companies, Inc.

Volunteer Job Schedule

Thank you for signing up to volunteer today. This will be our work schedule.

Hours	Job	Volunteer	Phone

232

© The McGraw-Hill Companies, Inc.

Certificate of Participation

_____
Name of Participant

has participated in _____
Program/Event

on _____.
Date

We proudly recognize your participation
in this fund-raising activity
at our school.

Thanks from all of us

at _____.
Name of School

Your participation makes a difference.

_____   _____
Administrator's Signature   Coordinator's Signature

© The McGraw-Hill Companies, Inc.

Pledge Form

Event		Date		Time	
Participant name				Age	Sex
E-mail				Phone	
Other information					

Sponsor name	Address	Pledge amount	Total pledge	Amount (with check number)
1.				
2.				
3.				
4.				
5.				
6.				
7.				
8.				
9.				
10.				
11.				
12.				
13.				
14.				
15.				

© The McGraw-Hill Companies, Inc.

17

Grant Writing

Have you ever considered seeking out money for a project near and dear to your heart? Have programs been cut due to budget constraints, and you want to find a way to keep them from being eliminated? Lack of funds is a large roadblock in education today. Additional funds can be obtained through various means, however, such as fund-raising, donations, and grant writing. Of the three, grant writing can potentially bring in the most funding for any single designated project. Grants can fund educational needs such as support materials, equipment, multicultural classroom libraries, science lab materials, academic learning games, technology software, computers, cameras, and art supplies. Grants can also fund something as large and comprehensive as a school program, for example, the hiring of physical education teachers and the purchase of equipment to facilitate a district-wide physical education program.

Below is a brief overview of the process.

Need

Identify your need first. This is important, because it is too hard to tailor a program to fit an exact grant; it is much easier to find a grant that meets your needs or matches your project. Why is this project or program needed?

Plan

Establish goals and objectives for your project or program. How does this meet the needs of your school and its students? How will you measure the results? What do you need to make this happen?

Fund

Research several grant opportunities in order to find one that matches your particular project. You should be able to refer to examples of grant proposals that have been approved by these funding sources in the past. When you prepare your own grant proposal, make sure that the specifics of your proposal are aligned with the grant you have selected.

Do

Implement the project. Follow all the requirements of the grant, such as the timeline, phases, and other obligations that are laid out in your commitment to the grant guidelines.

Thank

Follow up with a report that details the difference that the grant funds made in your school. Provide measurable results as required by the funding agency or organization and as evidenced by the positive impact of the project. Express appreciation.

© The McGraw-Hill Companies, Inc.

Through the Eyes of the Funder

Imagine that you had a million dollars and were giving it away. You really wanted to help schools bring the arts back into the classroom. You envisioned what that would look like, what you would want to see the money spent on, how such a program would be set up, and what end results you would want to see. If two hundred teachers applied to receive your funding, how would you make your selection? View your own project through the eyes of the funder as you prepare your grant proposal to compete with possibly hundreds of other grant applications. As a funder, you would want to see your money well spent. You would also want to see follow-through and results! Below is a list of what you, as the funder, would most likely want to see before giving your money away.

Commitment

Without a doubt, you would want to see a strong level of commitment from those who would receive your money. Is the school supportive? Is the school prepared to carry out their plan?

Evidence of a Need

You would want your money to go where it is needed. You would want clear-cut evidence of this need.

A Plan

You would want to see a solid plan of action that fits your own vision for how you would want your money spent.

The "Wow"

You would want to see something in the application that sets it apart from others, something that really impresses you. Is there an aspect, idea, or innovation that makes this application more appealing, yet still realistic? You want to be "wowed."

Organization

You would want to see organization, not only in the plan, but in the actual application. The neatness and professionalism of its presentation are evidence of this.

Follow-through

If you give this money to the project or program, will there be follow-through? Will your funds be put into action right away? Will there be benchmark goals throughout the school year to evaluate progress? Will it continue beyond the plan set forth in the grant? Will the school secure its own funds (or matching funds) for the project or program so that it can continue after your financial contribution has been spent? Is there a team of dedicated instructors who will see this through?

Viewing your project through the eyes of the funder is a great way to approach the grant. Keep the following considerations in mind as you prepare to write a grant proposal. If *you* wouldn't fund your project or program, why should anyone else? Always ask, would *I* fund this project or program if *I* had the money?

© The McGraw-Hill Companies, Inc.

Grant-writing Tips

Every grant situation is different. Do what works best for you and your school.

The Internet as a Valuable Resource

Use the Internet. There are a variety of websites that help with grant writing as well as with locating funding sources. Funding sources may include governmental, civic, educational, non-profit, and philanthropic organizations. The majority use the Internet to promote their goals and services. Researching online will get much of the legwork done. For some funding sources, it may also be that the only way to submit your proposal is online.

Don't Reinvent the Wheel

Don't hesitate to approach teachers, administrators, and parents to help with the process. There is a good chance that much of the information required for a grant proposal has already been written and exists on someone's computer somewhere on your school campus.

If At First You Don't Succeed …

Don't get discouraged if your application is rejected. You may have submitted an excellent grant proposal, having completed every step, every request for information—and did all of it thoroughly. Keep in mind that funding sources have a budget for the year and can only fund a certain number of requests. If your application is rejected, be sure to find out why. Most funding sources make their scoring system available. You'll be able to see which components of your proposal had weaker scores and where you were strongest. This can be very helpful when revising your proposal for another granting source.

Stand Out!

Try to think of new and creative ways to write your grant proposal so that it appears not just new and original, but also imaginative—and, of course, educational. This doesn't mean that you shouldn't use an idea that's already been done, but do add your own spin on things and try to be reasonable and realistic.

© The McGraw-Hill Companies, Inc.

Don't Be Greedy

When it comes to budget, don't ask for too little, but don't ask for too much, either. You want to be reasonable and realistic here. Determine your costs well in advance of choosing your funding source, and be prepared to give a detailed description of where and how your money will be spent.

Know the Hand That Feeds

Research the different funding sources to find out what kinds of projects each source will and will not fund. You don't want to spend time writing the grant proposal only to find out that they never fund that type of project.

It Takes a Village

One of the best ways to accomplish writing a grant proposal quickly and successfully is to pull together a grant team— a group of teachers, administrators, staff members, the librarian, and parents who are interested in being a part it. If any members of this team have already written a grant proposal, they will be an excellent resource! They would not only have experience, but they should also have their grant proposal to refer to.

The "grant team" can meet with you during the grant-writing period to discuss and review, as well as divide and conquer, the grant proposal. It is always good to have someone who is willing to edit, someone who is willing to do some research, someone who is willing to organize the text according to the funding source's format, and someone who is willing to do a bit of everything (usually the person who is seeking the grant money in the first place). Having this team together from the beginning is a big asset; it allows you to make the best use of each person's strengths throughout the entire process.

Know Your Audience

Consider your audience. Does your proposal meet the mission of the funder? Is it a good fit? Consider, too, the readers of the grant proposal, those who will be evaluating it. Is your proposal something that will appeal to this audience? Know your audience, and deliver.

© The McGraw-Hill Companies, Inc.

Follow Through!

Applying for a grant involves commitment, and you need to follow through. This includes more than just following the plan. It involves training those involved, monitoring progress, and documenting with measurable results—and even photographs—as the project progresses. After the project has been completed and the grant commitment fulfilled, follow through with a final report on the results, including a financial accounting. A thank-you letter is important, too, and a nice touch.

Save Everything

Save everything you have compiled in writing this grant proposal. Start a school grant resource file, either in hard copy or on designated flash drives, in which you include grant information received from other teachers, whether their proposals were successful or not. Having this information available saves time and gives you background information for your next proposal.

Prove It!

Don't just say you need something, back it up!

1. Explain in detail what the money will be used for. For example, if students need more technology, don't just say it's because "other schools have computers and our students need to be able to compete." What will they do with those computers? Give examples to justify your need.

2. Explain how the teachers, students, and staff will be trained to use the materials for your project (if that is applicable). Funders want to fund projects that can be supported by more qualified people than just yourself.

3. Give background and qualifications of any participating teachers. Include credentials, certificates, and résumés that show every participant's ability to successfully take on this project.

Do As You Are Told

Follow the guidelines. Read and reread them carefully to make sure that you include everything that is needed in your grant proposal.

© The McGraw-Hill Companies, Inc.

Components of a Grant Proposal

There are some components required for most grant proposals that you may want to sketch out even before finding your funding source. It might seem to you that you are doing more work than necessary if it turns out that not all of this information is needed for your specific grant proposal. However, you might need it eventually if you are not approved by your first funding source and have to choose another. Use the templates in this chapter to assist you. The following key components, listed alphabetically, are common to most grant proposals, and thinking about them early on will help you organize the information that you need to gather for the grant-writing process.

Assessment (Measurable Results)

What benchmarks will you have in place in order to monitor the progress of your project? Will you have a checklist of due dates? Will each of the project's goals be evaluated by you and an administrator throughout the project? How will you know that your goals are being met? How will you measure this? Without these assessments, one cannot make adjustments to the project if something is not working right initially.

Background Need

Explain how you came to need the funding for this project. Is one of your current and important programs in jeopardy of being cut due to budget constraints? Are you about to lose a necessary staff member because of budget cuts, or are you in need of a staff member for a particular project? Be as concise as possible, and use text from district letters or administration communications that will back up and strengthen your need. Document the need for your project with demographic information, test results, and anecdotal evidence if you have it.

Budget Costs

Research and determine the initial funding needed for your grant proposal's project or program, and think about what will be required for the project or program to continue after the grant funds are exhausted. When organizing your budget, be realistic and reasonable. Remember to include costs for required materials, supplies, and personnel. Having this information in hand will make it much easier to locate appropriate funding sources and to complete the grant application when the time comes.

© The McGraw-Hill Companies, Inc.

Goals

Describe the ways in which the project is going to meet your goals. When developing goals, make them tangible. Be sure they are specific and measurable. What do you expect the actual outcome or product to be? This can be written as a mission statement, or you can begin with an overall summary of your intended goals and then list each individual goal and its objectives as a bullet point, possibly with a short annotation.

Introduction

An introduction should introduce your school, its demographics, and why the project you want funded is so important. Share a little about yourself and your experience as a teacher so that they know you are qualified to use their money effectively for the project they are being asked to fund.

Methods

How will you achieve your project goals? Give a step-by-step breakdown of your methods for accomplishing this. You may choose to put each step on a timeline.

Summary

Make this as brief and clear as possible. Think carefully about what your project is really about and how the finding will be used. Remember that not all grantors will understand the "lingo" you might use, so have a lay person read it as well. If you can summarize your grant proposal in a short paragraph, it's a good sign that you know exactly what you are asking for.

© The McGraw-Hill Companies, Inc.

Grant-writing Resource Documents

In the next several pages we provide some resource documents for you to use as you plan and write your grant proposal. You may be able to use them "as is," or you may want to customize any or all of them for your own specific project.

Grant Survey *page 245*

Begin with a survey when planning to write a grant. This will help you see what grants the school has received in the past, who was involved, and what the current needs are. It will help you focus on your next grant proposal or idea. Complete the survey; share and discuss the results.

Grant Researcher Organizer *page 246*

This organizer will help you research grant opportunities that potentially fit the needs of your school and the proposed project or program. For each funding source, include the contact information, deadlines, funding amount, and a brief description of the kinds of grants that fit the funding source. This should be an ongoing list; add to it as you hear about new grant opportunities.

Grant Inventory Worksheet *page 247*

At a faculty meeting toward the beginning of the school year, circulate a grant inventory worksheet so that you can compile a list of grants that teachers have written or participated in before. Save this as a resource for future planning.

Grant Application Worksheet *page 248*

This worksheet is a sample of what may be required for your grant proposal. Use this form to gather information. A grant proposal might be several pages long, and it typically has a cover page for general information.

School Profile Organizer *page 249*

The school profile organizer should be completed with your school's information. Many grant proposals require information such as test scores or subsidized lunch program data. Having this information already gathered will help you when it's time to complete your grant proposal. Continue information on the back if necessary.

© The McGraw-Hill Companies, Inc.

Introduction/Overview Organizer *page 250*

Use this organizer to help you articulate your thoughts. Keep in mind any word count restrictions for your specific grant proposal. The information gathered here may be requested as separate items or it may be appropriate to weave it into a single narrative paragraph, depending on the grant application. This organizer is a way to organize some basic grant information in one place so you'll have it when you need it. When you are actually completing the grant proposal, be sure to put it in the format required for that specific funder.

Needs Statement Worksheet *page 251*

Your needs statement may be embedded in your overview or introduction. It needs to be well thought-out and carefully worded. The needs statement makes the case—in its most succinct form—for why you are seeking funding. Use this worksheet to help you develop three needs statements that fit your project, get feedback on them, and then select the one that best fits your project and the grant proposal itself.

Goals Organizer *page 252*

This organizer will help you outline your project goals and their objectives. Your project goals may stand alone in the grant proposal or they may be embedded in your introduction or overview. The statements outlining your goals need to be focused and specific to your project; make sure these goals are supported by the grant.

Methods and Design Organizer *page 253*

Use this organizer to help you in the design and methodology of your project. What exactly is your project? What tools will you use? How will you set it up? Who will be involved? Make sure that your project is well organized and that it aligns to the requirements of the funder. Keep it realistic. Don't overplan just because you think it will look impressive. What you want is a project that, if funded, will yield results.

© The McGraw-Hill Companies, Inc.

Measurable Results Organizer *page 254*

You will need to show documentation for measurable results for any grant. That is why the project is funded: The funder wants to see the return on investment. This organizer is designed to help you plan your methods for determining measurable results. These can be actual assessments, test scores, or observations. The results should clearly demonstrate gains that support your stated goals. A successful project will show gains. Not everything is successful though, and that is understandable. You want to have a well planned means of showing all measurable results—both positive and negative. Decide on several assessment methods that may be a good fit, and then choose the best one for your particular project and grant.

Budget Planner *page 255*

The budget is the estimated or projected cost of your project. How much will this cost? Is the budget current? Is it realistic? Is it enough? The budget for your grant proposal needs to be very specific. Many grant applications include budget submission forms with line items for each category of expenditure. Don't pad your budget or add too many extras; just request what you need to achieve the project's goals. You will also have to be flexible. Can you make it work if less funding is awarded or if prices change? This is very important, and you must anticipate the possibility.

Expenditure Tracker *page 256*

This tracking form can be used to account for all grant expenditures and the dates of purchase. Keep this for your records, with all invoices and receipts.

Activity Tracker *page 257*

This tracking form can be used to detail all of the activities that are outlined in your grant proposal. Keep it for your records.

Timeline Planner *page 258*

Some grants require a timeline as part of the proposal. When are your proposed goals going to be fulfilled? What are the projected dates for the completion of each phase or step of this project? It is a good idea to develop a timeline when you are planning your project, whether it is required for the proposal process or not. Include your own deadlines for grant writing and submission as well as the projected dates for completion of phases of the project itself.

© The McGraw-Hill Companies, Inc.

Grant Survey

What grants has the school received? Who has written them? Were they successful? Why? Briefly reflect on any grants your school has participated in and complete the form below as much as possible. This can be done individually or in a group discussion.

Grant	Writer(s)
Project/Program description	
Successful ☐ Yes ☐ No Why?	

Grant	Writer(s)
Project/Program description	
Successful ☐ Yes ☐ No Why?	

List 3 needs of the school or your class that could use the support of outside funding.

1.

2.

3.

Brainstorm about your next grant. (Briefly outline a project that could address one of the needs listed above.)

Project or Program

Goal

Materials

Possible funding source(s) (Discuss or search online.)

© The McGraw-Hill Companies, Inc.

Grant Research Organizer

Grant source, contact information (name, contact information, URL)	Deadline	Amount	Description

© The McGraw-Hill Companies, Inc.

Grant Inventory Worksheet

If you have written a grant proposal or participated in a grant-funded project, please provide the information requested below.

School			District	Group	

Grant	Teacher	Program/Project	Dates	Location	Funding amount
	☐ Writer ☐ Participant				
	☐ Writer ☐ Participant				
	☐ Writer ☐ Participant				
	☐ Writer ☐ Participant				
	☐ Writer ☐ Participant				
	☐ Writer ☐ Participant				

© The McGraw-Hill Companies, Inc.

Grant Application Worksheet

Complete the information below as much as possible.

Project/Program title

Lead applicant/teacher(s)   ☐ Single applicant   ☐ Additional teachers

Targeted grade levels	Program numbers _____ Students _____ Teachers	Grant request (the funding amount you are seeking)

School name			
Street	City	State	Zip
Website/e-mail	Phone	Fax	

School district ☐ Public ☐ Private	Local district County/Province

Lead teacher name			
Credentials (credentials, certificates, résumé)			
Street	City	State	Zip
E-mail	Phone	Fax	

Second teacher name			
Credentials (credentials, certificates, résumé)			
Street	City	State	Zip
E-mail	Phone	Fax	

Third teacher name			
Credentials (credentials, certificates, résumé)			
Street	City	State	Zip
E-mail	Phone	Fax	

Program overview/introduction

Needs statement

Goals (with specific objectives)

Project methods and design

Measurable objectives

Budget

© The McGraw-Hill Companies, Inc.

School Profile Organizer

School name

Street   City   State   Zip

Website/e-mail   Phone   Fax

School district	Local district
☐ Public ☐ Private	County/Province
Annual operational budget (include applicable school year)	Grants received
Administrator/Principal	Assistant administrator/principal

Staff numbers _____ Teachers _____ Resource teachers _____ Teacher assistants

School demographics (ethnicity of student population by percentage)

_____% _____ _____% _____ _____% _____

_____% _____ _____% _____ _____% _____

Special programs (for example, Speech, Tutoring, Drop-out Intervention, particularly any directly related to grant)

After-school program _____ Number of students served

List any subsidy programs (for example, Title I)

Assisted lunch program _____ Number of students receiving

Other

Awards/Honors (include name and year received)

School year	Test	Scores				

Other

© The McGraw-Hill Companies, Inc.

Introduction/Overview Organizer

The Introduction or Overview of your grant proposal is a brief persuasive narrative that introduces your project. Include an overview of the background, the problem, and the solution. This summary leads into the need and may be coupled with the need. Choose your words carefully. Have others proof, edit, and revise.

Introduction (Topic sentence/Introduce project (could be two sentences: (1) Problem: "In today's schools....", (2) Project definition: "This project is specifically designed to....")

Buzz words (Words that you have selected to support your project. Examples are included below; brainstorm and add to the list.)

Actions: empowers, improves, demonstrates, teaches, instills, provides, reduces, develops, …

Events or skills: reading, play, math, behavior, aptitude, math computation, …

Support

Statement 1 that supports the project.

Statement 2 that supports the project.

Statement 3 that supports the project.

Summary (Wrap up your introduction. Restate why this project is important. Maybe add a research statement. The reader should clearly understand the importance of this project and why the project should be funded.)

© The McGraw-Hill Companies, Inc.

Needs Statement Worksheet

Targeted population	Specific needs	Evidence

Be specific. What is the need? What evidence supports the need? Who is affected?

Needs statement version 1

Needs statement version 2

Needs statement version 3

© The McGraw-Hill Companies, Inc.

Goals Organizer

Considerations
- Are my goals specific to my project?
- Are my goals supported by the grant?
- Are my objectives measurable?

Goal	Objectives
Goal 1	1.
	2.
	3.
Goal 2	1.
	2.
	3.
Goal 3	1.
	2.
	3.

© The McGraw-Hill Companies, Inc.

Methods and Design Organizer

Project title

Goal

Schedule

_____ Weeks _____ Total hours

Targeted students

Total number _____

	Monday	Tuesday	Wednesday	Thursday	Friday	Saturday	Total hours
A.M.							
P.M.							

Teachers/Instructors

Materials (Include curriculums, book series, technology, etc.)

Brief model of operation (What will a day look like? How will it be monitored? What routine will be established?)

Time	Activity	Description

253

© The McGraw-Hill Companies, Inc.

Measurable Results Organizer

Grant title

Grant goals

Assessment/Test	Score		Description	Date
	Pre	Post		

Observation	Score		Description	Date
	Pre	Post		

© The McGraw-Hill Companies, Inc.

Budget Planner

Grant title				Date	

Class/Object	Description (include source, page, etc.)	Quantity	Unit price	Tax	Total expenditure

© The McGraw-Hill Companies, Inc.

Expenditure Tracker

Support with invoices and receipts.

Grant title				Date received	
			Total grant budget		
			Total outside/additional/matching funds		
Class/Object	**Description** (include source, page, etc.)	**Quantity**	**Unit price**	**Tax**	**Total expenditure**

© The McGraw-Hill Companies, Inc.

Activity Tracker

Keep for your records.

Activity (grant-related activities)	Description (include description of activity, participants, location, materials used)	Date	Goal (goal or objective targeted)

© The McGraw-Hill Companies, Inc.

Timeline Planner

List all events that have been included as part of your grant proposal (for example, grant planning, writing, and submission dates, project start date, purchases, project events, project end date, etc.).

Grant title			Date
January	**February**	**March**	**April**
May	**June**	**July**	**August**
September	**October**	**November**	**December**

© The McGraw-Hill Companies, Inc.

18

Preparing for a Formal Evaluation

You have now clearly reached the point in your teaching career when you are seen, referred to, and consider yourself a Master Teacher. You are no doubt an expert at lesson planning and have built many theme-based units. Nevertheless, even the most experienced teachers would do well to review the planning of a structured and specific lesson plan prior to a formal evaluation.

If it is your year to be formally evaluated, you will want to meet with your administrator early in the year to set up your first observation date, time, and lesson idea.

In this section, you will find a glossary of terms, a generic lesson plan format, and lesson examples that can be used to "wow" the administrator who comes to observe you. These materials might also serve as a discussion piece for you with teachers you are mentoring. Whatever your purpose, this is a valuable resource that you can use as a reference for organizing solid lessons.

Important Preparation Tips

✔ Those of you who identify as "traditional" teachers might feel most comfortable with the typical 5-, 7-, or 9-step lesson plans of the past. Feel free to continue with that style if you prefer, but try to include additional contemporary elements such as standards, assessments, extensions, English Language Development (ELD) considerations, special needs accommodations, and technology components.

✔ Pay attention to the room environment. Check your bulletin boards for current student work, focus standards, and appeal. Have the students' desks cleaned out and make sure the rest of your room is clean and organized.

✔ Professional appearance is important: Dress appropriately and hold yourself with confidence. If possible, try to practice your lesson in advance so you know you'll be pacing yourself well.

✔ Have student portfolios, district assessments, and other important documents in clear view so that your administrator has immediate access to them, because this may be required for your formal evaluation.

© The McGraw-Hill Companies, Inc.

7-Step Lesson Plan

There are several different types of lesson plans in existence and, in addition, many variations to them. It's always a good idea to check with the administrator who will be doing a formal evaluation to see if there is a particular format that your evaluator prefers. While most teachers are allowed to use any lesson plan format they choose, some administrators require a specific type of lesson plan. In most cases, using a 5-, 7-, or 9-step lesson plan will work out well, since these have been used successfully over time.

Throughout this section, we refer to the 7-step plan, but it is not the only plan recommended. While this lesson plan format is well understood in the teaching profession, be aware of the importance of incorporating additional components, such as differentiating instruction, using technology, and including modifications for those with special needs. A formal evaluation can sometimes be stressful, but with a supportive administrator it can be very useful, and it can serve as a chance to improve and to polish your skills.

1. Anticipatory Set and Scaffolding

Grab student attention, then relate new objectives to past learning.

2. Presentation and Procedure

List the sequential steps for the lesson you will model.

3. Guided Practice

The students and teacher work together to carry out an example or activity to match the objective.

4. Check for Understanding

Use a quick and simple assessment to confirm students' understanding.

5. Independent Practice

Students work independently on a task that meets the objective.

6. Assessments, Homework, or Project

Use an effective method to make sure students continue to understand the objective.

7. Content Standard

Refer to your state standards and list the standard that you will be teaching in this lesson.

© The McGraw-Hill Companies, Inc.

Evaluation Lesson Checklist

Here are some simple reminders to review while preparing for your formal evaluation. This checklist is one that you can use while planning the actual lesson.

☐ Check with your administrator to see if you are on the list for a formal evaluation for the current school year.

☐ Meet with your evaluator and discuss what he or she is expecting to see (or would like to see). Ask if a specific lesson plan format is required. Good administrators will likely give you the freedom to plan any lesson as long as it is aligned to the state standards.

☐ Plan your lesson while keeping in mind all the mastered skills you have in your repertoire. Remember to take into account the three types of learners—auditory, visual, and kinesthetic.

☐ Type up or write out your lesson plan. Your evaluator will want the opportunity to look it over, so submit it to your evaluator in advance.

☐ You should be aware of all union rights and regulations regarding a formal evaluation, no matter where you are in your teaching career or how good or bad your relationship with your administrator may be.

☐ Share this information with other teachers—a teacher you are mentoring, your student teacher, a friend—so that they can be better prepared for their own evaluation. If a friend of yours is also being evaluated, it's often nice to do some planning together.

☐ Great lessons often contain elements such as a great literature piece, hands-on activities for the students, and rigorous learning geared toward the state standards.

☐ Good planning coupled with a sense of trust between you and your administrator should make your evaluation go very smoothly. If your administrator seems to be unsupportive of your teaching, gently remind him or her that the objective of an evaluation is to provide teachers with support in their teaching in any way necessary.

© The McGraw-Hill Companies, Inc.

Lesson Plan Labels

Each section below includes a listing of labels that can be used to identify the different steps in your lesson plan. Not all sections are necessary for every lesson. Use the glossary on page 266 to help identify the labels that are most appropriate for your lesson. You can use all of them or a handful of them to meet your lesson plan needs.

Heading

- Class identification
- Unit identification
- Standards
- Goals
- Materials and equipment

Introductory Steps

- Anticipatory set
- Advanced organizer
- Purpose
- Objectives
- Behavioral objectives

Teaching Steps

- Input
- Procedures
- Instruction
- Model (may also be combined with Procedures and/or Instruction)
- Check for understanding (may also be combined with Procedures and/or Instruction)

Assessment Steps

- Guided practice (may also be combined with Procedures and/or Instruction)
- Check for understanding
- Closure
- Independent practice
- Assessment

Follow-up Steps

- Extension activities
- Follow-up activities
- Provide for student differences
- Management
- Technology
- Home connection

© The McGraw-Hill Companies, Inc.

Lesson Plan Label Descriptions

Heading

Class identification

Teacher's name, grade, regular, ELL, bilingual

Unit identification

Title of lesson and timeline (number of minutes)

Standards

List all state or district standards that apply to your lesson

Materials and equipment

What materials will you need to teach the lesson? Audio, visual, or tactile materials? Be prepared! Be prepared!

Introductory Steps

Anticipatory set

Something catchy and quickly related to the topic to grab student attention—something to hook students' interest. Pictures, objects, animals, puppets, books, stories, colors, realia, costumes. Focus the learner and establish transfer from past learning.

Purpose

Inform students of the objective for today built from yesterday's lesson or objective. Why do students have to learn what you are going to teach? Funnel the students. Connect yesterday's lessons to today's.

Objectives

List student learning outcomes that will be accomplished in the lesson. Do not list teacher behaviors or student activities here. Specific and observable objectives should be listed. Minimum level of adequate performance should be stated, for example, "By the end of the lesson, students will be able to use at least 5 of the 8 vocabulary words in individual sentences."

263

© The McGraw-Hill Companies, Inc.

Teaching Steps

Input

What will you be doing to teach the topic, issue, or subject? Examples are lecture, read-aloud, video, questioning, children teaching children.

Model

What are the lesson steps? What are the student learning activities (listed in chronological order)? How will you show the children what is to be learned? What will you use and how will you use it to model the process and outcome of the lesson objective? Provide examples using equipment or materials the students may use later. Involve students.

Check for understanding

What quick activity can you have students do to show that they understood the lesson and are ready to move on? Have students provide a rationale for why and how they solved a specific problem. Monitor, monitor, monitor!

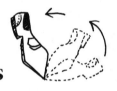

Assessment Steps

Guided practice

What is it that you and the students will be doing together to meet the objectives? Elicit overt responses that demonstrate behavior that meets the objectives. Students offer ideas and work with the teacher to achieve the objectives. Mass practice while students are still under the teacher's guidance.

Check for understanding

What quick activity can you have students do to show that they understood the lesson and are ready to move on? Have students provide a rationale for why and how they solved a specific problem. Monitor, monitor, monitor! How are you going to do this?

Closure

This is a chance for students to digest what they have learned. It is "think time," not a time for verbal response. "I want you to think about the map we just went over. Can you see the trails? Think about the people involved in the Westward Movement and how they traveled the trails." Use key terms to reinforce the subject matter.

Independent practice

This is where the student completes your objective. Give directions. The students are no longer working with you or the whole group at this point. They are working alone while the teacher monitors students carefully. Complete objectives! Complete objectives!

© The McGraw-Hill Companies, Inc.

Assessment

List all the formal and informal methods that you will use to determine whether students are getting the concept or not. State this in terms of observable student behavior and ways for the teacher to collect data that shows the students' understanding or mastery of the concept.

Follow-up Steps

Extension activities

What follow-up activities will you assign for homework? What other class activity will you do to reinforce the lesson? What challenging activities will you assign to promote higher-level thinking for the same concept?

Provide for student differences

What materials will you need to make sure all students are able to grasp the information in the lesson (for example, audio, visual, or tactile materials)? List any follow-up activities for students who need further practice in addition to the primary follow-up activity (for example, decodable books for struggling and/or emergent readers, flash cards for basic math skills, books at independent reading level). How will you meet the needs of English Language Learners, students with disabilities, and students with different levels of abilities?

Technology

What software will your students be working with for the lesson? How will students be using the computer to enhance their learning for the lesson? What website will be accessed for the lesson?

Home connection

How might you involve the parents of your students in the classroom for this lesson? Send notes home describing the new unit or lesson.

© The McGraw-Hill Companies, Inc.

Glossary of Terms Used in Lesson Plans

Advanced organizer

- A discussion, chart, diagram, book, or concept exercise that frames the key concepts of the lesson.
- *See* Anticipatory set.

Anticipatory set

- Something catchy and quickly related to the topic to grab student attention. It's something to hook students' interest.
- Pictures, objects, animals, puppets, books, stories, colors, realia, costumes.
- An activity that sets up the lesson and helps connect students to previously learned concepts or life experiences.

- This must be something that will make all students want to find out what is going to happen next.
- Something that will make students want to participate.
- Something to focus the learner and establish transfer from past learning.

Assessment

- List all the formal and informal methods that you will use to determine whether students are getting the concept or not.
- State in terms of observable student behavior and ways for the teacher to collect data that shows the students' understanding or mastery of the concept.

Behavioral objectives

- What are you going to teach?
- List student learning outcomes that will be accomplished in the lesson.
- State objectives in specific cognitive or performance student behavioral outcome language, for example, "By the end of the lesson students will be able to...."
- Do not list teacher behaviors or student activities here.
- Specific and observable objectives should be listed.

- Minimum level of adequate performance should be stated, for example, "By the end of the lesson, students will be able to use at least 5 of the 8 vocabulary words in individual sentences."
- *See* Objectives.

© The McGraw-Hill Companies, Inc.

Check for understanding

- Have students do something to demonstrate what they have learned.
- Have students do a quick activity to show that they understood the lesson and are ready to do it on their own.
- Have students provide a rationale for why and how they solved a specific problem.
- Use signals to represent agreement or disagreement.
- Monitor, monitor, monitor! How are you going to do this?

Class identification

- Teacher's name.
- Grade.
- Regular, English Language Learner (ELL), bilingual.

Closure

- This is a chance for the students to digest what they have learned—"think time," not really a time for verbal response. "I want you to think about the map we just went over. Can you see the trails? Think about the people involved in the Westward Movement and how they traveled the trails."
- Take just a few minutes to bring the whole group back together after independent practice to wrap up the lesson.
- Use key terms to reinforce the subject matter.
- Post-test.

Extension activities

- What follow-up activities will you assign for homework?
- What other class activity will you do to reinforce the lesson?
- What challenging activities will you assign to promote higher-level thinking for the same concept?
- *See* Follow-up activities.

Follow-up activities

- What follow-up activities will you assign for homework?
- What other class activity will you do to reinforce the lesson?
- *See* Extension activities.

© The McGraw-Hill Companies, Inc.

Goals

- List all state or district standards that apply to your lesson.
- List all unit goals that are addressed by the lesson.
- *See* Standards.

Guided practice

- The children and teacher go through the lesson activities together; after this step, the children work without the teacher.
- Students offer ideas and work with the teacher to reach the objectives.
- Teacher and children work together.
- Mass practice while the student is still under the teacher's guidance.
- Elicit overt responses that demonstrate behavior that meets the objectives.
- Provide specific knowledge of results.
- Teacher is present to provide assistance and give immediate feedback.

Home connection

- How will you involve the parents of your students in the classroom for this lesson?
- Send notes home describing new unit or lesson.
- Permission to discuss questionable topics.

Independent practice

- The student completes your objective.
- Give the directions, and have two to four students repeat the directions back to you. Then let the children do the activity independently.
- The students are no longer working with you or the whole group at this point. They are working alone.
- Teacher monitors students carefully.
- Complete objectives! Complete objectives! Complete objectives!

Input

- What will you be doing to teach the topic, issue, or subject?
- What lesson steps will you be doing (for example, lecture, read-aloud, video, questioning, children teaching children)?
- What are the student learning activities (listed in chronological order)?
- Develop skill, step by step.
- *See* Procedures.

© The McGraw-Hill Companies, Inc.

Instruction

- Provide information.
- Pre-test.

Management

- How will you differentiate instruction?
- Safety concerns such as goggles or close-toed shoes.
- How will you meet the needs of differing ability levels and English Language Learners (ELLs)?

Materials and equipment

- What materials will you need to teach the lesson (audio, visual, or tactile materials)?
- What audio or visual equipment might you need to teach the lesson?
- Be prepared! Be prepared! Be prepared!

Model

- How will you show the children what is to be learned?
- What will you use to model the process and outcome of the lesson objective, and how will you use it?
- Provide examples using equipment or materials that the students may use later.
- Involve students.

Objectives

- What are you going to teach?
- List student learning outcomes that will be accomplished in the lesson.
- State objectives in specific cognitive or performance student behavioral outcome language, for example, "By the end of the lesson students will be able to...."
- Do not list teacher behaviors or student activities here.
- Specific and observable objectives should be listed.
- Minimum level of adequate performance should be stated, for example, "By the end of the lesson, students will be able to use at least 5 of the 8 vocabulary words in individual sentences."
- *See* Behavioral objectives.

© The McGraw-Hill Companies, Inc.

Procedures

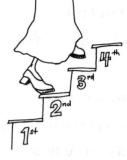

- What are the student learning activities (listed in chronological order)?
- What are your lesson steps?
- *See* Input.

Provide for student differences

- What materials will you need to make sure all students are able to grasp the information in the lesson, for example, audio, visual, and tactile materials?
- List any follow-up activities that will be assigned to students who need further practice in addition to the primary follow-up activity (for example, decodable books for struggling and/or emergent readers, flash cards for basic math skills, books at independent reading level).
- How will you meet the needs of English Language Learners, students with disabilities, and students with different levels of abilities?
- *See* Management.

Purpose

- Inform students of the objective for today based on yesterday's lesson or objective.
- Why do students have to learn what you are going to teach?
- Funnel the students. Connect yesterday's lesson to today's.
- What is the reason for teaching this subject matter?

Standards

- List all state or district standards that apply to your lesson.
- List all unit goals that are addressed by the lesson.
- *See* Goals.

Technology

- What software will your students be working with for the lesson?
- How will students be using the computer to enhance their learning for the lesson?
- What website will be accessed for the lesson?

Unit identification

- Title of unit or theme, for example, Friendship, Heritage, Fossils.
- Quarter.
- Week number.
- Pacing, or the lesson timeline.

© The McGraw-Hill Companies, Inc.

Teacher Evaluation Overview

This section will help you use the checklist and reflection components that follow as you prepare for a formal teacher evaluation.

• Classroom Environment Checklist

• Teacher Self-evaluation Checklist

• Teacher Self-reflection

Start by going through the checklists; these serve as reminders of what administrators will be looking for in your classroom. It's always good to do a quick check, though as a master teacher you likely have most if not all of this covered.

After you have gone through the checklists, give yourself time for reflection and rank yourself on the ten items listed. This is a page used only for self-reflection, so be honest, objective, and critical of yourself and your teaching practice; it's for your eyes only. Write down some of your strengths and an area where you would like to improve. List a few teachers who might provide expertise to help you with your "needs improvement" area. This page is designed to help you reflect on what you are already doing as a way to plan for the future.

Teacher Self-evaluation Checklist

Below is a checklist for you to use in prep... evaluation. It is very lik...

...e lesson you will teach for your formal
...a place in your classroom.

...mpression, even when
...in the room.

...m, choosing a new bulletin board
...urrent and it is easy to keep up with.
...hould be displayed. A typical list
...tle, rubric, teacher comments, and

...keep records of students'
...from seeing this type of folder.

...best work, it gives

...r year provide you with
...administrators appreciate.

...ble. You may want to keep
...d practice to have these

...nother
...rade

...n or classroom rules.
...action with students and

...f your answer is "yes,"

Classroom Environment Checklist

The environment in your classroom will be a key factor in your formal evaluation. While you want your room to showcase your students' strengths and your goals, you also want it to have a unique presence. Your room should be a reflection of all of this. As a master teacher, this is most likely a natural part of the process and it simply highlights the excellent instruction you provide.

☐ Furniture arrangement facilitates instruction and easy circulation.
☐ Independent reading area is arranged for student comfort and accessibility.
☐ Bulletin boards display current student work and content standards.
☐ Captions on boards promote critical thinking.
☐ Emergency bag is up-to-date and in a visible place.
☐ Content inside students' desks is arranged neatly.
☐ Bookcases are arranged neatly.
☐ Tops of students' desks are neat and clean.
☐ Class schedule is posted.
☐ Floors are clean and free of debris.
☐ Teacher's desk is neat and organized.
☐ Closets are clean and free of clutter.
☐ Weekly lesson plans are visible.
☐ Worktables are clean and the sink area is dry and orderly.
☐ Charts and graphs are used freely (print-rich environment).

...reflection tool to be used after you have
...ecklist. Be critical of your teaching
...ment. Self-reflection is critical; there's
...teaching practice, even if you are a

...t score; 5 is the highest) with regard
...your score and write it below.

...following thoughts:
...-10

...hile since you revised your teaching practice.
...d time to visit others and see what they are
...p the students engaged and excited. It's time
...pdating your repertoire with college or
...ework and some creativity.

...rengths are present; it's time to look at
...are missing. You are on your way; refine
...uild on your strengths. Gain confidence.

...hard work are paying off; stretch yourself
...weak areas.

...nd was always your path. Help others
...you have found.

...on, and practice have given you wisdom
...ime. You are the master!

271

© The McGraw-Hill Companies, Inc.

Classroom Environment Checklist

The environment in your classroom will be a key factor in your formal evaluation. While you want your room to showcase your students' strengths and your goals, you also want it to have a unique presence. Your room should be a reflection of all of this. As a master teacher, this is most likely a natural part of the process and it simply highlights the excellent instruction you provide.

- ☐ Furniture arrangement facilitates instruction and easy circulation.
- ☐ Independent reading area is arranged for student comfort and accessibility.
- ☐ Bulletin boards display current student work and content standards.
- ☐ Captions on boards promote critical thinking.
- ☐ Emergency bag is up-to-date and in a visible place.
- ☐ Content inside students' desks is arranged neatly.
- ☐ Bookcases are arranged neatly.
- ☐ Tops of students' desks are neat and clean.
- ☐ Class schedule is posted.
- ☐ Floors are clean and free of debris.
- ☐ Teacher's desk is neat and organized.
- ☐ Closets are clean and free of clutter.
- ☐ Weekly lesson plans are visible.
- ☐ Worktables are clean and the sink area is dry and orderly.
- ☐ Charts and graphs are used freely (print-rich environment).

© The McGraw-Hill Companies, Inc.

Teacher Self-evaluation Checklist

Below is a checklist for you to use in preparation for the lesson you will teach for your formal evaluation. It is very likely that these items already have a place in your classroom.

☐ **1. Clean room environment**

A clean, inviting, child-centered room makes a good impression, even when things get hectic. Each item should have its own place in the room.

☐ **2. Current student work displayed**

Current bulletin boards are important. Try to rotate them, choosing a new bulletin board every two to three weeks. This way, the work will stay current and it is easy to keep up with. Check with your school for recommendations on what should be displayed. A typical list might include standards, open-ended questions, board title, rubric, teacher comments, and rubric score.

☐ **3. Student work sample folders**

Collecting samples of each student's work is a good way to keep records of students' performance. Both administrators and parents will benefit from seeing this type of folder.

☐ **4. Student portfolio box**

When students have a portfolio box to use for storing their best work, it gives them a way to reflect on their own progress in the class.

☐ **5. Current lesson plans**

Your lesson plans should show evidence of planning; it's good if current lesson plans are available for viewing.

☐ **6. Long-range lesson plans**

The lesson plans that you have developed for an entire month or year provide you with some direction for your class; they also show forethought that administrators appreciate.

☐ **7. Assessments**

Every teacher has preferred assessments that are trusty and reliable. You may want to keep a folder for each student that includes basic assessments. It's good practice to have these assessments drive your instruction.

☐ **8. Grade book**

Detailed documentation for grades—whether in a grade book or another format—is important. It is invaluable if it's necessary to explain a grade to the administration or at parent teacher conferences.

☐ **9. Discipline plan and class rules**

It's important for an administrator to see evidence of a discipline plan or classroom rules. Rules do not necessarily need to be posted in a classroom. Your interaction with students and their behavior provide evidence that they exist.

☐ **10. A room good enough for your child**

Would you want your own child to be a member of this class? If your answer is "yes," then you are ready.

© The McGraw-Hill Companies, Inc.

Teacher Self-reflection

This document is a scoring and reflection tool to be used after you have reviewed the Self-evaluation Checklist. Be critical of your teaching practice and classroom environment. Self-reflection is essential; there's never an end to developing your teaching practice, even if you are a master!

Rate yourself on a scale of 1 to 5 (1 is the lowest score; 5 is the highest) with regard to each of the items on the checklist, then total your score and write it below.

1. Clean room environment		Review the following thoughts:
2. Current student work displayed		**Score of 0–10** It's been a while since you revised your teaching practice. This is a good time to visit others and see what they are doing to keep the students engaged and excited. It's time to consider updating your repertoire with college or district coursework and some creativity.
3. Student work sample folders		
4. Student portfolio box		
5. Current lesson plans		**Score of 11–20** One or two strengths are present; it's time to look at the things you are missing. You are on your way; refine and practice. Build on your strengths. Gain confidence.
6. Long-range lesson plans		
7. Assessments		**Score of 21–30** Knowledge and hard work are paying off; stretch yourself just a bit in your weak areas.
8. Grade book		
9. Discipline plan and class rules		**Score of 31–40** Above and beyond was always your path. Help others to find the place you have found.
10. A room good enough for your child		
Your score		**Score of 41–50** Perfection, precision, and practice have given you wisdom far ahead of your time. You are the master!

My strengths are

An area I would like to improve is

List a few teachers who could provide expertise.

© The McGraw-Hill Companies, Inc.

Teacher Responsibilities

Here is a reminder of all the things you take care of during the school day, week, and year. Thank you for taking on this multifaceted job while encouraging high student achievement! Job well done!

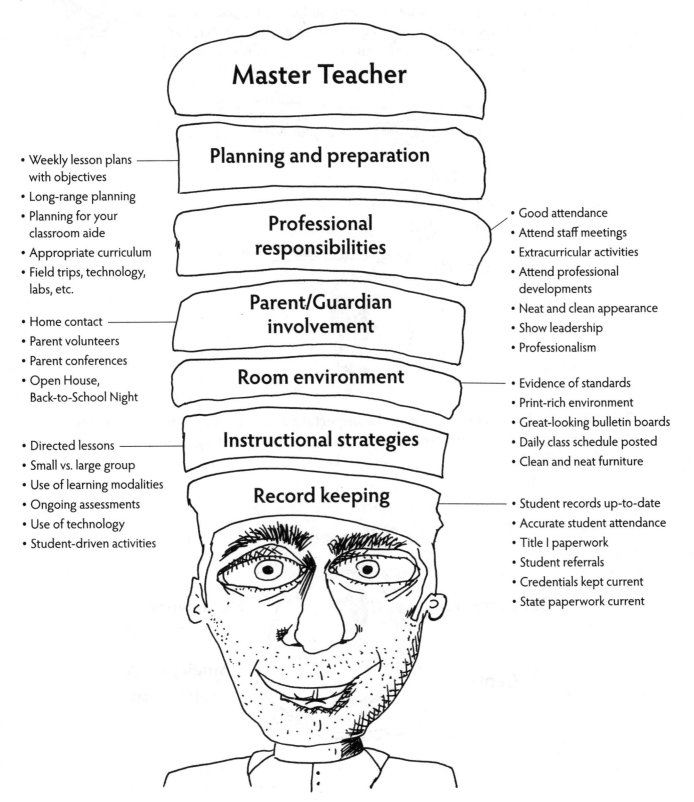

Master Teacher

Planning and preparation

- Weekly lesson plans with objectives
- Long-range planning
- Planning for your classroom aide
- Appropriate curriculum
- Field trips, technology, labs, etc.

Professional responsibilities

- Good attendance
- Attend staff meetings
- Extracurricular activities
- Attend professional developments
- Neat and clean appearance
- Show leadership
- Professionalism

Parent/Guardian involvement

- Home contact
- Parent volunteers
- Parent conferences
- Open House, Back-to-School Night

Room environment

- Evidence of standards
- Print-rich environment
- Great-looking bulletin boards
- Daily class schedule posted
- Clean and neat furniture

Instructional strategies

- Directed lessons
- Small vs. large group
- Use of learning modalities
- Ongoing assessments
- Use of technology
- Student-driven activities

Record keeping

- Student records up-to-date
- Accurate student attendance
- Title I paperwork
- Student referrals
- Credentials kept current
- State paperwork current

© The McGraw-Hill Companies, Inc.

Time Management

Classrooms move at a fast pace, making time management a critical part of the success of a master teacher's daily plan. Most of you already know that having good time management skills allows you to get through the scheduled activities on your agenda. This is what helps you pace the school day and cover the material that should be taught in each class that day. If time management is already one of your strengths, feel free to refresh yourself and review!

The illustration below shows some of the important areas related to time management in the classroom. Attention to these areas can bring your teaching game from an A to an A+.

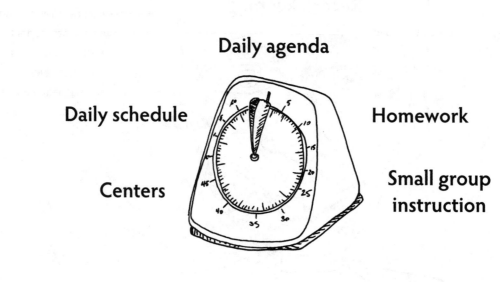

© The McGraw-Hill Companies, Inc.

Daily Schedule and Daily Agenda

You should have a specific place in your classroom where you display the daily agenda, daily schedule, and homework. Your formal teaching evaluation is not simply about the lesson plan and the delivery of the lesson. Your administrator will look at the whole picture, and your daily schedule and agenda are an important part of that.

The daily schedule and agenda could be written on the board, or a typed copy might be placed on a specified section of a bulletin board where students know to refer to it. The following is an example of a third grade schedule and agenda. It includes time periods and subject areas, but those could change on a day-to-day basis, depending on the skills you are working on each day. Time periods can also be affected by events such as assemblies and enrichment pull-out classes, so try to be flexible.

Daily Schedule

The daily schedule is a broad overview of your daily activities, subjects, and time periods.

Daily Schedule

8:15–10:00	Language Arts (Reading, Writing, Spelling, Grammar)
10:00–10:20	Recess
10:20–11:00	Continue with Language Arts (Reading, Writing, Spelling, Grammar)
11:00–12:15	Math
12:15–1:00	Lunch
1:00–1:30	P.E.
1:30–2:00	Science, Social Studies, Art, or Music
2:00–2:30	Social Studies, Science, Art, or Music
2:30–2:40	Explain homework, collect backpacks, and dismissal

© The McGraw-Hill Companies, Inc.

Daily Agenda

The daily agenda is more in-depth than the daily schedule. Having a detailed agenda is especially good for upper-grade students, with the necessary transition times from one subject to the next. Using an egg timer is a good way to keep the day moving. Always set it for 2 to 4 minutes earlier than the scheduled end-of-class time to allow for the closing of one subject or topic and a transition to the next.

Daily Agenda

8:00–8:15	Morning intake (attendance, lunch count, collect homework, organize backpacks).
8:15–8:30	Daily oral review. Correct the sentences on the board for punctuation and capitals.
8:30–9:00	Read aloud *The Very Hungry Caterpillar* by Eric Carle and complete journal entry.
9:00–10:00	Language Arts Centers (Spelling Sentences for Words #1–5 in Center #1, Grammar Practice Worksheet with the Verb "to be" in Center #2, Independent Reading pages 34–39 in Language Arts book in Center #3, and Answer the "Author's Questions" on page 39 in Center #4).
10:00–10:20	Recess.
10:20–11:00	Peer editing for essay on the Butterfly Lifecycle. Then re-write essay with new edits. Pull small groups and individuals needing help.
11:00–11:10	"Do Now" math review from yesterday's lesson.
11:10–11:30	Teach or model today's math lesson on multiplication.
11:30–12:15	Math Centers (Create Multiplication Flash Cards for 4s at Center #1, Create Multiplication Word Problems at Center #2, and Complete #1–31 Odd on pages 27–28 in Student Book in Center #3.).
12:15–1:00	Lunch.
1:00–1:30	P.E. Interval Training.
1:30–2:00	Finish the hanging mobile for the Butterfly Lifecycle in your Science groups.
2:00–2:30	Continue working on Social Studies map of California.
2:30–2:40	Explain homework and collect backpacks.
2:40	Dismissal.

© The McGraw-Hill Companies, Inc.

Homework

In addition to the general Daily Schedule and the Daily Agenda, you will want to post a Homework list so that students are always aware of what they need to turn in each day. If they missed an assignment, they need to know what to make up. Below is a sample.

1. *Put spelling words in alphabetical order.*
2. *#2–30 Even on pages 27–28 in Math book.*
3. *Re-write peer-edited essay on the Butterfly Lifecycle.*

Homework

Monday Oct 3, 2009
☐ Spelling Words 3x ea.
☐ Math Addition Problems
☐ Draw Parts of a Butterfly #1-20
Tuesday Oct 4, 2009
☐ Spelling words ABC order
☐ Math Addition P. 26 #20-40
☐ Write the life cycle of Butterfly

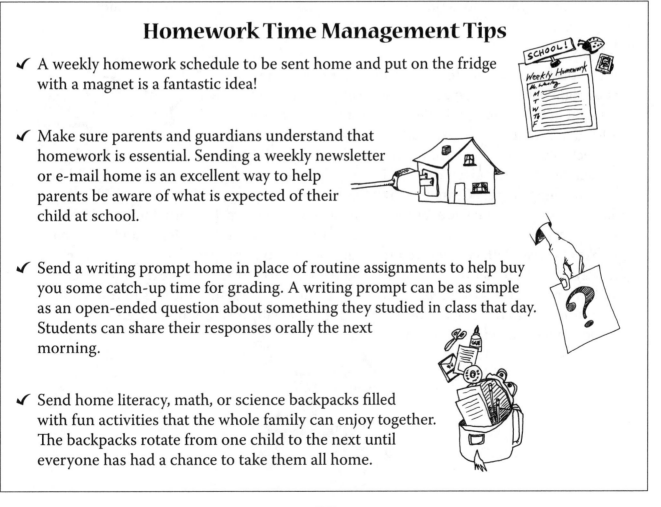

Homework Time Management Tips

✔ A weekly homework schedule to be sent home and put on the fridge with a magnet is a fantastic idea!

✔ Make sure parents and guardians understand that homework is essential. Sending a weekly newsletter or e-mail home is an excellent way to help parents be aware of what is expected of their child at school.

✔ Send a writing prompt home in place of routine assignments to help buy you some catch-up time for grading. A writing prompt can be as simple as an open-ended question about something they studied in class that day. Students can share their responses orally the next morning.

✔ Send home literacy, math, or science backpacks filled with fun activities that the whole family can enjoy together. The backpacks rotate from one child to the next until everyone has had a chance to take them all home.

© The McGraw-Hill Companies, Inc.

Small Group Instruction

If you incorporate small group instruction into your classroom, it is important to have a designated area where you meet with individual students or small groups of students to help them with specific skills or projects. Be sure that you can still see the rest of the class when you are meeting in this area; place your chair so that you face the students who are at their seats or at other centers. This allows you to monitor the whole class while working with small groups or individuals. A kidney-shaped table allows easy access both to your small group and to those working without you. Keep this table organized, with necessary and relevant materials displayed. Administrators will want to have a picture of what you do there even if it isn't a part of your formal evaluation.

If you choose not to have a table and chairs for small group instruction, you can use a rug area or set up a small circle with student chairs. If you have simultaneous small groups working cooperatively, be sure that each student understands where he or she should go (for example, Table 1, Table 2, etc., or the Writing Center, the Computer Center, etc.) It is important for administrators to see that small group activities are well organized, so be clear in your instructions to make sure that there are no misunderstandings.

Centers

If you plan to incorporate centers into your daily schedule, you might want to organize them according to curricular area. As seen in the sample Daily Agenda, you can create 15- to 20-minute rotating groups. Students need to carry only their  subject folder and pencil from table to table; they will find the necessary materials at each table for the given centers. For example, in Language Arts, students would find their Spelling Words, Grammar Practice Worksheet, Language Arts Reading Book and the "Author's Question" at four Language Arts centers. In Math, they would find index cards for their flash cards, sample multiplication word problems, and their math books at three Math centers. You need to teach them to prepare for transitions, and to stay on task so that they can finish and be ready to move to the next center after 15 to 20 minutes. Having centers organized and preparing the students to transition well from one to the other is very important, especially if your administrator will be observing you during this time.

280

© The McGraw-Hill Companies, Inc.

Sample Lesson Plan: Auto-Bio-Poem

The following is a sample lesson plan for a wonderful lesson that principals love to observe and evaluate, especially at the beginning of the year when you are getting to know your students. At the end of this chapter, you will find a sample template, which is also filled out with the information included here. This template is helpful to have and easy to use, especially if it has been some time since you had to organize a lesson plan in this way. For the Independent Practice assignment in this lesson, we present the Auto-Bio-Poem format, as well as a sample of a completed Auto-Bio-Poem.

Auto-Bio-Poem

Mrs. Kashala Alexander
Grades 2–12
Poetry
45 Minutes

Content Standards

2.0 Writing Applications (Genres and Their Characteristics)

Students write compositions that describe and explain familiar objects, events, and experiences. Student writing demonstrates a command of standard American English and the drafting, research, and organizational strategies outlined in Writing Standard 1.0.

Using the writing strategies of grade three outlined in Writing Standard 1.0, students do the following:

2.1 Write narratives

    a. Provide a context within which an action takes place.

    b. Include well-chosen details to develop the plot.

    c. Provide insight into why the selected incident is memorable.

2.2 Write descriptions that use concrete sensory details to present and support unified impressions of people, places, things, or experiences.

Vocabulary

Autobiography—memoirs, life story, history of your life

Biography—account or chronicle of another person's life

Poetry—verse, lists, rhymes, etc.

Materials

Paper and pencil

Auto-Bio-Poem format—found at http://wside.k12.il.us/tms/Tech2/Auto.html

© The McGraw-Hill Companies, Inc.

Set

Read aloud *I Like Myself* by Karen Beaumont (2nd- to 3rd-grade level), then show an example of your auto-bio-poem for the children to listen to, read, and use as a reference for their own. Read your auto-bio-poem aloud, then go back to it and compare it to the necessary elements for an auto-bio-poem.

Purpose

The purpose of this lesson is to have the writer analyze himself or herself to provide an introduction to the rest of the class.

Objective

By the end of the lesson students will be able to

a. analyze themselves
b. inform themselves
c. introduce themselves

by writing a poem that focuses on several personal traits and transcribing them in a closed poetry format.

Model

After sharing your own auto-bio-poem with the class, compare each of the lines in your poem to each of the lines in the format.

Guided Practice

Have a student come to the front of the class; guide the student through the process of an auto-bio-poem. Do this for the first five lines, then encourage the student to finish it at his or her desk.

Check for Understanding

Have students review each of the elements of the poem with you orally. You will answer any concerns about the requirements.

Independent Practice

Each student will write his or her own 14-step auto-bio-poem using the format as a guide (it can be either on a handout or written on the board as a reference). Your auto-bio-poem is also a good reference point.

Closure

Have volunteers share their poem with the class.

© The McGraw-Hill Companies, Inc.

Homework

Ask students to choose a family member to write a bio-poem about. Use the same format, but the student will write about a family member instead of himself or herself.

English Language Learners (ELLs)

Students who speak English as a second language may want to write in their primary language or have you transcribe their responses in English.

Extension Activity

Have students draw a self-portrait using color pastels or colored pencils. Use this as the cover sheet for their auto-bio-poem.

© The McGraw-Hill Companies, Inc.

Sample Lesson Plan

Title *Auto-Bio-Poem*	Unit *#4*	Grade level *3rd*
Teacher *Mrs. Kashala Alexander*	Suggested time *45 minutes*	

1. Anticipatory Set and Scaffolding
Grab students' attention, then relate new objectives to past learning.

Read aloud "I Like Myself" by Karen Beaumont (2nd- to 3rd-grade level), then show an example of your auto-bio-poem for the children to listen to, read, and use as a reference for their own. Read your auto-bio-poem aloud, then go back to it and compare it to the necessary elements for an auto-bio-poem.

Objective
By the end of the lesson, students will be able to
a. analyze themselves
b. inform themselves
c. introduce themselves
by writing a poem that focuses on several personal traits and transcribing them in a closed poetry format.

2. Presentation and Procedure
List the sequential steps for the lesson you will model.

The teacher will grab students' interest by reading the story "I Like Myself."
Share the auto-bio-poem format with the class.
After sharing your own auto-bio-poem with the class, compare each of the lines in your poem to each of the lines in the format.
Students will work to create their own poem with the class.
Students will create their own poem using the handout as a guide.
Students will illustrate their poem and read it aloud to the class!

3. Guided Practice
The students and teacher work together to carry out an example or activity to match the objective.

Have a student come up to the front of the class; guide the student through the process of an auto-bio-poem. Do this for the first five lines, and then encourage the student to finish it at his or her desk.

4. Check for Understanding
Quick and simple assessment to confirm student understanding.

Have students review each of the elements of the poem with you orally. You will answer any concerns about the requirements.
Have volunteers share their poem with the class.

© The McGraw-Hill Companies, Inc.

5. Independent Practice

Students work independently on a task that meets the objective.

Each student will write his or her own 14-step auto-bio-poem using the format as a guide (it can be either on a handout or written on the board as a reference). Your auto-bio-poem is also a good reference point.

6. Assessment, Homework, or Project

What method will you use to be sure students continue to understand the objective?

Have students choose a family member to write a bio-poem about. Using the same format, the student will write about the family member.

Have students draw a self-portrait using colored pencils or color pastels. Use this as the cover sheet for their auto-bio-poem.

7. Content Standards

2.0 Writing Applications (Genres and Their Characteristics)

Students write compositions that describe and explain familiar objects, events, and experiences. Student writing demonstrates a command of standard American English and the drafting, research, and organizational strategies outlined in Writing Standard 1.0.

Using the writing strategies of grade three outlined in Writing Standard 1.0, students do the following:

2.1 Write narratives

a. Provide a context within which an action takes place.
b. Include well-chosen details to develop the plot.
c. Provide insight into why the selected incident is memorable.

2.2 Write descriptions that use concrete sensory details to present and support unified impressions of people, places, things, or experiences.

8. Modifications, Special Needs, Technology

Students who speak English as a second language may want to write in their primary language or have you transcribe their responses in English.

Students can publish their autobiography poems on the computer and add different fonts and clip art.

© The McGraw-Hill Companies, Inc.

Lesson Plan Template

Title		Unit	Grade level
Teacher		Suggested time	

1. Anticipatory Set and Scaffolding
Grab students' attention, then relate new objectives to past learning.

Objective

2. Presentation and Procedure
List the sequential steps for the lesson you will model.

3. Guided Practice
The students and teacher work together to carry out an example or activity to match the objective.

4. Check for Understanding
Quick and simple assessment to confirm student understanding.

© The McGraw-Hill Companies, Inc.

5. Independent Practice
Students work independently on a task that meets the objective.

6. Assessment, Homework, or Project
What method will you use to be sure students continue to understand the objective?

7. Content Standards

8. Modifications, Special Needs, Technology

© The McGraw-Hill Companies, Inc.

Auto-Bio-Poem Format

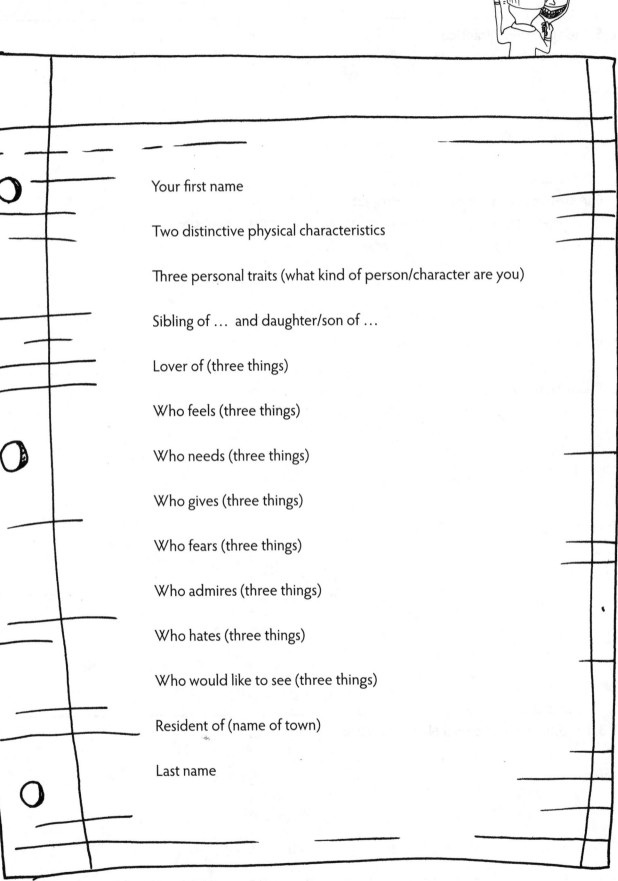

Your first name

Two distinctive physical characteristics

Three personal traits (what kind of person/character are you)

Sibling of … and daughter/son of …

Lover of (three things)

Who feels (three things)

Who needs (three things)

Who gives (three things)

Who fears (three things)

Who admires (three things)

Who hates (three things)

Who would like to see (three things)

Resident of (name of town)

Last name

© The McGraw-Hill Companies, Inc.

Sample Auto-Bio-Poem

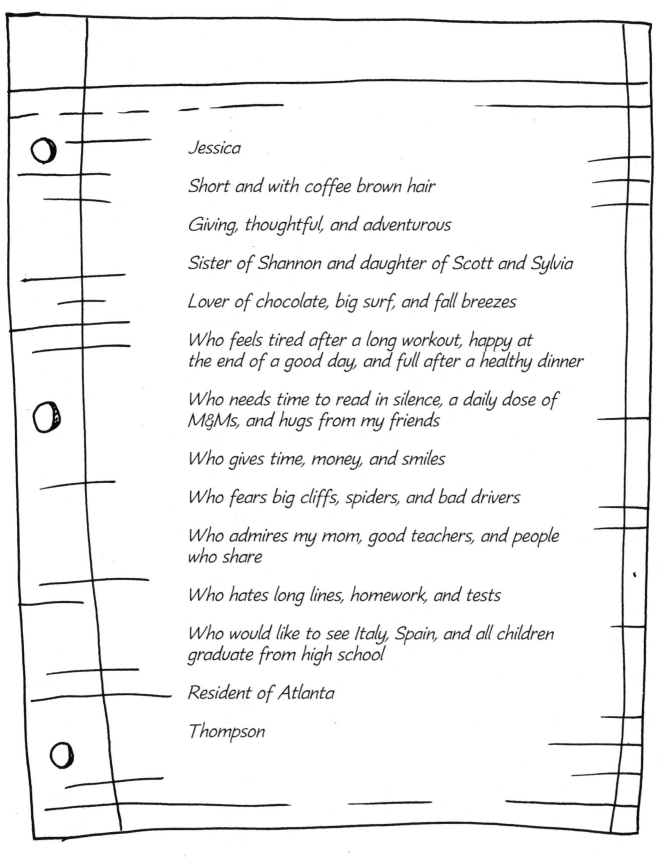

Jessica

Short and with coffee brown hair

Giving, thoughtful, and adventurous

Sister of Shannon and daughter of Scott and Sylvia

Lover of chocolate, big surf, and fall breezes

Who feels tired after a long workout, happy at
the end of a good day, and full after a healthy dinner

Who needs time to read in silence, a daily dose of
M&Ms, and hugs from my friends

Who gives time, money, and smiles

Who fears big cliffs, spiders, and bad drivers

Who admires my mom, good teachers, and people
who share

Who hates long lines, homework, and tests

Who would like to see Italy, Spain, and all children
graduate from high school

Resident of Atlanta

Thompson

© The McGraw-Hill Companies, Inc.